SVG

For Designers:

Using Scalable Vector
Graphics in Next-Generation
Web Sites

About the Authors...

Bill Trippe is president of New Millennium Publishing, a Boston-based consulting practice formed in 1997 (www.nmpub.com). Bill has more than 20 years of technical and management experience in electronic publishing, content management, and SGML/XML and related technologies. He brings a unique blend of strategic and hands-on knowledge of the products and trends that are shaping the publishing and content technology marketplace. In addition to his role at New Millennium, Bill is associate editor of The Gilbane Report, the XML columnist for Transform, a consulting associate with the consulting and market research firm CAP Ventures, and a regular contributor to the magazine, *EContent*. He recently co-authored *Digital Rights Management: Business and Technology* (Hungry Minds).

Kate Binder is a publishing production expert with experience in book, magazine, newspaper, and online publishing. She is a partner in Prospect Hill Publishing Services (www.prospecthillpub.com), located in Nashua, NH, with a diverse client list that includes Houghton Mifflin Company, Pearson Technology Group, Rockport Publishers, *Quilting Arts* magazine, Muska & Lipman Publishing, PennWell Corporation, and Internet Biz.Net. In addition to consulting on production issues, Kate has written about electronic publishing tools and techniques for *PEI* and *eDigital Photo* magazines, among others, and is the author of several books, most recently *The Complete Idiot's Guide to Mac OS X* (Alpha Books).

SVG

For Designers:
Using Scalable Vector
Graphics in Next-Generation
Web Sites

Bill Trippe & Kate Binder

McGraw-Hill/Osborne

New York   Chicago   San Francisco   Lisbon   London   Madrid   Mexico City
Milan   New Delhi   San Juan   Seoul   Singapore   Sydney   Toronto

Publisher
Brandon A. Nordin

Vice President & Associate Publisher
Scott Rogers

Acquisitions Editor
Marjorie McAneny

Project Editor
Monika Faltiss

Acquisitions Coordinator
Tana Allen

Technical Editor
Andrew Watanabe

Copy Editor
Dennis Weaver

Proofreader
Nancy McLaughlin

Indexer
Jack Lewis

Computer Designers
Kelly Stanton-Scott
Carie Abrew
Elizabeth Jang

Illustrators
Michael Mueller
Lyssa Wald

Series Design
Kelly Stanton-Scott

Cover Design
Greg Scott

Cover Illustration
Hank Osuna

McGraw-Hill/Osborne
2600 Tenth Street
Berkeley, California 94710
U.S.A.

To arrange bulk purchase discounts for sales promotions, premiums, or fund-raisers, please contact **McGraw-Hill**/Osborne at the above address. For information on translations or book distributors outside the U.S.A., please see the International Contact Information page immediately following the index of this book.

SVG For Designers: Using Scalable Vector Graphics in Next-Generation Web Sites

1234567890 FGR FGR 0198765432

ISBN 0-07-222529-7

This book was composed with Corel VENTURA™ Publisher.

For Christian and Nathaniel, who reminded Dad
not to work too much and instead take a break
here and there with a game of catch.
—*Bill Trippe*

For all those who taught me that it's important
to know how things work so you can use
them right: Dad, Alex, Paul, and all the rest.
—*Kate Binder*

CONTENTS AT A GLANCE

CONTENTS

I Understanding SVG

II Creating SVG Graphics

III   SVG in Context—Flash, Web Design, and Dynamic SVG

Acknowledgments

This book took shape over a several-month period in which SVG emerged, took shape, and began to find practical use on the Web. Because the topic is still so new, we had to think long and hard about how best to present the topic and what primary audience to address. We arrived at the idea of a book on SVG aimed at graphic designers; this differs markedly from most other books on the topic, which are really addressed at web developers and computer programmers. We decided instead to focus on explaining SVG to readers who already understand all the aesthetic and production issues in play, but who need to better understand the technical underpinnings of SVG.

Our acquisitions editor, Margie McAneny, was incredibly helpful to us in thinking this through, formulating a proposal, and organizing the material for this audience. She then teamed us with the perfect technical editor for both the topic and our approach, Andrew Watanabe. Andrew combines a designer's instincts with a rich understanding of SVG. As an early adopter of SVG, he is far ahead of the curve on how SVG is already being used and will be used in the future. As a result, his comments and corrections to our draft chapters were invaluable. In the end, though, we had to make the final call on some questions and issues. In particular, we held to our interpretation of how the various browsers, notably Internet Explorer, interact with SVG. So, we take all responsibility for any errors or omissions.

The rubber meets the road when you write and start to turn in chapters. Tana Allen from McGraw-Hill was very helpful with all the details of manuscript and artwork development, and patiently reminded us (well, reminded Bill) when we were late with different portions of the book. Project editors Monika Faltiss and

Jody McKenzie did a fine job of combing through complex text, code, and illustrations, and the book is a better product thanks to them.

A number of people helped with research. Dan MacAlpine, Bill's friend and colleague at New Millennium Publishing, was instrumental in the research and thinking for both Chapter 1 and the concluding chapter. He was also a great sounding board as some of the overall ideas for the book were developed. Jennifer Richtarek did much of the groundwork for Chapter 8, and Marc Dashevsky provided the servers, technical expertise, and good humor to get us through all the installation and testing of the server-side products. Paul Crook reviewed Chapter 2, and helped with the example XML and XSLT files.

All of the vendors were very helpful when we contacted them. They provided software, sample files, reviewer's materials, and technical support. It was nice, of course, that they were so supportive of our efforts, but it was even more satisfying to experience how enthusiastic some of them were for the very subject of SVG itself. It is clearly a passion for some of these folks, and it was nice sharing that passion. We would especially like to acknowledge Scott Michaels from Savage Software and Jonathan Manktelow from GraPL.net for their time.

S*VG For Designers* is intended to be precisely what the title suggests—a practical introduction to this important new technology—aimed at you, the working graphic arts professional who needs to produce materials for the Web. As this new graphics format gains acceptance, designers and production professionals will need to know how to generate and use SVG graphics in their designs, and they'll be asked to help integrate SVG into content management and web automation systems.

SVG For Designers gives you the information you need to accomplish these tasks, showing the code structure behind SVG and the tools available to create, modify, and implement SVG graphics in web and other applications. We have made the assumption that you will want to use the tools and workflows you have become accustomed to, so this book focuses on using common popular tools that you are familiar with, while also introducing certain specialized tools that may improve performance and productivity.

The audience for *SVG For Designers* includes web designers and illustrators who want to keep up with rapidly changing web technology. We have made the further assumption that you seek to know why and how to use SVG in your work, but that you don't want to wade through an encyclopedic guide to the technology. In *SVG For Designers*, you'll find the application-specific information you need to keep moving ahead.

This book is organized into three distinct but interrelated parts. Part 1, "Understanding SVG," introduces you to SVG, how it is used, and what its advantages are for web site development. It then describes the technical underpinnings of SVG by introducing you to the eXtensible Markup Language (XML), and how XML is used as the basis of SVG. By the end of Part 1, you will be able to create, modify, view, and troubleshoot basic SVG files.

Part 2, "Creating SVG Graphics," really forms the heart of the book. It walks you through the SVG features and capabilities of commonly used drawing applications, such as Adobe Illustrator and CorelDRAW. It assumes that you likely have some prior experience with these tools, but that you are newer to using these tools to create SVG files. It also introduces you to specialized tools for creating SVG, such as JASC's WebDraw. By the end of Part 2, you will be creating complex, professional-quality SVG drawings.

By this point in the book, you should be proficient in using tools to create SVG drawings. Part 3, "SVG in Context—Flash, Web Design, and Dynamic SVG," then provides the necessary context for working with SVG. It begins by addressing the questions that are perhaps foremost in your mind—how does SVG compare to Flash, and when would you use one or the other? It then walks you through the basics of building web pages that *incorporate* SVG, as well as how you could build pages that are *entirely* SVG. We then discuss the set of products that can be used to generate SVG automatically, on the server side if you will, and review the functionality of three of them at some length. The book then concludes with a discussion of the future of SVG, which we think is only beginning to emerge.

Appendixes include a lengthy walk through of the SVG syntax, and a catalog of all of the source files used in the creation of this book. All of the supporting materials are also available online at www.svgfordesigners.com. We had the working graphic arts professional in mind when we wrote this book, and we think the most useful feature of the book is the large number of working code examples. Our intent is for you to be able to use these, modify them, create your own, and take off with them. We are very confident that this book will provide the theoretical and practical background you need to begin working with—and being productive with—the exciting new technology of SVG.

part I

Understanding SVG

chapter 1

The SVG Standard

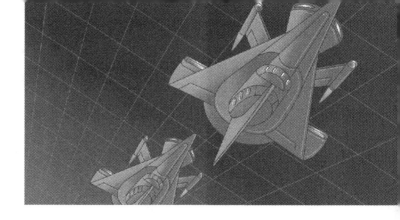

Since the mid-1980s, people working in publishing, the graphic arts, and web design and production have enjoyed a small number of significant, groundbreaking new technologies. Nearly 20 years ago, the introduction of WYSIWYG desktop publishing (What You See Is What You Get) was one of the first such breakthrough technologies. Prior to WYSIWYG, publishers and graphic artists couldn't see the finished product until the page had been pasted up or even printed. Copy was typeset using a sometimes bewildering set of codes and commands, leaving designers and editors working in the dark until galleys were produced and pasted up. Artwork, especially photos and anything else requiring color or gray scale, was photomechanically reproduced and worked into the layout at the last minute, usually by skilled craftspeople working under special conditions. We take it for granted now, but WYSIWYG-based desktop publishing, such as that shown in Figure 1-1, suddenly made it possible to see a whole page on a computer screen—to make small changes or totally reconfigure the layout right on a computer.

Along with WYSIWYG came PostScript printing, notably moderate-priced laser printers. These devices brought high-quality printing into an office setting, including output to plain paper instead of specialized papers and films. Together, desktop publishing, PostScript, and laser printing brought the entire workflow for publishing into a normal office setting, allowing graphic designers, writers, editors, and production staff to collaborate effectively and efficiently.

Then the early '90s brought the cross-platform communication revolution. In May 1991, Tim Berners-Lee developed the first version of HTML, instantly making the Hypertext Markup Language the latest communication breakthrough. The HTML language made it possible to read documents from any computer across the

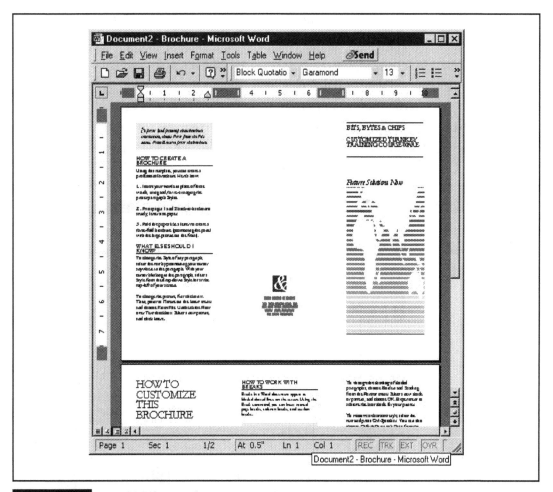

FIGURE   1-1   *WYSIWYG publishing allows the designer to see all elements in position.* ■

rapidly growing World Wide Web. Right on the heels of HTML, another break-through made documents even more accessible. In 1992, Adobe released Carousel, the first commercial application of PDF—the Portable Document Format. PDF, as we now know so well, allows all of the graphical and layout elements of a document to be perfectly reproduced in a portable file that can be viewed on any computer and printed on essentially any printer. Strategically, PDF was Adobe's response to the stunning overnight acceptance of HTML among business and personal computer users. But PDF, while allowing the user to read documents across all platforms, also serves the needs of the publishing professional. As Figure 1-2 shows, with its enhanced graphics capability and its ability to maintain the original page design and layout, PDF has also become the predominant method graphics professionals use for delivering final copy to printers.

In the interim, many supporting technologies have emerged to help enhance each of these applications. Electronic fonts, for example, are key to all of these primary technologies, as are tools for color management and image editing. HTML

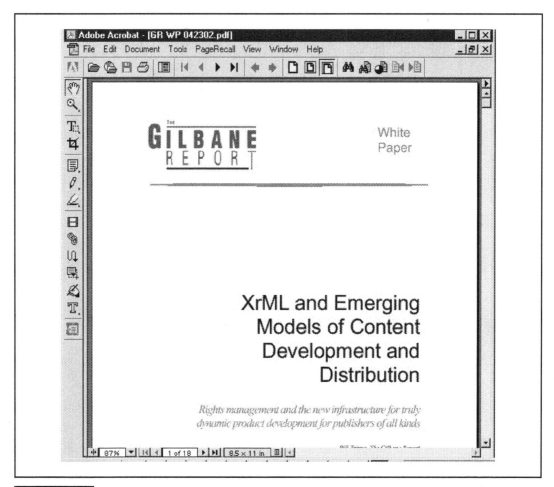

FIGURE 1-2   *Adobe's Acrobat application allows documents to be turned into PDF and then displayed or printed from virtually any computer.* ∎

benefits from a dizzying array of supporting technologies, including scripting languages for interactivity, cascading style sheets, and even tools for animation. Yet we would argue that, since the advancement of HTML, no new fundamental technology has emerged to change how web pages are rendered. That is, most web pages are still done with HTML tags, supported by scripts and static graphical objects like GIF and JPG tags.

Now Scalable Vector Graphics (SVG) has emerged, with all the potential to be the next fundamentally new technology for production and design professionals. SVG-based graphics and web pages can save time and money, improve quality, and revolutionize the way web graphics convey information. Moreover, SVG will be able to do this with minimal new costs for software and training, and will result in a better workflow for web production and for organizations that combine web and print production.

Bringing Vector Graphics to the Web

SVG holds this promise for a few simple reasons. First, vector graphics are a necessary complement to the bitmap graphic formats such as JPG and GIF that now dominate the Web. Vector graphics mean better quality and greater precision for many types of illustrations and artwork, especially technical illustrations and other kinds of artwork created by computer-aided design programs. Second, SVG brings an industry standard approach to creating vector graphics on the Web. Up until now, there have been only proprietary methods for creating vector graphics. Third, and, perhaps most importantly, the SVG standard provides more than vector graphics handling, as it allows for the incorporation of vector graphics, bitmap graphics, text, style sheets, and scripts. Users of SVG cannot only create stand-alone illustrations; they can also create and exercise greater control over the design of entire web pages. They can also flexibly incorporate other text, other graphics, data, and scripts. And finally, because SVG files are text files, they can be easily generated and manipulated, allowing for applications like data-driven graphics and personalization.

SVG gives the graphic designer, using virtually the current standard industry toolbox, the power to create live web images. Unlike bitmap images, SVG images can dynamically update as the designer, the web developer, or the end user enter or change data and otherwise interact with the web image. SVG files can be scripted to automatically take this information and modify the existing graphic or regenerate the graphic. Importantly, SVG often provides this flexibility using less disk space and memory, providing faster upload and download times, and putting more creative control into the graphic designer's hands than current static bitmap technology.

A Hypothetical SVG Application

To see how SVG might revolutionize graphics, commerce, and information flow on the Web, let's take a look at a common web transaction—buying tickets for an event. With bitmap technology, a fan generally sees a map of the stadium or arena and then has to choose via the static, unchanging map on the screen. SVG, on the other hand, can be used to create an image of exactly the seats the fan is buying, in, say, a seating chart of the stadium; SVG can also be used to create an image that simulates the view that the fan will have of the event.

In this scenario, we have a baseball fan whose father is visiting from out of town for two weeks in August. The fan wants to take his dad to a game. The dad, being elderly, needs easy access to the aisle and to rest rooms. The fan would prefer a day game. The fan isn't a millionaire, so he would need to purchase the lower- and moderate-priced seats. He's only been to this ballpark a few times himself, so he'd like to see how fans rate the seats and what type of view he and his dad would have from each seat. Obviously, he wants two seats together.

With standard bitmap files, it would be impossible—or at least extremely difficult—to create enough graphics to meet this fan's needs to visualize so many details. The web site would have to anticipate each question this fan planned to ask and then create a graphic to help answer the question before the fan even logged on. For this one fan alone, the web site would need to have at the ready potentially hundreds of bitmap files to even begin to answer his questions and show the views and seating plans he is interested in.

Not so with SVG. A live text file on the web site, the SVG can dynamically update an infinite number of times, depending on the data fed into it. Just as the

HTML itself is text and can be generated on the fly and intermingled with script and code, SVG is also textual. SVG is, in fact, based on XML. Because it is XML-based, SVG can be liberally mixed with other formats such as XHTML and scripting languages such as JavaScript. Entire web pages can be rendered with SVG, or individual components such as graphics.

Back to our baseball fan—the basic SVG graphic is a map of the stadium, similar to any map of any stadium through which fans buy tickets. But, this map is different. The map changes as the data behind the map changes, depending on the information the fan wants to see.

Moving from the overall map of the stadium, the SVG-based graphic first changes by showing small "thumbnail" drawings of the seats available for the two weeks the fan's dad is visiting (the first two weeks in August).

Two weeks is a long time, so the fan asks what teams will be playing during that period, and then selects a set of games for the Texas Rangers, Aug. 10–14. The SVG document then changes again, showing only thumbnails for seats available for those dates. The fan then types in other needs: proximity to a men's room, access to the aisle. The SVG document changes again, the thumbnails showing seats available that meet the fan's criteria. The fan specifically asks for a day game. The graphic then shows seats available for two day games, Aug. 11 and 12. The graphic displays seats for those two days. He decides to go with upper box seats and the map morphs again, showing only those seats that meet all his criteria. The fan then settles on several options, clicking on each of several pairs of seats; with each click, the graphic zooms in on the specific seats and automatically displays a typical view of the field from each seat and an overall fan rating of the seat. The fan then selects his seats, pays, and exits.

Finally, the fan can even print out a view of the seats that he can take with him to the game so he can find the seats more easily.

Meanwhile, the SVG-enabled web site remains ready for the next fan and the next set of parameters. This fan only wants Sunday games and to sit in the bleachers behind the home bullpen…

Comparing the SVG Approach with the Traditional Web-Based Approach

Compare the SVG ticket-buying experience with options available on a web site with conventional graphics and the advantages SVG offers become even more obvious.

Some web sites don't even offer a floor plan for the arena or stadium because the downloads take so long—remember, SVG uses far less memory than do bitmap graphics so downloads are much faster and easier.

If the site does offer a floor plan, it is static—a mere picture of the seating. It never changes. Fans can't zoom down to a pair of seats and get a view of the field from those seats. They can't get pop-up graphics that give more information about the stadium or the specific seats. Instead, the fan must move on to another page to receive additional information. Fans don't receive real-time, up-to-date information regarding the availability of seats as other fans are buying their tickets. They can't print out the stadium or arena map, if it exists, because the bitmap graphic is prohibitively large for downloading (100 to 150KB), can't be effectively zoomed, and likely won't reproduce accurately on their printer, see Figure 1-3.

SVG, on the other hand, provides all these features and more. For the end user, SVG-based graphics are

- *Higher graphic quality*, for the screen as well as for printing.

- *Zoomable* (Using Adobe SVG Viewer, if you zoom in on, say, the seats you've selected and the nearest entrance, you can print out this exact view to take with you to the venue.)

- *Searchable*, allowing you to quickly find seat JJ-398 because the text label is actually text and not rendered pixels; copy and paste any pertinent info such as directions, phone numbers, etc. that may be embedded in the layout.

- *More informative* (Dynamically updated content shows information that is up-to-the-minute current—that is, seating availability.)

- *Interactive* (ToolTips on mouseover, drill-down for more detailed info right on the graphic, as opposed to having to read info from another window or page.)

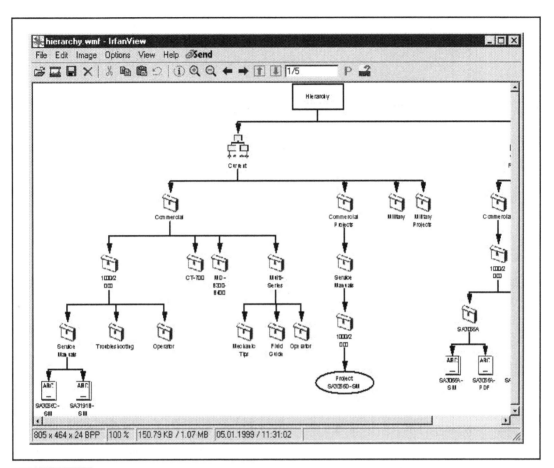

FIGURE 1-3   *Complex illustrations, once captured in bitmap format, are then very unsatisfactory to zoom.* ■

Just as importantly to the graphic designer and developer, SVG allows for richer, more detailed graphics on the web page even as it makes the site more accessible to the user, see Figure 1-4.

■ SVG graphics are overall much faster because the download is smaller (vectors are more efficient than rasters)—zoomed in views are *not* new downloads, but simple transformations that take place on the client side (as well as additional data that may be hidden on first load, but is revealed on interaction or animation).

■ SVG graphics can be richer looking, as there are a great number of filter effects that can be applied (filter effects create raster-style blurred drop shadows or 3-D bevels, custom font faces that allow text to remain as text for accessibility).

■ SVG graphics are manageable as an asset much like HTML. A designer can style a graphic using the same cascading style sheet (CSS) as for the rest of the site. For example, background color for the graphic may be a color specified in the style sheet for the entire site. Say for a Giants game, the primary colors should be orange and black. The SVG image can dynamically be made orange and black by a simple change to the style sheet along with other elements in the HTML—a simple change cascades through the SVG along with the HTML.

■ These SVG assets can be reused for multiple applications. (As suggested earlier, the graphic can be customized for different events; you can also use the same graphic for printing brochures, handouts, tickets, or other devices such as handheld browsers.)

Other Details to the Application

Adobe created just such a demo application for SVG years ago, and used the floor-plan graphic to illustrate a ticket that the user could print directly from the web site. (The Adobe demo included an SVG-generated barcode on the ticket to potentially prevent fraud.) The customized ticket would include the route from the entrance of the stadium to the ticketholder's seat. Text descriptions for directions to the venue, to the seat, and information about the event would be in SVG so that this info could be copied and pasted, or used for applications such as "send an e-mail to a friend" so that they know where you'll be.

Finally, it would be fairly straightforward to customize this application for mobile devices such as a Palm Pilot or PocketPC. For example, a simpler version of the graphic could be customized via CSS. Custom fonts could be removed, filter effects could be removed or simplified, and the color palette could be customized for the smaller device.

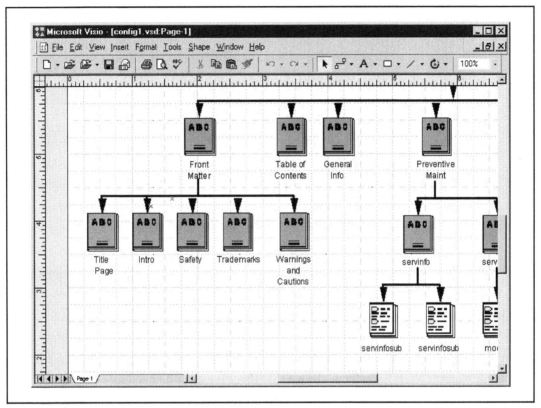

FIGURE   1-4   *Complex illustrations, when rendered in vector form, can be much more effectively zoomed and panned.* ■

SVG's Potential Impact

The preceding example shows only one way in which SVG can help advance commerce on the Internet. Imagine graphics that change at the user's whim. The implications for everything from financial services to catalog sales are tremendous. SVG-based graphics would give consumers more choices and more confidence in those choices because SVG gives the consumer control and more ability to visualize the transaction they are making. And e-commerce is only one potential application (more are discussed at the end of this chapter). The potential applications are endless.

In September of 2001, the World Wide Web Consortium (W3C) published the W3C *Recommendation* for SVG 1.0, paving the way for software developers to begin, in earnest, developing products that support SVG. Adobe, Sun, Corel, and IBM, among others, are all over it. Adobe, significantly, has already built SVG capabilities into major products like Illustrator and GoLive, and they claim to have distributed over 35 million copies of their SVG Viewer.

The very presence of a format for vector graphics on the Web is significant. For all its promise as a graphical user interface and publishing medium, the Web has relied too heavily on bitmap graphical formats like GIF and JPG. Bitmaps have inherent limitations—they tend to be static and difficult to reuse, and they often need to be optimized for the particular screen resolution of the displaying device. As a result, most web sites are laden with single-use graphic files, and there is little use of graphics to personalize the presentation of material. Moreover, with the growth of non-PC devices such as PDAs and cell phones, the limitations of heavy bitmaps become even more pronounced.

In an interview with the technology web site www.cnetnews.com, Chris Lilley, graphics activity lead for the W3C, commented on the importance of vector graphics on the Web. "Flash has shown that there is a definite need for vector graphics," said Lilley. "What people have found is they have existing XML infrastructure. So by using the same XML infrastructure for graphics as they are using for text and data, you can use the same tools. That's very powerful—it means it's no harder to have a graphical view of something than it is to have a textual view."

Until now, the vector images that exist on the Web have largely been rendered as Macromedia Flash illustrations and animations. Yet for all the "flash" of Macromedia's authoring tools, the format has never proliferated all that widely. Microsoft Internet Explorer has included support for its own vector format, VML, but that format has not caught on at all. An open standard that can be created by many tools is the obvious solution. This is especially true in the culture and approach of the Web, which has been based on open standards, most of which developed under the auspices of the W3C.

Advantages of SVG

General-purpose and specialized illustration programs have used vector graphics for years. In that sense, there's nothing new about the vector graphics aspect of SVG. Adobe Illustrator, among other programs, is based on vector graphics, as are specialized programs like AutoCAD. The revolution comes when this technology meets the Web. Suddenly a whole world of improved, nearly three-dimensional documents opens up—live documents and graphics that designers can change and manipulate without having to regenerate a whole new set of graphics, graphics that morph at the whim of consumer demand, graphics that download in significantly less time than current bitmap graphics.

This combination of speed, versatility, and artistic control gives the graphic designer a dramatically more powerful, perhaps even a revolutionary creative tool. Instead of static web images, drawn and created one at time, SVG gives the graphic designer the power to create and change multiple web images simply by entering new data.

Advantages of Quality and Performance

Not only does SVG give the graphic designer a faster, vastly more powerful web display, it also provides higher-quality graphics that will print more clearly and maintain a consistent resolution no matter the screen quality upon which they're viewed, no matter the size, no matter the dpi. That's the scalable part of scalable vector graphics. The image conforms to the new scale regardless of media, size, or screen quality.

Moreover, in the case of SVG graphics, less typically means more. While the bitmap formats GIF and JPG have excellent compression, the compression varies depending on the kind of illustration. Consider a very simple black-and-white illustration of a ruled line. This would actually compress very well in a GIF image, in this particular case, the GIF is going to be about 1/7 the size of the SVG image, because in this case the GIF uses compression to say, "Make a black pixel, then make 999 more just like it." SVG: 811 bytes, GIF: 51 bytes. Bitmap compression works best when you have a lot of adjacent pixels of the same color, as in this example.

The size advantage comes in with more complex documents, particularly those that use built-in SVG filters and primitives, because then you can say "make a circle with a blur" instead of having to spell out every pixel in a different shade of gray. In the case of the image in Figure 1-5, which shows a circle with a blur applied to its stroke, the SVG image is 1280 bytes, and the GIF is 6489 bytes—a significant size advantage for SVG in this instance.

SVG images then are sometimes smaller and sometimes larger than corresponding bitmap images, so SVG won't give an advantage every time. What this means, though, is that designers would have the option of creating a complex image in one format or another, and then actually using the one that offers the best compression.

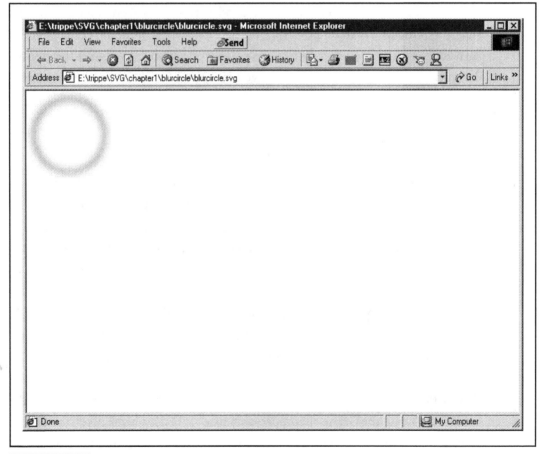

FIGURE 1-5 *Example of image that compresses better in SVG* ∎

It also means that some images that have traditionally been very large and hard to download can now be dramatically smaller and thus much more useful and easier to deploy.

SVG also provides several other practical benefits to the graphic designer:

- Use of familiar graphic-design software, most notably Adobe Illustrator and Corel Draw, to manipulate and create these files. While there are special tools for creating SVG images (and this book covers several of them), many people will want to use the tool that they already use for image preparation. Because SVG is a standard, support for it has already been built into several major products.

- Better work flow and less labor for graphic designers. An illustration created for print today needs to be separately saved in another format, often with different characteristics, for deployment on the Web. If the image changes, the entire workflow typically needs to be repeated, leading to tedious, expensive, time-consuming rework.

- Because SVG images can be managed as assets, and because SVG supports programming models such as the Document Object Model (DOM), designers can work in parallel with web site developers. While the developers are creating and updating the relevant code and data, the designer can be creating and updating the illustrations and animations. This is an improvement over situations where the work must be done in serial fashion—where first the designer works, then the developer, and so on.

SVG and Data-Driven Graphics

The fact SVG images can be data-driven—that is, the software creates images directly from the data provided—gives SVG graphics one of its biggest practical advantages over bitmap technology. While there are tools for creating bitmaps on the fly, they are typically limited to single-purpose tools, such as a tool we've used for creating math symbols directly from MathML-encoded data.

SVG files are XML-encoded text files, and, as you will see in coming chapters, human readable and human malleable. Just as it is easy for a savvy production person to change, for example, the size and style of text in an HTML file, it is similarly easy to make that kind of change in an SVG file. As a result, making SVG files "data driven" is really a matter of generating or regenerating the appropriate text string. Chapter 2 introduces you to XML encoding and to the basics of SVG, but to give you an idea of how SVG encapsulates text and graphics rendering in a text string, see the following:

```
<line x1="64" y1="189" x2="156" y2="189"
 style="fill:none;stroke:rgb(0,0,0);stroke-width:2"/>
```

As will be explained more in Chapter 2, this line of SVG instructs the software to draw a line, beginning at x,y position 64,189 and ending at x,y position 156,189. It goes on to describe the width of the line, whether it is filled or not, and in what color it should be rendered. If this string existed in a text file, it would be straightforward to edit; if a program were generating it, it would be straightforward to generate a slightly different string; and so on.

With the data encoded in SVG, any software that can interpret the SVG will generate the graphic. And once that the program generates the image, it can then be easily regenerated if the underlying data changes. The SVG-compliant software will automatically alter it to match new information. This feature alone will save graphic designers and the graphics department untold hours of labor. No more re-drawing an entire graphic or set of graphics when a detail changes. Just plug in the new numbers and a new graphic displaying the new information can be generated.

Data-driven graphics will be especially useful for web sites that track industries with rapidly changing statistics. Financial sites come to mind. Investors demand a wide range of financial information—interest rate changes from the Fed, stock prices, unemployment data, and a myriad of other always-changing statistics. Investors also demand varying snapshots of such data—differing frequencies, levels of detail, and so forth. Providing a graphical view of such data would be a significant advantage for a financial web site. SVG opens up the possibilities for the kinds of graphics that can be employed on a site, and how dynamically and flexibly they can be modified and displayed.

SVG and Interactive Graphics

One step beyond creating a data-driven graphic is to make a graphic interactive for the user. With a little bit of scripting, for example, a data-driven chart can easily be made interactive. For example, the seating chart described above is an excellent example of interactivity. The base SVG file, as we described it, is the stadium seating chart. By adding certain information—the dates for desired games—the base drawing can be regenerated, and then regenerated again when additional information is added (the price the fan is willing to pay, the need for proximity to the aisle, and so forth).

The early examples of SVG on the Web point to this kind of application. At the time we were writing this chapter, some of the better early SVG-driven sites are http://www.gis-news.de/svg/samples/karlsruhe/index.htm and http://www.dbxgeomatics.com/SVGMapGallery.asp?Language=EN.

Adobe's site (www.adobe.com/svg) also uses SVG for interactivity; one simple but effective graphic allows you to click on and view the name of a chemical to see its three-dimensional structure, and another allows you to see what an Airbus jet looks like with various exterior lights turned on and off.

SVG and Personalized Graphics

If interactive graphics are one step beyond data-driven graphics, personalized graphics are perhaps one step beyond interactive, or perhaps are a kind of interactive graphic. They imply some amount of interactivity in the same way personalized web text does. With a personalized web site such as www.amazon.com or my.yahoo.com, you have "opted in" and agreed to be profiled, at least to the extent that your browser passes on some information (through a cookie, for example). Or, you may have more explicitly provided some information from past orders, or by filling out a profile, or perhaps even by storing some data there. Either way, the web site is somehow able to identify you, and customize, or personalize, the experience for you accordingly.

Typically, such personalization is textual. The site www.amazon.com, for example, greets the return customer with "Hello (your name here)," and then proceeds to list "Your recommendations," "Your book store," and so forth. As shown in Figure 1-6, some of these personalized lists include graphics—a screen shot of a book cover, for example—but the graphic presentation itself is static from user to user. What if, instead, certain personalized graphics could be generated automatically? For example, as authors, we might like to see a customized bar chart showing all our books sold, by day, with certain colors displayed for sales exceeding certain thresholds. Or a buyer with an outstanding gift certificate might want to see a running balance, displayed as a graphic of a dollar bill with the precise balance showing.

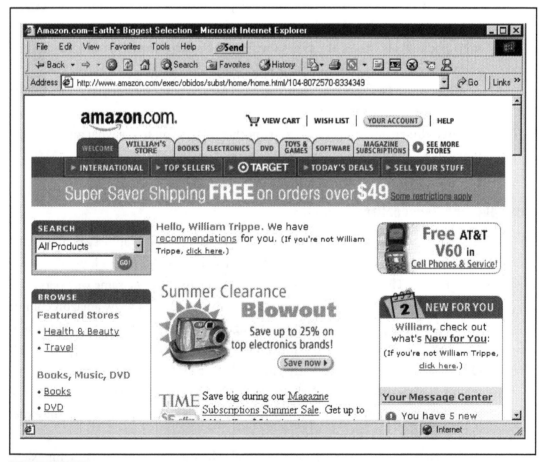

FIGURE 1-6   *Personalization such as with Amazon.com can be useful, but it is limited to the textual elements only.* ■

"Personalization" does not have to be just textual. It can target a specific individual or audience by

- *Demographic*   The customer who bought the box seats at the ball game gets the high-end local Mercedes ad included on their SVG ticket, while the customer who bought the cheap seats gets the $1 off coupon for a beer.

- *Culture*   The color red may be in poor taste in one culture, so it is replaced by something more suitable.

- *Language*   SVG's "systemLanguage" attribute can be used to detect the user's language and display text content in the correct language.

- *Accessibility*   Properly tagged content is readable by screen readers so that the visually impaired get as much info and interactivity from the graphic as anyone else. Note that not all screen readers can read SVG content—this is a plug-in-to-browser issue.

Potential Applications

Beyond the e-commerce potential discussed in the sports event scenario earlier, SVG-based graphics provide great possibilities for scientific and medical illustration, engineering documents, architectural plans—virtually any profession or academic field in which data-driven graphics help people understand information. Professions using heavy technical documentation have been slow to use the Web as publishing medium, precisely because browsers can't handle large, complex illustrations that are best rendered as vector graphics. SVG-based graphics typically require less disk space and memory, and are thus are more easily Web navigable.

Technical illustration is a good example of the kind of application that can take good advantage of SVG. An automotive manufacturer we have worked with does all of their parts illustrations in a sophisticated CAD-CAM system. When they are ready to publish the parts catalog in print and on the Web, they convert the CAD drawings to TIFF for the print catalog and to GIF for the online catalog. If an illustration changes, they need to go all the way back to the CAD system and regenerate the illustration in both formats. The GIF files are less than satisfactory for the Web, however, as they are often too big and unwieldy. The lower-resolution display available through the browser, and the more limited screen size, make it very difficult to satisfactorily view a large-format, detailed illustration (see Figure 1-7).

SVG-based graphics can allow, among other things, for the technical illustration to be created once and stored in a single format. The same file can drive both print and web display, and a change can be made to the single file and easily deployed to the systems that need it. Finally, because SVG graphics scale to the display, they can be more effectively rendered, zoomed, and printed.

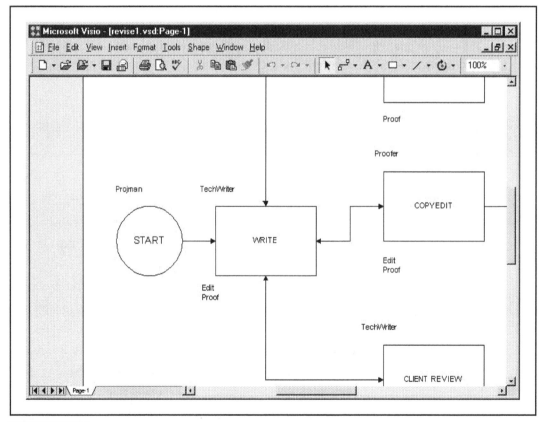

FIGURE 1-7   *With SVG, a larger, detailed technical illustration, such as a workflow diagram, can be very effectively viewed on the Web.* ∎

Conclusion

Ultimately, SVG will prove itself in how it is used in real-world applications. The compelling thing is that SVG is an entirely open, entirely textual format. It can be easily generated from a database for applications such as dynamic page serving. It can also be modified on the fly for such applications as personalization.

If you visit the Adobe site, (or any other SVG-powered site) you'll confront one of the few things standing in SVG's way—it requires that you download a browser plug-in. We expect this requirement to go away in some future version of Internet Explorer, which should add SVG rendering. In the meantime, this lack of browser support will create some hesitancy in the market. However, Adobe does have a track record of creating a product that people are willing to separately download and use; when last we checked, Acrobat had reached more than 110 million downloads.

The other practical challenge is a relative lack of tools for creating SVG, but this is changing quickly. As mentioned above, though, Adobe is building SVG support into their products, as is Corel. Perhaps more significantly, database vendors and content management companies are adding SVG support, as they understand how central SVG is likely to become to web development and publishing.

chapter 2

Understanding XML

XML, or eXtensible Markup Language, is arguably the most important development in web technology since HTML. Ironically, though, it has remained the almost exclusive province of programmers and database developers. This differs markedly from HTML, which is a ready tool for design and production personnel, many of whom are now as well versed in web production as they are in print production.

This lack of full understanding of XML among design and production personnel has had a small but noticeable impact on how XML is being used. XML has become largely a tool for programmers to use in such technical componentry as server-to-server communication and database interfacing. While this is not a bad thing, it is a decidedly different thing from how XML was conceived, which was as the next step in web markup—to move beyond HTML and to an *extensible* markup language that would allow developers to conceive and implement web sites that have rich semantic meaning. This semantic meaning would come from developers developing and extending their markup—principally their tags (more properly called *elements*) and attributes.

We think this will change over time, though, and that design and production personnel will use XML more in the course of their web site development. There is a growing list of design-focused technologies that use XML as their core, with SVG being perhaps the most important one to date. This chapter, then, serves as an *introduction* to XML. As such, it is not meant to be an exhaustive discussion about XML, as there are many good books that handle XML in detail, such as *XML: A Beginner's Guide* by David Mercer and *XML: The Complete Reference* by Heather Williamson (both published by Osborne/McGraw-Hill, 2001). Instead, this chapter has two goals:

- To convey enough essential information about XML to help you understand how XML is used as the underlying technology for SVG.

- To demonstrate XML in action, along with some methods for displaying XML in web browsers.

These two things together will provide the necessary foundation for understanding SVG, along with enough other background to give you ideas for using XML elsewhere in your web applications.

Just Enough XML

XML may be the latest, greatest thing, but it has its roots in mature technology that has been solving problems since the days of mainframes and minicomputers. Indeed, XML is already five years old, and is itself the progeny of a technology called *SGML*, the Standard Generalized Markup Language, which has been an International Standards Organization (ISO) standard since the mid-1980s.

SGML and XML both have the same goal, which is to give content developers and programmers a means by which they can tag data for both meaning and structure. Where HTML is really a markup language for formatting data for browser presentation, SGML and XML both have this more abstract goal of allowing developers to develop tag sets that structure and describe the *meaning* of content.

XML versus HTML

Take, for example, how you might format a list of addresses in HTML. I happen to like the list-like formatting you get with the definition list <DL> and accompanying Definition tag <DD>, so I could create some HTML like this:

```
<html>
<head>
<title>Sample Address List</title>
</head>
<body>
```

```
<H1>Sample Address List </H1>
<DL style="FONT-FAMILY: Courier; FONT-SIZE: 12pt">
<DD><B>Jones, Casey</B><BR>
844 Rush St.<BR>
Chicago, IL 60611 </DD></DL>
<DL style="FONT-FAMILY: Courier; FONT-SIZE: 12pt">
<DD><B>Public, John</B>
10 Main St<BR>
Anytown, CO 80000 </DD></DL></body>
</html>
```

On most browsers, that HTML will appear as shown in Figure 2-1.

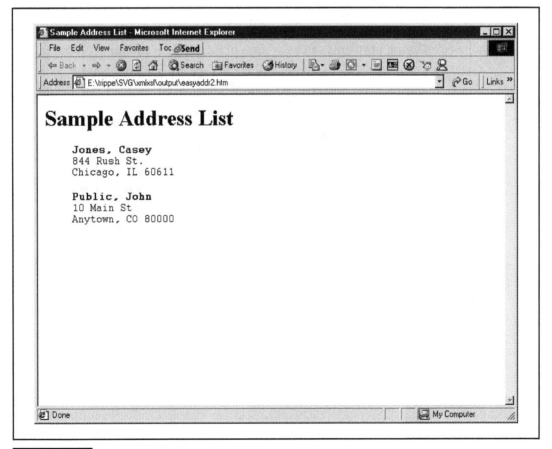

FIGURE 2-1   *HTML display of the sample address list* ∎

No harm, no foul, right? The HTML displays perfectly well, doesn't it? Well, yes, it does. And if this were the only thing you were ever going to do with this address list, you would be fine. However, many—perhaps even most—applications require information to be reused. What works on the web site might not work in the printed directory, or on the handheld presentation, and so on. And beyond these issues of *multimedia publishing and presentation* are even subtler issues of *application integration*. The name and address list may need to move from my copy of Microsoft Outlook to your copy of Act!, or from one Human Resources database to another, and so on.

This is where XML comes in, along with its ability to allow developers to invent markup languages that capture the real structure of the data and to apply meaningful element names ("tags") to the data. Here is what the address list might look like in XML:

```
<?xml version="1.0" standalone="yes"?>
<ADDRESSES>
      <TITLE>Sample Address List</TITLE>
      <ADDRESS>
           <LAST>Jones</LAST>
           <FIRST>Casey</FIRST>
           <STREET>844 Rush St.</STREET>
           <CITY>Chicago</CITY>
           <STATE>IL</STATE>
           <ZIP>60611</ZIP>
      </ADDRESS>
      <ADDRESS>
           <LAST>Public</LAST>
           <FIRST>John</FIRST>
           <STREET>10 Main St</STREET>
           <CITY>Anytown</CITY>
           <STATE>CO</STATE>
           <ZIP>80000</ZIP>
      </ADDRESS>
</ADDRESSES>
```

We will explain the details of this XML file more in the next section, but a few things are worth noting:

- The specific tag names for the data—"last," "first," street," and "state."

- The hierarchical structure. The overall document is one unit ("addresses") consisting of a "title" and a set of "address" elements.

- The file itself is carefully formed—all the start and end tags are there, they are all in one case (in this instance, uppercase), and there are no tags that incorrectly overlap (for example, the end tag for "city" appears before the start tag for "state" begins. In XML parlance, this is known as "well-formed" XML, and this is a requirement for XML files to be successfully processed.

- Most importantly, *the complete lack of formatting information.*

XML's Advantages over HTML

Well if XML is so great, why does it just sit there, unformatted? As we will demonstrate later, XML data needs some kind of style sheet to be displayed as anything more than as text and markup. At first blush, this would seem to be a limitation more than an advantage, but in fact, this separation of content from format is extremely powerful for content development and for applications of all kinds. By separating content from format, you are creating content that can be reused liberally. The XML-encoded address list is ready to be published in print, in various flavors of HTML, in wireless formats such as WAP, and in many other formats that we don't even know about yet.

In addition to separating content from format, XML is also more machine-readable and machine-processable than HTML. Think back to our discussion of "well-formed" XML, and its rules for the precise organization of files. This differs markedly from HTML, which is much more forgiving of mistakes such as missing end tags, incorrectly formed tags, and missing quotes around attributes. XML must be at least well formed, thus making it more machine-processable than HTML and other publishing formats. The strict rules governing an XML file make the job of a computer program that handles the file that much easier.

In fact, developers can make XML files more than well formed. XML files can be made to conform to even stricter rules and organization by applying either a Document Type Definition (DTD) or an XML schema to the processing. DTDs and schemas do essentially the same thing, which is to describe a formal set of rules for the XML markup. They define which elements will appear, in what contexts they can appear, and in what order they appear relative to one another. Both DTDs and schemas are viable ways to add this kind of validation to your XML, with DTDs being the more established technology. For example, a DTD for the address list we have been analyzing might look something like this:

```
<!DOCTYPE ADDRESSES [
    <!ELEMENT ADDRESSES (TITLE, ADDRESS+)>
    <!ELEMENT TITLE (#PCDATA)>
    <!ELEMENT ADDRESS (LAST, FIRST, STREET+, CITY, STATE, ZIP)>
    <!ELEMENT LAST (#PCDATA)>
    <!ELEMENT FIRST (#PCDATA)>
    <!ELEMENT STREET (#PCDATA)>
    <!ELEMENT CITY (#PCDATA)>
    <!ELEMENT STATE (#PCDATA)>
    <!ELEMENT ZIP (#PCDATA)>
]>
```

Let's look at this in enough detail to understand how a DTD can apply more stringent rules to XML data. For example, examine the following line:

```
<!ELEMENT ADDRESSES (TITLE, ADDRESS+)>
```

This line declares that the file containing addresses must start with the <ADDRESSES> tag, which must then contain a <TITLE> element followed by one or more <ADDRESS> elements. (The "+" symbol following ADDRESS indicates that the element must occur once and can occur more than once; the absence of a symbol after TITLE indicates that it must appear exactly once.)

Let's look at the next line, which defines what the address element itself can contain:

```
<!ELEMENT ADDRESS (LAST, FIRST, STREET+, CITY, STATE, ZIP)>
```

The "+" symbol, as with ADDRESS+ above, indicates that the STREET element can appear one or more times. (A question mark would mean that it could appear zero or one times; see summary below.) This would allow, for example, a person to include more than one line of their street address. The following table contains some basic XML syntax:

Symbol	Meaning
?	Element can appear zero or one times.
+	Element must appear once, and can appear more than once.
*	Element can appear zero, one, or more times.
,	Separated elements appear in the order listed.
|	Separated elements can appear in either order.

The last sort of element type declarations you need to understand are ones that declare the content of an element is not other elements, but in fact is text. Thus

```
<!ELEMENT LAST (#PCDATA)>
<!ELEMENT FIRST (#PCDATA)>
```

These two lines indicate that the elements LAST and FIRST both consist of text.

If we were to look at a fragment of our XML file from above, then, we would see that it in fact conforms to the rules of this DTD we have presented:

```
<?xml version="1.0" standalone="yes"?>
<ADDRESSES>
      <TITLE>Sample Address List</TITLE>
      <ADDRESS>
            <LAST>Jones</LAST>
            <FIRST>Casey</FIRST>
            <STREET>844 Rush St.</STREET>
            <CITY>Chicago</CITY>...
```

Note that this XML is following the rules of the DTD. In other words, this file is "valid," which is the more stringent form of XML data beyond being "well formed." When XML data is valid, it conforms to the rules of a DTD or schema. Such validity allows for even more processability. A program can first interpret the rules of the DTD and *then* process the data. Because of the formal rules in the DTD, such a program can then know precisely what data will be in the file, and can process the data based on knowing the full data structure, including the parent/child and sibling/sibling relationships that exist in the data. As such, the XML data can be manipulated quite flexibly. A script could be written to select and somehow process only the last names, only the first names, or the first names with phone numbers, and so forth.

Elements and Attributes

We've introduced the more formal name "element" to refer to the tags that appear in an XML file. In fact, tags often include both elements and *attributes*, which should be very familiar from any HTML work you have done. For example, the tag used for linking in HTML (the "a" element) makes significant use of the attribute "href":

```
<A HREF="target.html">
```

In XML terminology, "A" is the *element*, "HREF" is the *attribute*, and "target.html" is the *value* of the attribute "href." Note also, as mentioned above, that XML is specific in its requirement that all attribute values be enclosed in quotes. If attribute values are not properly enclosed in quotes, the XML file is not well-formed and will fail to process.

Understanding XML and Style Sheets

So far we have discussed XML—how it is different from HTML, and what advantages it has over HTML. The next important aspect of XML, as it relates to design and production staff, is how it ends up published in a browser window.

An XML file, without any kind of style sheet, is very uninteresting when presented in a browser window, as shown in Figure 2-2.

To provide some styling for a browser presentation, you have the option of marrying your XML with either cascading style sheets (CSS) or an eXtensible style sheet language (XSL). For our example, we will use XSL style sheets, which will format the data much as the original HTML file we showed above.

In fact, XSL is a bit of a misnomer. There are in fact two kinds of XSL—XSLT, which stands for XSL *Transformations,* and XSL-FO, which stands for XSL Formatting Objects. We'll provide examples of both, which will give you an idea of the flexibility of XML and XSL.

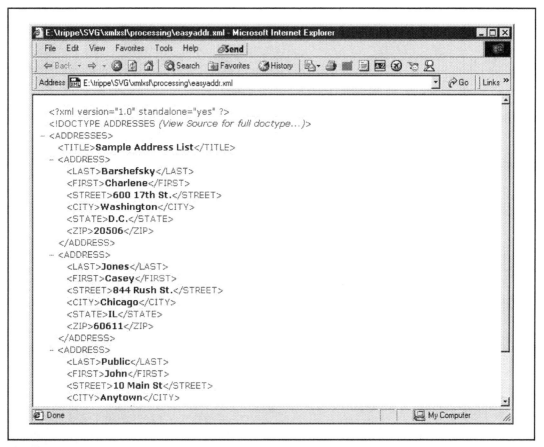

FIGURE 2-2 *XML file displayed in Internet Explorer with no style sheet* ∎

As we've said, on its own, XML data just sits there—tidy, well-organized and self-describing—but it still just sits there. Yet XML is an expanding technology not for what it does itself; it is important because of the many related technologies and standards now coming to light. At the very least, you need to be able to format data for presentation and shape it into any other necessary forms. This is where XSL comes in, and, in particular its offshoot language, XSLT.

This talk of *transformation* probably seems too abstract, or too precious. But, in fact, the word "transformation" has been used with XML since its inception and earlier than that with SGML, XML's predecessor. The question about XML data always has been, "What can I do with it?" The first answer has always been, "Transform it into something else," such as HTML for a web presentation or PDF for print.

What does XSLT Do? The World Wide Web Consortium (W3C) Recommendation describes XSLT as "a language for transforming XML documents into other XML documents." As such, it is not intended to be a general-purpose language for transforming XML into anything and everything. There are already many XSLT-based products and other tools for such applications as moving data between XML and EDI systems, XML and common document formats, such as Microsoft Word, and XML and relational database structures.

The concepts are pretty straightforward. As we've shown, XML data can be traversed, among other ways, as a hierarchy, or tree structure. For instance, you can think of the address list as one big tree, with each address being a branch, and elements of each address being smaller branches, and so on. In this example, you could use XSLT to traverse the addresses to select and manipulate each name and phone number, or each name and ZIP code, or each name, phone number, and ZIP code.

Now to make this XML data viewable in, say, a browser window, you would need to somehow transform this data to HTML tags and text. The following style sheet does precisely this:

```
<?xml version="1.0"?>
<!—Sample XSLT stylesheet - Address list XML to HTML —>
<xsl:stylesheet xmlns:xsl="http://www.w3.org/1999/XSL/Transform"
                version="1.0">
<xsl:output method="html" encoding="ISO-8859-1"/>

<!— root rule —>
<xsl:template match="/">
<HTML>
 <HEAD>
  <TITLE>
    <xsl:value-of select="ADDRESSES/TITLE"/>
  </TITLE>
 </HEAD>
 <BODY BGCOLOR="#FFFFFF">
  <H1>
    <xsl:value-of select="ADDRESSES/TITLE"/>
```

```
   </H1>
   <xsl:for-each select="ADDRESSES/ADDRESS">
    <DL STYLE="font-family:Courier; font-size:12pt;">
     <DD><B><xsl:value-of select="LAST"/><xsl:text>, </xsl:text></B>
      <B><xsl:value-of select="FIRST"/></B><BR/>
      <xsl:value-of select="STREET"/><BR/>
      <xsl:value-of select="CITY"/><xsl:text>, </xsl:text>
      <xsl:value-of select="STATE"/><xsl:text> </xsl:text>
      <xsl:value-of select="ZIP"/>
     </DD>
    </DL>
   </xsl:for-each>
  </BODY>
 </HTML>
 </xsl:template>
 </xsl:stylesheet>
```

There's a great deal going on in this brief code example. Let's look at key elements of it so you understand XSLT's key features.

The first few lines basically declare that this is an XSL style sheet, which is going to output HTML (xsl:output method="html").

```
<?xml version="1.0"?>
<!—Sample XSLT stylesheet - Address list XML to HTML —>
<xsl:stylesheet xmlns:xsl="http://www.w3.org/1999/XSL/Transform"
                version="1.0">
<xsl:output method="html" encoding="ISO-8859-1"/>
```

The style sheet then goes into a series of rules that essentially output HTML tags and text that has been selected from the XML source file. This is a key concept, and is first illustrated with the following:

```
<HTML>
 <HEAD>
  <TITLE>
    <xsl:value-of select="ADDRESSES/TITLE"/>
  </TITLE>
 </HEAD>
```

When processed, this style sheet will output the HTML tags shown, together with the text (from the XML file) contained in the TITLE element. Thus, the text, "Sample Address List" that occurs within the TITLE element will be included here, resulting in an output stream as follows:

```
<HTML>
 <HEAD>
  <TITLE>
    Sample Address List
  </TITLE>
 </HEAD>
```

In other words, the HTML file that is produced by running this XSL file on the XML file would begin with the HTML as shown above. The XSL file continues, with a slightly more complex rule for how it is going to handle each of the address elements:

```
<xsl:for-each select="ADDRESSES/ADDRESS">
 <DL STYLE="font-family:Courier; font-size:12pt;">
  <DD><B><xsl:value-of select="LAST"/><xsl:text>, </xsl:text></B>
   <B><xsl:value-of select="FIRST"/></B><BR/>
   <xsl:value-of select="STREET"/><BR/>
   <xsl:value-of select="CITY"/><xsl:text>, </xsl:text>
   <xsl:value-of select="STATE"/><xsl:text> </xsl:text>
   <xsl:value-of select="ZIP"/>
  </DD>
 </DL>
```

The key to understanding this part of the style sheet is to understand the first line: `<xsl:for-each select="ADDRESSES/ADDRESS">`

This is a for-each statement, which programmers know to mean, "for each of the elements that follow…" and is usually followed by some kind of a "do statement". In this case, the elements that will be acted will be each "address": each address will be processed accordingly. The "do" statement for each address will be for the style sheet to emit HTML tags, together with text from the child elements of the address element.

Thus, the XSL code

```
<DD><B><xsl:value-of select="LAST"/><xsl:text>, </xsl:text></B>
 <B><xsl:value-of select="FIRST"/></B><BR/>
 <xsl:value-of select="STREET"/><BR/>
 <xsl:value-of select="CITY"/><xsl:text>, </xsl:text>
 <xsl:value-of select="STATE"/><xsl:text> </xsl:text>
 <xsl:value-of select="ZIP"/>
```

will result in the following output in the HTML file for each address in the XML file:

```
<DL STYLE="font-family:Courier; font-size:12pt;">
<DD><B>Jones, </B><B>Casey</B><BR>844 Rush St.<BR>Chicago, IL 60611</DD>
</DL>
```

The resulting HTML file is shown in full here, and then, in Figure 2-3, as it would be displayed:

```
<HTML>
<HEAD>
<META http-equiv="Content-Type" content="text/html; charset=ISO-8859-1">
<TITLE>Sample Address List</TITLE>
</HEAD>
<BODY BGCOLOR="#FFFFFF">
<H1>Sample Address List</H1>
<DL STYLE="font-family:Courier; font-size:12pt;">
<DD><B>Jones, </B><B>Casey</B><BR>844 Rush St.<BR>Chicago, IL 60611</DD>
</DL>
<DL STYLE="font-family:Courier; font-size:12pt;">
<DD><B>Public, </B><B>John</B><BR>10 Main St<BR>Anytown, CO 80000</DD>
</DL>
</BODY>
</HTML>
```

It's worth reminding you at this point that you don't need to learn XSL to learn SVG. Indeed, the basic XML syntax you have learned already is enough to enable your understanding of SVG. At the same time, though, it is worth understanding this basic principle of XSL, and how it can be used to manipulate XML. Why?

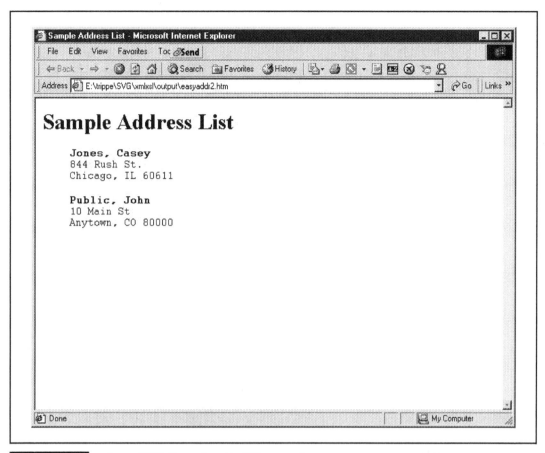

FIGURE   2-3   *Output HTML file produced by XSL processing* ∎

- XSL is already the primary mechanism for manipulating XML data. Even if you don't end up writing XSL programs yourself, it will be good for you to understand how XML data can be manipulated.

- This example here is only one of potentially unlimited ways that the single XML file could be transformed into HTML. It could be converted using different HTML tags, or it could even be converted with different parts of the XML file being used. For example, one HTML version could be created with first and last names only, one with last names and phone numbers only, and so forth. The possibilities, even in this simple file, are endless.

Learning More about XSL

Processing XSL requires a specialized tool, and there are many of them available. Indeed, since there are both XSLT and XSL-FO to deal with, there are in fact specialized tools for each. For an excellent starting point, see the XSL resources section on the web site www.xml.com (http://www.xml.com/pub/rg/XSL).

For these examples, we processed the XML and XSL on a Windows machine using Microsoft's MSXSL.EXE Command Line Transformation Utility (see http://msdn.microsoft.com/downloads/default.asp?URL=/downloads/sample.asp?url=/MSDN-FILES/027/001/485/msdncompositedoc.xml). This is a command-line wrapper that takes advantage of XSL processing code that is installed with Microsoft Internet Explorer. It allows you to, as in these examples, use XSL to process XML files into various output HTML files.

If you would like to learn more about XSL, we suggest you consider one of the following books:

- *The XML Bible*, by Elliotte Rusty Harold (Hungry Minds, 2001)

- *XSLT Quickly*, by Bob Ducharme (Manning Publications, 2001)

- *XSLT*, by Doug Tidwell, (O'Reilly and Associates, 2001)

Understanding Namespaces

A namespace is a clever little bit of technology that, in short, allows developers to mix different types of data into a single file. This is important, as web pages are already complex mixes of HTML and code (for example, JavaScript), and are beginning to add additional kinds of data, such as XML. With the advent of specialized XML vocabularies like SVG and MathML (XML for creating equations), web pages are going to become increasingly complex. Namespaces are a method to formally tell the processing software, such as the browser, that a web page contains more than one kind of data.

Namespaces do this by adding a system of prefixes to elements and attributes. Here's a simple example of a web page that combines data with elements from two sources—from the HTML DTD and from a specialized DTD for recipes:

```
<?xml version="1.0" encoding="UTF-8"?>
<h:html xmlns:nmp="http://www.nmpub.com/recipes"
        xmlns:h="http://www.w3.org/HTML/1998/html4">
 <h:head><h:title>Favorite Pastas</h:title></h:head>
 <h:body>
  <nmp:recipe>
   <h:title>Chicken, Broccoli, and Ziti</h:title>
   <h:ul>
      <h:li><nmp:ingredient>Lots of Chicken</nmp:ingredient></h:li>
      <h:li><nmp:ingredient>Lots of Broccoli</nmp:ingredient></h:li>
      <h:li><nmp:ingredient>Lots and lots of Ziti</nmp:ingredient></h:li>
      </h:ul>
  </nmp:recipe>
 </h:body>
</h:html>
```

In the above example, the element names preceded by "h:" come from the HTML DTD, which can be found at the URL listed in the third line (http://www.w3.org/HTML/1998/html4). The elements preceded by "nmp:" come from the specialized recipe DTD that can be found at the URL listed on the second line (http://www.nmpub.com/recipes).

Thus, the following elements are HTML:

- <h:head> (the HTML *head* tag)

- <h:title> (the HTML *title* tag)

- <h:body> (the HTML *body* tag)

- <h:ul> (the HTML *unordered list* tag)

- <h:li> (the HTML *list item* tag)

The remaining elements are XML elements from the recipe DTD:

- <nmp:recipe> (the *recipe* element)

- <nmp:ingredient> (the *ingredient* element)

A less than technical way of explaining this is to say that a namespace is a way of saying, "the following element comes from..." (fill in the blank—"this HTML," "this XML DTD," and so forth) It is intended to deal with the confusion when a web page combines elements from several sources, and the different types of data need to be processed differently. The browser, for example, needs to know that some elements are to be interpreted as HTML and rendered accordingly, and others are to be interpreted as SVG and thus handled differently, and so on.

Looking Under the Hood at SVG Files

As we discussed in Chapter 1, SVG is significant for many reasons, not the least of which is that complex, high-quality illustrations can now be rendered from concise, human-readable text files. This opens the door to many applications, ranging from data-driven graphics to interactive illustrations and animations. But before one learns to run, one must learn to crawl. This section walks you through the basics of the SVG file format, focusing on the core syntax of the files and the creation of basic illustrations.

To get started, download the appropriate Adobe SVG Viewer (available at http://www.adobe.com/svg/viewer/install/) for your computer and operating system. We also recommend you do some of these early examples with a favorite text editor (for example, Notepad or SimpleText) in order to understand how to write simple SVG content. We will discuss how to use illustration tools to design sophisticated graphics later in this book.

The Primary Tags, Including <svg>, <g>, <text>, and <style>

Authors of programming books like to begin to explain a new language by showing how one would write a simple program using the new language. The classic example is a program that does nothing more than print the expression, "Hello, World!" Here, then, is the SVG version of this programming classic:

```
<?xml version="1.0" standalone="no"?>
<!DOCTYPE svg PUBLIC "-//W3C//DTD SVG 1.0//EN"
```

```
"http://www.w3.org/TR/2001/REC-SVG-20010904/DTD/svg10.dtd">
<svg width="200" height="200">
      <text fill="rgb(255,0,0)" font-size="24" font-family="Arial"
      x="30px" y="60px">Hello, World!</text>
</svg>
```

It doesn't get any simpler than that. This bit of code is going to create an image measuring 200 pixels by 200 pixels, and begin a text string at an x,y position of 30,60. It will then create red text, 24 points high, using the font-family Arial, and spell out "Hello, World!" as shown in Figure 2-4.

If you've downloaded the SVG Viewer from Adobe, you can enter the above code in a text file, name it smallworld.svg, point your browser at it, and view the same file you see in the figure. You can also load this code into an SVG editing or creation tool, such as Jasc WebDraw, if you already have one.

FIGURE 2-4   *Example SVG, "helloworld.svg"* ∎

Some Simple Examples of SVG

Let's look now at a slightly more complex example, where we combine text with a simple figure—in this case, a rectangle with color. Here is what the SVG code would look like:

```
<?xml version="1.0" standalone="no"?>
<!DOCTYPE svg PUBLIC "-//W3C//DTD SVG 1.0//EN"
    "http://www.w3.org/TR/2001/REC-SVG-20010904/DTD/svg10.dtd">
<svg width="200" height="200">
    <text x="82px" y="55px" style="fill:rgb(0,0,0);
    font-size:30;font-family:Arial">SVG?</text>
    <rect x="58px" y="97px" width="108" height="76"
    style="fill:rgb(0,0,255);stroke:rgb(0,0,0);
        stroke-width:0"/>
</svg>
```

And Figure 2-5 shows what the resulting image would look like.

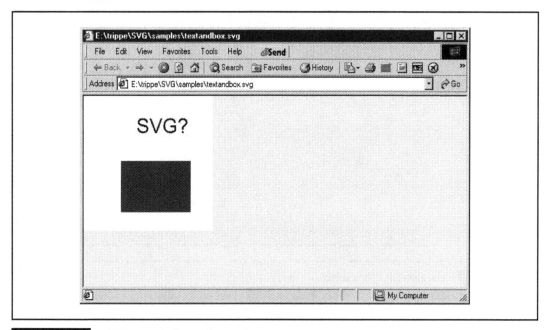

FIGURE 2-5   *SVG example, "textandbox.svg"* ∎

Let's look at this code in detail. The first two lines simply indicate this is an XML file that is going to follow the SVG DTD. In other words, these two lines formally declare that this is an SVG file:

```
<?xml version="1.0" standalone="no"?>
<!DOCTYPE svg PUBLIC "-//W3C//DTD SVG 1.0//EN"
 "http://www.w3.org/TR/2001/REC-SVG-20010904/DTD/svg10.dtd">
```

The next line then begins the SVG image itself, and declares that it is going to be 200 pixels by 200 pixels. Note that the file later finishes with the close SVG tag.

```
<svg width="200" height="200">
```

The next line should be familiar from our "Hello, World" example. It indicates some text is going to begin at x,y position 82,55, in font-family Arial, with a point size of 30.

```
<text x="82px" y="55px" style="fill:rgb(0,0,0);
 font-size:30;font-family:Arial">SVG?</text>
```

Finally, we have our first bit of graphical rendering, a rectangle. This line indicates that a rectangle is going to be drawn beginning at x,y position 58,97, with a width of 108 pixels and a height of 76 pixels. The rectangle will be drawn in solid blue (fill:rgb(0,0,255)), with no border (stroke-width:0).

```
<rect x="58px" y="97px" width="108" height="76"
 style="fill:rgb(0,0,255);stroke:rgb(0,0,0);stroke-width:0"/>
```

Another Example, with Additional Elements

Let's take the same example above, the text and box, and add one more simple element to it—in this case, a ruled line. The code would be as follows:

```
<?xml version="1.0" standalone="no"?>
<!DOCTYPE svg PUBLIC "-//W3C//DTD SVG 1.0//EN"
 "http://www.w3.org/TR/2001/REC-SVG-20010904/DTD/svg10.dtd">
<svg width="200" height="200">
<text x="82px" y="55px" style="fill:rgb(0,0,0);font-size:30;
```

```
font-family:Arial">SVG?</text>
<rect x="58px" y="97px" width="108" height="76"
 style="fill:rgb(0,0,255);stroke:rgb(0,0,0);stroke-width:0"/>
<line x1="64" y1="189" x2="156" y2="189"
 style="fill:none;stroke:rgb(0,0,0);stroke-width:2"/>
</svg>
```

And Figure 2-6 shows what the resulting image would look like.

The line rendering adds exactly one line to the SVG file, which you may be able to interpret already:

```
<line x1="64" y1="189" x2="156" y2="189"
 style="fill:none;stroke:rgb(0,0,0);stroke-width:2"/>
```

This line indicates that a black line (stroke:rgb(0,0,0)) will be drawn beginning at x,y position 64,189 and continuing to x,y position 156,189 (x2... y2...).

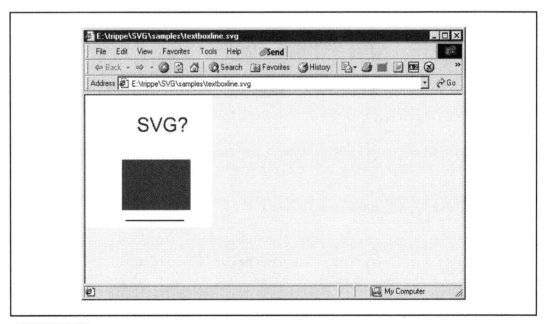

FIGURE 2-6 *SVG Example, "textboxline.svg"* ∎

Creating and Displaying an SVG File

Part 2 of this book will give you detailed instructions for creating and editing SVG files in several commercial editing products. This section gives some basic guidelines for creating and editing SVG files in a text editor, viewing them in the Adobe SVG Viewer, and troubleshooting basic problems with files you have been editing.

SVG files are text files, and thus can be created and saved in any text editor. On a Windows system, you could use Microsoft Notepad or a favorite HTML editor; on a Macintosh system, you could use SimpleText (pre-OS X), TextEdit in OS X, or the ever-popular BBEdit (www.barebones.com); on a UNIX or Linux system you could use vi, emacs, or any conforming text editor. Most of the examples in this chapter were created with Microsoft Notepad, and the results viewed in the Adobe SVG Viewer. A few were created with the Jasc WebDraw editor. Finally, some of them were opened and touched up with Altova's XML Spy, which is a general-purpose XML editor that also can create and edit SVG files, and has a built-in version of the Adobe SVG Viewer.

A few guidelines to keep in mind:

- Be sure to save the files with the .svg extension.

- Develop some good habits for formatting your files. For example, include a carriage return before the start of a new tag.

- Learn how to comment your SVG files, and comment liberally. SVG comments take the same form as HTML or XML comments, beginning with "<!—" and ending with —>"; thus a valid comment would take the form

```
<!– this is a comment –>
```

As shown here, the basic structure of an SVG file includes the opening XML processing instruction, the *document type declaration* that invokes the SVG data model, and the opening SVG tag:

```
<?xml version="1.0" standalone="no"?>
<!DOCTYPE svg PUBLIC "-//W3C//DTD SVG 1.0//EN"
```

```
"http://www.w3.org/TR/2001/REC-SVG-20010904/DTD/svg10.dtd">
<svg width="200" height="200">
```

The SVG file then needs to conclude with the ending SVG tag:

```
</svg>
```

The first lines establish to the processing application that the file is an SVG file, and conforms to the SVG DTD (http://www.w3.org/TR/2001/REC-SVG-20010904/DTD/svg10.dtd). The SVG tag itself then has two required attributes, width and height.

Anything else you add to the file then comes between the start SVG tag and end SVG tag.

- Experiment first with small simple files as shown above. By the time you are working with and developing longer files, you will probably want to use a commercial editing application.

- All the files listed in this chapter are available for download at www.svgfordesigners.com/chapter2.

- Assuming you have installed the SVG Viewer from Adobe (available at http://www.adobe.com/svg/viewer/install/), you should be able to view any SVG file through your browser.

Modifying, Redisplaying, and Troubleshooting an Existing SVG File

Modifying and redisplaying an SVG file should be straightforward. You should be able to save the SVG file and refresh the browser to load the newly saved file.

Troubleshooting is not always as straightforward, depending on the type of error and the complexity of the file. Consider the following code, which is identical to the file "textboxline.svg" shown above, except that it is missing closing quotes on one of the attributes:

```
<?xml version="1.0" standalone="no"?>
<!DOCTYPE svg PUBLIC "-//W3C//DTD SVG 1.0//EN"
 "http://www.w3.org/TR/2001/REC-SVG-20010904/DTD/svg10.dtd">
```

```
<svg width="200" height="200">

<!- this is a comment ->
     <text x="82px" y="55px" style="fill:rgb(0,0,0);

      font-size:30;font-family:Arial">SVG?</text>
     <rect x="58px" y="97px" width="108" height="76"
      style="fill:rgb(0,0,255);stroke:rgb(0,0,0);
           stroke-width:0"/>
     <line x1="64" y1="189" x2="156" y2="189"
      style="fill:none;stroke:rgb(0,0,0);stroke-width:2/>
</svg>
```

Note that the last attribute value, for "style" in the "line" element is missing the closing quote that should appear after the numeral 2. If you attempt to view this in the Adobe Viewer, the image will display, minus the ruled line at the bottom, but without an error message. However, once you mouse over the image, or right-click it, you will see on the status bar at the bottom of the screen, "not well-formed: line 12, column 0." If you were to then count lines (or had a line count displayable in your editor), you would see that line 12 is actually where the close SVG tag appears. The error is not there, but on the line prior to it, where the attribute value was not properly quoted.

You can see, then, that a specialized tool for editing the SVG may be in order—not that these are always perfectly helpful. For example, JASC WebDraw issues the following error message for that same error:

```
Line 12, Column 2: A '<' character cannot be used in
attribute 'style', except through &lt;
```

Note this tool is also complaining about line 12, even though the error is on line 11. It does, though, suspect the problem has something to do with the style attribute. Specifically, it is complaining about the "<" character at the beginning of line 12 as if it were part of the style attribute. (Believe it or not, this is more helpful, as it should suggest to you that the parser doesn't consider the style attribute to be properly closed. And if you remember your rules for creating well-formed XML, you'll remember that all attributes need to be properly quoted. Still, this probably seems like a lot of trouble over a missing quote...)

This difficulty in troubleshooting is one of the reasons we devote several chapters of this book to using various commercial tools for creating and editing SVG files. However, if you want to use a text or code editor, we recommend you use one that helps you properly quote attribute values, and that prompts you for closing tags. An XML editor like XML Spy will also check for validity and give you the kinds of error messages that Jasc WebDraw produces.

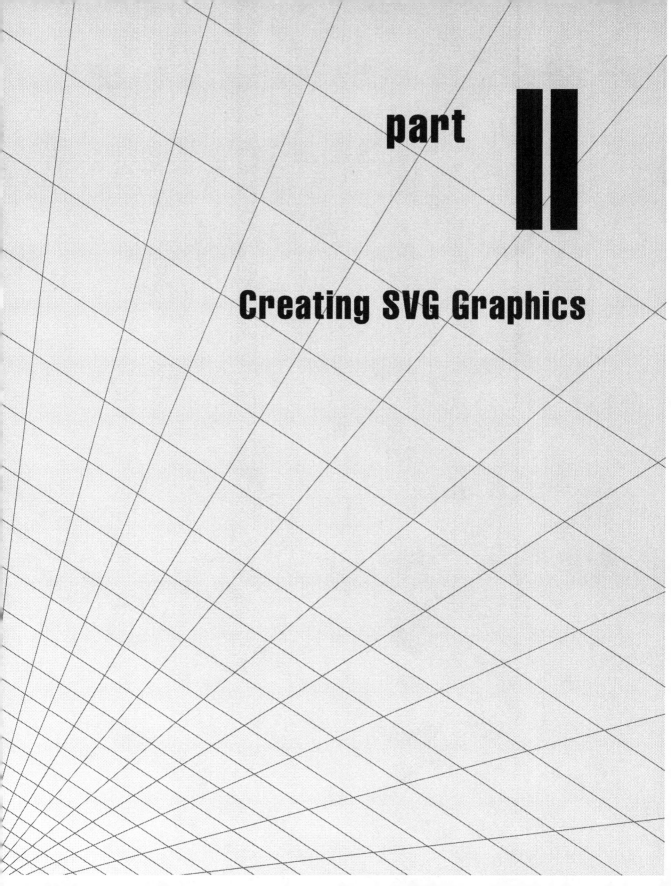

part II

Creating SVG Graphics

chapter **3**

Creating SVG Images
with Jasc WebDraw

As the only full-fledged drawing program designed specifically for creating SVG images, Jasc WebDraw should be part of every web designer's toolkit. It runs on Windows only, and is at version 1.1 as this book is written.

WebDraw is the only illustration program that reads and writes SVG natively, rather than importing and exporting SVG images, and it combines a fairly complete collection of standard drawing tools with some special SVG features, including

- Source view, where you can see and edit the underlying SVG code
- The Properties palette, which displays the values of all an object's attributes
- An object-based animation timeline in which you can specify object properties that change over time, producing an animated effect

Because WebDraw's native format is SVG rather than a proprietary format, you can open any SVG image in WebDraw, edit it, and save it. This enables you to work with images created in Illustrator or any other SVG editor. You can also open WebDraw images in any other SVG editor with no translation required.

If you've used a conventional drawing program such as CorelDRAW or Adobe Illustrator before—or even if you haven't—you'll have no trouble learning how to use WebDraw's tools and palettes to create new images and edit existing ones. This chapter provides a quick tour of the program's windows, palettes, and menu commands, then walks you through WebDraw's preferences settings. After that, we'll go on to creating drawings in WebDraw and adding special SVG features to them.

This chapter isn't designed as a complete tutorial for WebDraw, and because WebDraw (like the other programs discussed in Part 2) is a WYSIWYG drawing program, this chapter doesn't address hand coding SVG images or modifying source code. Rather, this chapter is intended to give an overview of the program's drawing capabilities to users who are familiar with illustration software in general. Before we go on, let's recap the basics of illustration programs.

About Illustration Software

As a class, illustration programs have a few things in common. They're based on the creation of vector objects—rather than raster images such as scans—and those objects are defined by Bézier curves. A mathematical concept that allows a curve to be described by giving the coordinates of each endpoint and two "control points" for each endpoint, the Bézier curve or something like it is used in all drawing programs. Such programs enable the user to create and modify shapes, apply strokes and fills to those shapes, and apply filters and transformations to those objects. Because vector images are defined mathematically, rather than one pixel at a time like raster images, they retain their sharp edges and smooth curves when they're increased in size, or when the user zooms in on them. They can also contain type as text, rather than letterforms created from pixels, so that the text within vector images can be both searchable and editable.

If you've used Adobe Illustrator, CorelDRAW, Deneba Canvas, or another drawing program, most of the techniques presented in this chapter will be familiar to you. If you're using a drawing program for the first time, you may need to refer to WebDraw's online help more often, and you may also find it helpful to read the company's WebDraw newsgroup at news://news.jasc.com/webdraw/.

WebDraw Basics

Illustrator and CorelDRAW users will find that WebDraw is a smaller, less complex program without some of the bells and whistles found in traditional illustration programs. For example, you won't find an equivalent to Illustrator's

PathFinder commands in WebDraw. But what you will find is a neat interface and tools that work logically. Here's a once-over of what you'll find when you start up WebDraw and begin exploring it.

The WebDraw Workspace

Much of WebDraw's interface, shown in Figure 3-1, will look familiar if you've used other illustration software programs. Its tools are intuitive, its menus are logical, and its workspace is neatly arranged. A few elements, such as the DOM palette, may seem alien at first, but even these have some parallels in such programs as Illustrator and CorelDRAW.

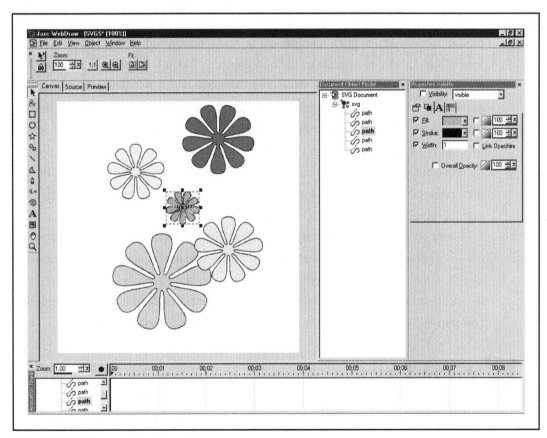

FIGURE 3-1 *WebDraw's interface includes elements of traditional illustration software as well as SVG-specific tools such as the DOM palette.* ∎

The Windows

The document window is where most of the action takes place in WebDraw. Its three tabs enable you to switch among three different views of a document (see Figure 3-2). When you're drawing, you'll use the Canvas tab to create images using drawing tools; this is the default view when you open a file. Here you can see the complete appearance of your objects, but you can't preview animations or Web links. To display a document's underlying SVG code, you can switch to the Source tab, which uses preference settings to display code in the colors and markup style of your choice. You can enter code directly in the Source tab, and changes made here are reflected immediately when you return to the Canvas tab. Finally, there's the Preview tab, where you can see the image as it will appear in Internet Explorer using the Adobe SVG Viewer. Here you can preview animations and test clickable links.

At the top-left corner of the document window's title bar is the Document Control icon. Clicking the icon displays a menu of common window-related commands: Restore, Move, Size, Minimize, Maximize, Close, and Next.

Below the document window you'll find the Animation Timeline, used for assigning times to animation events. For more information about using the Animation Timeline, see "Adding Animation" later in this chapter.

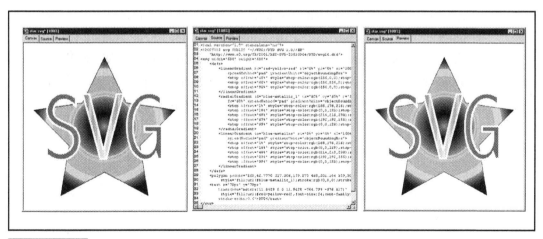

FIGURE   3-2   *Each tab shows a different view of the same document.* ∎

The Palettes

WebDraw's palettes can all be shown or hidden via the View menu, but when you first start up the program you'll see all of them.

The Tool Options bar appears above the document window; its options change depending on the currently active tool.

Note   *Turn to "Working with WebDraw's Tools," later in this chapter, for more information about the Tool Options bar's settings.*

Like the Tool Options bar, the Properties palette is context-sensitive; its contents vary depending on the selected object. It contains four tabs:

- **Attributes tab**   View and change the values of all editable attributes of the selected object. Attributes may include object ID, size, position, corner radius, and so on. Some objects may only have ID attributes.

- **Fill and Stroke tab**   Access settings for the selected object's fill (solid color, gradient, or pattern) and stroke (width and color).

- **Font tab**   Change the font settings for a selected text object.

- **Miter tab**   Edit an object's line cap style, line join style, and miter limit settings to determine the appearance of line ends and corners.

Each SVG object has a visibility setting: Visible, Hidden, Collapse, or Inherit. Hidden objects still exist in the document, but they're completely transparent. Collapsed objects are visible on the canvas but not in a web browser. And objects marked "inherit" take their visibility property from the objects or groups that contain them. You can set the visibility property for an object at the top of the Properties palette, as shown in the following illustration.

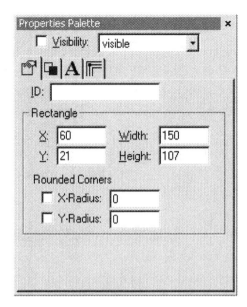

Two other palettes assist you in moving around a document and dealing with its component objects. The first of these, the overview window, displays a thumbnail view of the current document and allows you to navigate within the document even when you are zoomed way in. The rectangle shows the current area visible in the document window; you can drag the rectangle to view different parts of the image. At the bottom of the overview window, the current zoom level for the document window is shown:

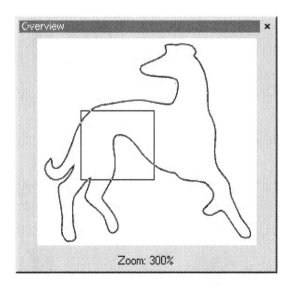

To work with a document's individual objects, you can use the DOM palette. This palette takes its name from the Document Object Model, which defines how the objects within a document are organized and how they can be referenced by other documents, including scripts. WebDraw's DOM palette lists each distinct object in a document in a hierarchical display that shows you the relationships between those objects. Each object's attributes and properties also appear in the DOM palette, and you can select them and then modify them in the Properties palette. Selecting an object in the DOM palette also selects it on the canvas. The DOM palette is shown here:

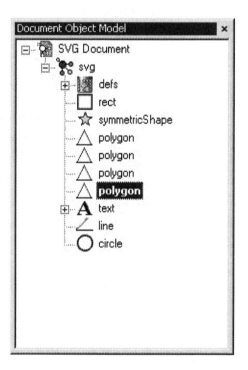

The Menus

WebDraw's menu commands are a fairly minimal set, containing mostly standard Windows commands that you need in order to work with any kind of document. Most of the program's functionality lies in its tools and palettes. Nonetheless, you'll need to know what's in the menus to get the most out of WebDraw. Here's a quick tour:

- **File**   In addition to the standard File menu commands such as New, Open, Close, and Save, you'll find three commands special to WebDraw: Export, which converts an SVG image to a JPEG or BMP raster image; Other Jasc Products, which enables you to jump to programs, including Paint Shop Pro, if they're installed; and Preferences. (To learn about setting WebDraw preferences, see the next section.)

- **Edit**   There are no unusual commands here—you'll see Undo, Redo, and a Command History, as well as cut and copy commands and selection commands.

- **View**   If you prefer, you can use the View menu's Mode commands to switch tabs in the document window. This menu also enables you to display a nonprinting grid, nonprinting guides, and rulers in the Canvas tab of the document window, as well as line numbers in the Source tab. The Send to Editor and Show in Browser commands display your artwork in the code editor or web browser of your choice, and the Toolbars/Palettes submenu enables you to hide or show palettes.

- **Object**   Here you can apply transformations and effects to objects, as well as rearrange their stacking order and alignment relative to each other. You can also group objects and assign them web links.

- **Window**   This menu contains standard commands for arranging windows on your screen and viewing any of the open documents.

- **Help**   WebDraw's help includes a Tip of the Day, a Read Me file, comprehensive textual help, and a link to the Jasc web site.

Setting Preferences

WebDraw's preferences are fairly straightforward. The most intriguing settings are those in the Tool Drag pane of the General Program Preferences, but be sure to take a look at all the preference settings. To set the General Program Preferences, choose File | Preferences | General Program Preferences to make changes to settings that affect the operation of WebDraw in general. The General Program Preferences dialog box has four panes.

File Locations   The name of this preference pane is a bit misleading—rather than keeping track of data files' locations, it enables you to choose external text editors in which you can edit SVG code, and web browsers in which you can preview SVG images. Text editors are useful for making global changes to code, such as switching one color for another or updating HTML links, and all web files should be previewed in multiple browsers to check for compatibility. After you've specified your choice of text editor and web browser here, you can choose View | Send to Editor or View | Show in Browser to transfer your open document to one of the specified programs. Here's a look at the File Locations pane:

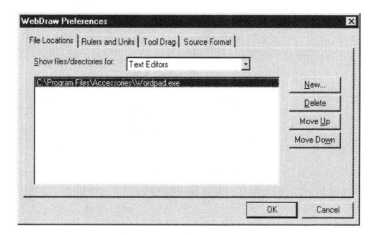

Rulers and Units   In this pane you can set the display units (inches, centimeters, pixels, points, millimeters, or picas) that will be used by rulers and dialog boxes. You can also choose a color for guides, and you can set the display units, spacing, and color for gridlines. Generally, it's best to stick with pixels for measurement units, because all other units vary in size depending on the user's monitor resolution. But you can set up your guides and gridlines to suit your own tastes and your project's requirements. The settings shown in the following illustration are the program's defaults:

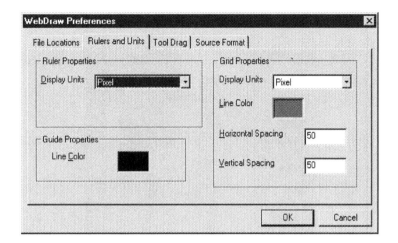

Note *The measurement units you specify in the Rulers and Units pane won't appear in the SVG image files you create; they're only intended to help you create images that must fit certain dimensions.*

Tool Drag   The Tool Drag preferences determine the behavior of the left and right mouse buttons when used alone and with modifier keys. To choose a behavior for each combination, first check the combination you want to use on the left, then choose an option on the right for what happens when you use the mouse in that way. The three behaviors you can affect are as follows:

- **Drag**   Choose whether the point at which you start dragging becomes the upper-left corner of the object or its center.

- **Shape**   Click Square to create symmetrical objects (squares and circles) regardless of the size of the shape you drag out.

- **Alignment**   This behavior rotates the selected object; choose Axis Aligned to rotate the object but not its bounding box, Free Rotation to rotate the object and its bounding box to any angle, or Constrained Rotation to rotate the object in degree increments you can specify.

The Tool Drag preferences pane is shown here:

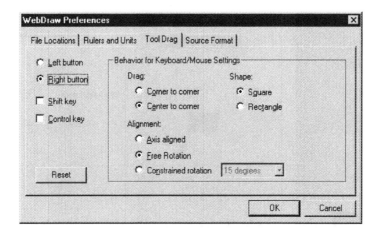

Source Format   These settings determine the text formatting used within the SVG files you create; they don't affect the images' appearance, just the way their code is written. You can choose a format for colors (Hexadecimal, Name, or RGB), an option for line breaks, and the way that text lines are indented and broken within the code. You can also opt to use CSS styles, XML styles, or both. The default settings in this tab, shown here, are best for most purposes:

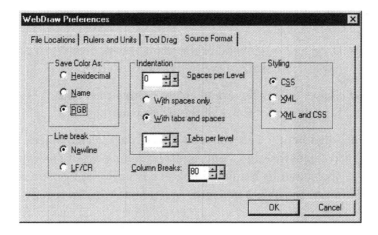

Setting Source View Preferences

Choose File | Preferences | Source View Preferences to open the Font and Color Settings dialog box, which contains formatting controls for each type of code text. Code formatting helps you distinguish different code elements when you're look-ing at a document in Source view. You can choose fonts, colors, and sizes for the code elements, and you can also set a background color and a default foreground color for text that's not covered by one of the code elements listed in the pick list on the left side of the dialog box. Before making changes here, it's a good idea to open an SVG image and take a look at it in the Source tab so you can see how the default settings look; they are shown here:

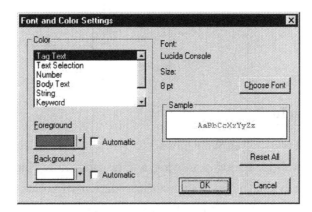

Working with WebDraw's Tools

By default, WebDraw's Tool palette is docked at the left side of the screen, but you can drag it into the middle of the screen to turn it into a floating palette that you can position wherever you want. Its tools fall into four fairly standard categories: object editing tools, object creation tools, tools for adding elements other than drawn objects, and navigation tools. Each tool has options that you can set using the Tool Options bar. Here's a look at the Tool palette:

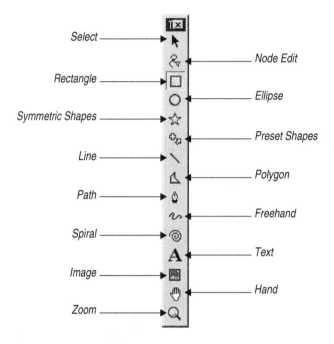

Object Editing Tools

The first two tools in WebDraw's Tool palette are the Select and Node Edit tools, used respectively for selecting, moving, and resizing entire objects and for doing the same to the individual nodes of each object—the corner points that define each shape. The settings on the Tool Options bar for the Select tool are the same as those for the Hand and Zoom tools (discussed later in this section). The Node Edit tool's settings are varied; they include Expansion % (used by the Expand Selected and Contract Selected commands), Duplication Offset (used by the Duplicate and Offset command), Segment Type, and buttons that close open paths and break closed paths.

Object Creation Tools

Object creation tools appear next on the Tool palette. These tools enable you to create prefab shapes and freehand shapes of any size by clicking and dragging in the canvas area. The available tools are as follows:

- **Rectangle** Creates rectangles and squares; options include fill and stroke style, stroke width, and corner style (square or rounded).

- **Ellipse** Creates ellipses and circles; options include fill and stroke style and stroke width.

- **Symmetric Shapes** Creates symmetrical polygons with acute or obtuse angles; options include fill and stroke style, stroke width, number of sides, and angle radius (for acute-angled shapes such as stars).

- **Preset Shapes** Creates shapes from a built-in library that includes arrows, stars, hearts, speech balloons, lightning bolts, and more. Options include fill and stroke style and stroke width.

- **Line** Creates straight lines. Options include fill and stroke style and stroke width.

- **Polygon** Creates open or closed asymmetrical polygons. Options include fill and stroke style and stroke width.

- **Path** Creates open or closed Bézier paths. Options include fill and stroke style, stroke width, and segment type (straight, standard "cubic" Bézier, or freehand Bézier).

- **Freehand** Creates open Bézier paths. Options include fill and stroke style and stroke width.

- **Spiral** Creates spiral paths. Options include fill and stroke style, stroke width, type (square or round), revolutions, number of edges (for square spirals), and expansion (whether the space between revolutions increases or stays consistent).

Tip *You can determine exactly how a tool behaves when you click on the Canvas and drag out a shape by choosing File | Preferences | General Program Preferences, then clicking the Tool Drag tab. Options include whether the mouse's starting point becomes the center or the upper-left corner of the resulting shape.*

Text and Image Tools

WebDraw's tools for adding elements other than drawn objects are the Text and Image tools, used for placing type and raster images such as scans, respectively, within an SVG drawing. See the "Adding Text and Raster Images to Drawings" section later in this chapter for more information about including text and images within SVG drawings.

Navigation Tools

Falling into the final category of tools are WebDraw's Hand and Zoom tools. You can click and drag with the Hand tool to move the current drawing around within the document window, and you can click with the Zoom tool to increase the view percentage.

Working with SVG Images in WebDraw

Now that you've taken the WebDraw tour, let's start creating some images. First, we'll create an image file, then we'll start creating some objects and applying fills and features to them. Finally, we'll learn how to add text, raster images, and animation to SVG images. Throughout this section, we'll use WebDraw's tools and techniques to build an example image. You can follow along by duplicating our image, or you can create your own.

Note *To duplicate the example image shown in this chapter, you'll need to download an image of a greyhound's head. You can find it at www.svgfordesigners.com/examples/greylogo.svg.*

Opening SVG Images

WebDraw can open any SVG image, regardless of how it was created. The procedure is straightforward. Let's start by opening the greyhound head logo image:

1. Choose File | Open or press CTRL-O.

2. In the Open dialog box, navigate to the greyhound logo image.

3. Click OK to open the image (see Figure 3-3).

The image's source code may offer clues about its originating program, as well as other information. For example, every SVG image created in Adobe Illustrator, including this one, contains the following code line:

```
<!- Generator: Adobe Illustrator 10, SVG Export Plug-In .
  SVG Version: 3.0.0 Build 76)  ->
```

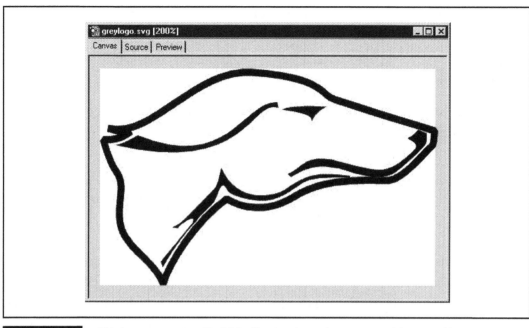

FIGURE 3-3 *This image was created in Adobe Illustrator by tracing a scan, and then saved in SVG format.* ■

Tip *Unlike Adobe Illustrator, WebDraw doesn't insert any extraneous information. If you want to strip an SVG image's code to its bare bones, you can open it in WebDraw, then copy its elements and paste them into a new WebDraw document. When the objects are pasted, their code is converted using WebDraw's preferences, and all the elements will be coded as though they had been created in WebDraw itself.*

Creating SVG Images

To create a new document, you must first decide what size the file will be. Follow these steps to create a new image file that will eventually be a web site splash screen:

1. Choose File | New or press CTRL-N.

2. In the New Image dialog box, set the measurement units to pixels and enter a Height value of 440 and a Width value of 600 to determine the size of the new image. You can use pixels, centimeters, millimeters, inches,

percent, picas, or points, and you can use different units for the width and height—for example, you can create a document that's 640 pixels wide by 2 inches deep.

3. Click OK.

If you click the Source tab of this new image, before you draw anything in the window, you'll see the following:

```
<?xml version="1.0" standalone="no"?>
<!DOCTYPE svg PUBLIC "-//W3C//DTD SVG 1.0//EN"
 "http://www.w3.org/TR/2001/REC-SVG-20010904/DTD/svg10.dtd">
<svg width="500" height="500">
</svg>
```

This is the basic code that every SVG image created by WebDraw contains; the only information you've contributed to it so far is the values of the WIDTH and HEIGHT attributes of the <svg> tag itself—in this case, WebDraw's default values of 500 pixels. As you draw in the Canvas tab, the corresponding source code is automatically added between the <svg> tag and its end tag (</svg>).

Tip   *If you're new to SVG, a fantastic way to learn more is to draw simple objects on the canvas and then check the Source tab to see what the code describing those objects looks like. Try creating a simple square or circle; look at its source code; then change the object's attributes and see how the source code has changed. Using this simple technique, you can begin to see how the objects you draw translate into SVG source code.*

Filling Objects with Colors, Gradients, and Patterns

Once you've drawn a shape, the Fill and Stroke tab of the Properties palette offers you a choice of stroke and fill options with which to color it. Both strokes and fills can be any of three types: a solid color, a gradient, or a pattern. You'll also see two other options in the Fill and Stroke pop-up menus: None and Inherit. None, reasonably enough, sets the color of the fill or stroke to none. The Inherit option is a bit more complicated.

Using the Inherit setting enables you to apply a fill or stroke to a group, symbol, clipping path, mask, or pattern such that every "child" object included within the "parent" group or element uses the same fill or stroke settings. To make use of this SVG feature, you need to complete two steps:

1. Select the objects (children) that you want to have the same fill or stroke attributes and choose Inherit for their fill, stroke, or both.

2. Choose Object | Group to group the objects. If you look at the Source tab after the group is created, you'll see that the objects are now nested within a parent <g> tag.

3. Apply the desired fill or stroke to the group (parent).

Any kind of fill and stroke combination can be inherited; you can also choose to have objects inherit the fill but not the stroke of their parent objects, or vice versa.

Coloring Objects with Solid Colors

You can fill or stroke an object with any RGB color. Clicking the color swatch next to Fill or Stroke opens a color picker in which you can choose colors from a basic palette or a color wheel or enter values in RGB, HSL, or hexadecimal values. The color picker is shown here:

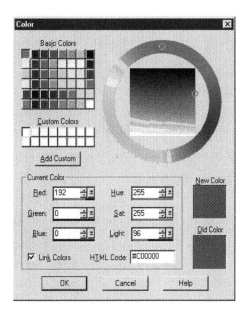

Coloring Objects with Gradients

Gradients used in an SVG document are defined within a <defs> element at the beginning of the document. Each gradient definition includes an ID attribute that gives the gradient a name; this name is then used to assign the gradient to objects. You don't need to know any of this to create gradients and apply them to objects, however.

If you choose Gradient from the Fill or Stroke pop-up menu, you can then click the gradient swatch to open the Gradient dialog box. SVG supports both linear and radial gradients, with several gradient styles predefined in the program. WebDraw allows you to create custom gradients with as many as 100 separate color stops; SVG itself sets no limit on the number of stops. The Gradient dialog box is shown here:

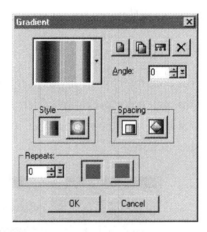

The Gradient dialog box contains three groups of controls. First, you can choose from the set of predefined gradients shown in the pop-up menu in the upper-left corner of the dialog box. If you want to modify the way a gradient is applied to the selected objects, you can use the second group of controls:

- **Angle** Rotates a linear gradient to any angle.

- **Style** Switches between linear and radial gradients.

- **Spacing** Determines whether the gradient is applied only within the object or to the entire workspace, with the object acting as a mask to display only the portion of the gradient that falls within its bounds.

- **Repeats** Determines the number of times the gradient is repeated within the selected object.

- **Repeat/Reflect** Determines whether a gradient repeats in the same direction or "flopped" if the number of repeats is greater than 1. These buttons aren't labeled—you'll find them next to the Repeats field.

Finally, you can edit the existing gradients and create your own named gradients that will then appear in the pop-up menu. To edit a gradient, choose the gradient from the pop-up menu in the Gradient dialog box and click the Edit Gradient button to open the editing dialog box, shown here:

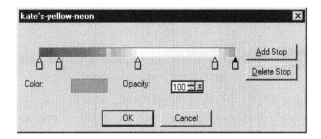

Each color stop on the gradient bar represents a color that's being used to create the gradient. Here there are only two colors, black at one end fading to white at the other end. You can add up to 100 colors to create chrome effects, spectrums, sunsets or sunrises, or any combination you like. Each color can be opaque (100-percent opacity), transparent (0-percent opacity), or somewhere in between. Here's how the controls in the editing dialog box work:

- To add a stop, click the Add Stop button.

- To delete a stop, click it once, then click the Delete Stop button.

- To move a stop, click it and drag it along the gradient bar.

- To edit an existing stop, click it once, then click the color swatch to open the color picker and change the color, or enter a new opacity value.

When you're satisfied with the changes you've made, click OK to return to the Gradient dialog box, where the pop-up menu will display the modified version of the gradient. If you like its looks, click OK again to apply the gradient to the selected objects.

You can also duplicate an existing gradient by clicking the Copy Gradient button next to the Create Gradient button at the top of the Gradient dialog box. Assign the new gradient a name and save it with a logical filename, then click OK.

Tip   *Play it safe by always copying a gradient before you edit its colors. That way you can go back to the original if you decide the copy isn't what you were looking for after all.*

If you want to create a gradient from scratch, click the Create Gradient button—the first of the four buttons at the top of the Gradient dialog box. Assign the gradient a name and save it with a logical filename, then use the editing dialog box to create your custom gradient. And finally, if you want to delete gradient, select it in the pop-up menu and click the Delete Gradient button.

Caution   *Be careful when you delete a gradient. You won't see a confirmation dialog box—the gradient is deleted immediately and it's not recoverable.*

Follow these steps to create a purple-to-white gradient background in the new file you created earlier in this chapter:

1. Use the Rectangle tool to draw a rectangle on the canvas. Don't worry too much about getting it to cover the entire canvas; we'll adjust its size and position in the next step.

2. Choose View | Toolbars/Palettes | Properties Palette to display the Properties palette.

3. With the rectangle still selected, click the Attributes tab on the Properties palette and enter the following values to align the rectangle correctly: X: **0**, Y: **0**, Width: **600**, Height: **440**.

4. Switch to the Properties palette's Fill and Stroke tab and click the gradient swatch to open the Gradient dialog box.

5. Click the New Gradient button and assign your gradient a filename and an object name (our example uses "purple-white" for both names), then click Save.

6. In the purple-white dialog box, click the left-hand gradient stop, which is black by default. Click the color swatch to open the color picker and change the swatch's color to the Web-safe HTML color 660099, then click OK.

7. Click the Add Stop button to create a new gradient stop, and set its offset value to 50 and its color to white. This additional white stop in the center of the gradient shortens the transition from purple to white.

8. Click OK to leave the purple-white dialog box.

9. Enter **90** in the Angle field, so that the gradient runs from the top of the rectangle to its bottom, rather than across. Then click OK to close the Gradient dialog box.

Keep this image open, as well as the greyhound head image you opened earlier; we'll use them both later in this chapter.

Filling Objects with Patterns

Using patterns to fill or stroke objects works similarly to using gradients. First, choose Pattern from the Fill or Stroke menu in the Properties palette. To choose a pattern, click the pattern swatch to open the Pattern dialog box. Here you'll see a pop-up menu showing the available patterns. You can also choose a spacing option. As with gradients, the spacing setting determines whether the pattern is applied only within the object or to the entire workspace, with the object masking (or hiding) the portions of the pattern fill that appear outside the object. The Pattern dialog box is shown here:

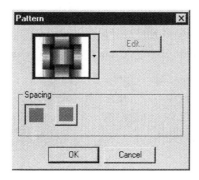

> **Note** At this writing, WebDraw doesn't include the ability to edit patterns and define your own patterns. Those features are supported by SVG and are planned for a future release of WebDraw.

Adding Text and Raster Images to Drawings

Although WebDraw is a vector drawing program, you can include both text and raster images within SVG image files.

Adding Text

Type retains its font and style when used in SVG images, and it remains text rather than becoming text-shaped objects, so it's editable and searchable. WebDraw supports only "point" text, meaning that each line of text must be a separate text object. Adding text to a drawing is fairly straightforward. Let's add the necessary type to the splash screen image we've been working on:

1. Return to the gradient image you created earlier in this chapter.

2. Switch to the Text tool.

3. In the Font tab of the Properties palette, set the point size (48) and font (Impact) for the type. Then switch to the Fill and Stroke tab and choose a fill color for the type (HTML Code: CC00CC).

4. Click anywhere in the document and enter the first line of text: **Tri-State Greyhound**.

5. Switch to the Select tool, then back to the Text tool again and repeat Step 4 with this text: **Adoption League**.

6. Switch back to the Select tool and align the two text lines (select both and choose Object | Alignment | Left), then adjust the vertical spacing between the two lines. Group them by selecting both and choosing Object | Group.

7. Follow Steps 2 through 4 to create another line of text, **W E L C O M E**, in 18-point Impact all caps. Choose Object | Align to Canvas | Center Horizontally to center the text within the image.

8. See Figure 3-4 for the image as it now stands.

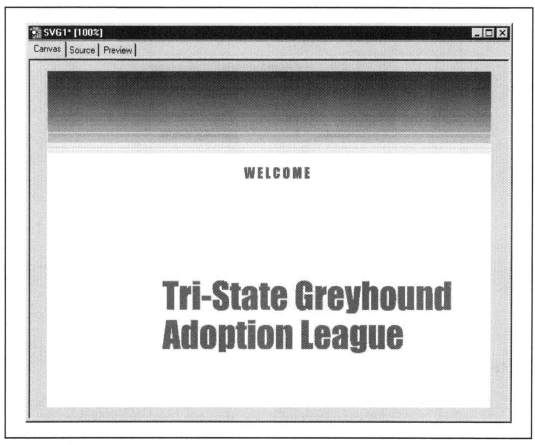

FIGURE   3-4   *The image now has a background and three lines of text; it still needs a logo and perhaps a filter effect or two.* ■

9. If you want to modify attributes of any of these text lines, switch back to the Select tool and change the Font or Fill and Stroke settings in the Properties palette.

To edit the text itself, select its entry in the DOM palette, then click the Attributes tab of the Properties palette and enter the new text as shown here:

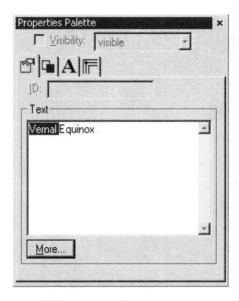

Adding Raster Images

Raster images imported into WebDraw are still nothing more than pixels, even though they're now part of an SVG image. For this reason, try to avoid resizing imported images upward.

Here's how to add raster images such as photos to a WebDraw document:

1. Switch to the Image tool.

2. Use the tool to define the location for the imported referenced image in one of these ways:

   ■ Click in the image to define the location for the imported referenced image's upper-left corner and import it at 100 percent.

   ■ Click and drag to define the area that will be occupied by the image and import it at that size and shape.

3. In the dialog box, choose an image file to import. The supported file formats are PNG, JPEG, and SVG.

You can resize an image after it's imported by pressing SHIFT and dragging a corner handle to increase or decrease the image's size.

Applying Filter Effects and Transformations

Filters and transformations are shortcuts to creating complex, sophisticated images from simple shapes and colors. The filter effects available within WebDraw are akin to filters you might apply to raster images in Adobe Photoshop or a similar program. Transformations, on the other hand, are a matter of pure geometry; they allow you to resize, reposition, and reshape objects.

Applying Filter Effects

SVG filters called "primitives" enable you to apply effects that look like classic raster effects—blurs, shadows, and the like—but they have a couple of big advantages. They're rendered on objects, on the fly, rather than only when an image is created. So, they look good at any display resolution and zoom percentage. And they don't affect the status of SVG objects; in other words, the objects aren't rasterized in order to apply the effects. That means that a circle is still a circle in the SVG code, even if it has a drop shadow—and, best of all, text remains editable, and searchable.

Importing Other SVG Images

You may have noticed that you can import SVG image files as well as raster images. Why would you do that? Well, for example, you can import a logo file that another artist is working on. WebDraw previews the file, but your SVG only contains the pointer to the image file rather than the image itself. You can complete your work without having to wait for the other content to be finalized. Importing SVG images comes in handy when you want to use the same element, such as a logo, in multiple images. If a change is made to the original, such as a new corporate color, all the files that reference that imported file are automatically updated too—as long as the original file remains in the same location it had when it was imported.

WebDraw's filter effects are actually combinations of SVG's built-in filters, which act as building blocks for more complex effects. For example, WebDraw's Bevel effect combines four different instances of SVG primitives: a Gaussian blur, a specular lighting effect, and two versions of the Composite primitive, which controls how the lighting effect interacts with the shape of the underlying object. You can choose from WebDraw's library of 15 filter effects, and you can modify the appearance of a filter once it's applied to an object by changing the primitives' settings in the Properties palette, shown here:

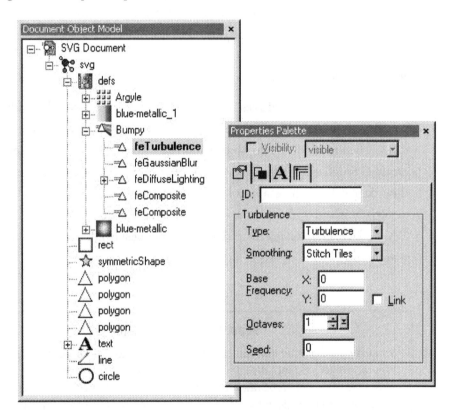

To finish up the splash screen image we've been working on, let's add the organization's logo and then apply a drop shadow to the logo and the text. Follow these steps:

1. Return to the greyhound head logo image, which you opened earlier in this chapter.

2. Choose Edit | Select All or press CTRL-A, then choose Edit | Copy or press CTRL-C.

3. Switch to the gradient image with text that you've been working on throughout this chapter.

4. Choose Edit | Paste or press CTRL-V to add the greyhound head image to the file.

5. Select the text and the greyhound head image; SHIFT-click to select more than one object. Group the four objects (Object | Group) and center them on the canvas (Object | Align to Canvas | Center Horizontally).

6. Choose Object | Apply Effect.

7. Choose the Drop Shadow effect from the pop-up menu.

8. Change the default settings for the effect as follows: Offset X: 4, Offset Y: 4, Blur Radius: 4, Shadow Opacity: 50.

9. Click OK to apply the effect. The final artwork is shown in Figure 3-5.

10. In the DOM palette, click the plus sign next to the <defs> entry; the palette now lists all the effects, gradients, and the like that have been used in the document, as shown here:

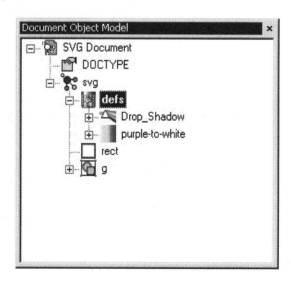

11. Click the plus sign next to the name of the effect you've just applied. Now you can see the list of primitives that together make up the effect.

12. Click one the the primitives and review its settings in the Attributes tab of the Properties palette. You can change any of these settings to alter the appearance of this instance of the filter. This illustration shows the settings for an instance of the Offset primitive, which determines the position of the drop shadow with respect to the object to which it's applied:

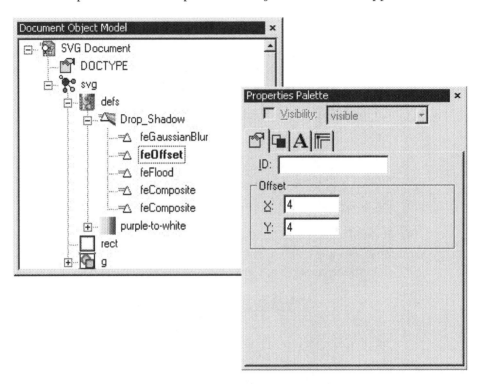

The final result of this exercise is shown in Figure 3-5.

To remove an effect entirely, select the object and choose Object | Remove Filter. If you've applied the same effect to more than one object in a drawing, but used different settings each time, you'll see more than one instance of the effect in the <defs>. WebDraw numbers each new instance of an effect, so the first bevel effect you apply will be called Bevel and the next one Bevel_1.

Applying Transformations

WebDraw offers only three simple transformations: rotation, flipping, and resizing. To apply rotate or flip a selected object, choose Object | Transformation and pick one of these options from the submenu:

- **Mirror**   Flips the object along a horizontal axis.
- **Flip**   Flips the object along a vertical axis.
- **Rotate Left 90**   Rotates the object counterclockwise.
- **Rotate Right 90**   Rotates the object clockwise.

These transformations work in relation to the object's center point. If more than one object is selected when you apply the transformation, they're transformed as a group around their common center point. There's no command to remove a transformation, but you can undo it by flipping or rotating the object back to its original orientation.

FIGURE   3-5   *The final artwork makes use of different SVG effects.* ■

The third available transformation is resizing. Of course, you can resize an object or group by dragging its corner point, but you can also automatically specify that a selected object or objects be sized to match another object. To perform this transformation, first select the object whose size you want to match, and then select any objects you want to resize. Choose Object | Make Same Size | Both. If you only want to match the first object's width, choose Object | Make Same Size | Horizontal; to match its height, choose Object | Make Same Size | Vertical.

When you use transformations, remember that each instance of a transformation is recorded separately—so if you resize an object three times, all three rotations are recorded in the file rather than just the object's final size. While it's conceivable that you would want to retrieve this information later on, most of the time it's just bulking up your image file unnecessarily.

Tip *You can remove extra transformations and other unneeded information by copying and pasting an image into a new, blank file.*

Adding Animation

Animation is created by changing an objects' appearance and location over time. In conventional raster formats, you have to create multiple images, each slightly different, in order to form an animation. In SVG, however, you can animate an image simply by telling it that you want it to change it color, location, or another aspect of its appearance at a specified time. Doing animation this way results in smaller files that are more easily edited. The standard by which SVG animation works is called Synchronized Multimedia Integration Language (SMIL) and is an open standard, like XML and SVG.

The key to animation in WebDraw is the Animation Timeline. To create animation, you pick a time on the timeline and make changes to the selected object. Then, when you play the animation, the object changes to display its new characteristics at that point in time. Transitions are smooth, with "tweening" so that the object appears to change gradually rather than suddenly.

You can use any editable property of an object in animating it, from its size and position to its color and filter effects. How you combine these properties to create dynamic animations is up to you. Here are the basic steps for creating an animated image in WebDraw:

1. Choose View | Toolbars/Palettes | Animation Timeline or press ALT-0 to display the Animation Timeline.

2. Position the object you want to animate at its starting point within the image.

3. Click the Record button on the Animation Timeline, as shown in this illustration:

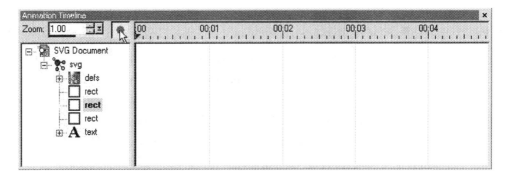

4. Click at the 00 point in the gray ruler at the top of the timeline to set the object's attributes at the beginning of the animation.

5. Click at the next time point in the timeline and make any changes to the selected object that you want to take effect by that point in time.

6. Continue setting time points and modifying the object until the animation is complete.

7. Click the Record button again to turn recording off.

8. Click the Preview tab to watch the animation play. You can also get a stop-motion preview by dragging the slider on the Animation Timeline.

Tip   *Remember, you can animate more than one object within a drawing.*

Saving SVG Images

Saving WebDraw files is very simple; there are only two options. To save the splash screen image file you've been working on throughout this chapter, follow these steps:

1. Choose File | Save (or File | Save As to save an existing file with a new name).

2. Enter a name for the new file (our file is named greysplash.svg) in the File Name dialog box. Note that you don't have to add the filename extension—WebDraw does that automatically depending on the file type you choose in the next step.

3. Choose a file type:

   - SVG

   - SVGZ

SVGZ is a compressed version of the SVG format that uses lossless compression. SVGZ files are significantly smaller than uncompressed SVG files, often by as much as 80%. The Adobe SVG Viewer plug-in displays both compressed and uncompressed SVG images with no noticeable difference in speed; other viewer software may not display SVGZ files correctly. Which you choose depends on how likely your users are to be using the Adobe plug-in.

Remember, because WebDraw uses SVG as its native format, WebDraw files are standard SVG files, not proprietary, and they can be opened and edited in any text editor or SVG-savvy illustration program. Similarly, SVGZ files use standard GZIP compression, so they can be decompressed by any utility that decompresses GZIP files; once decompressed, they are regular SVG files.

Tip *If you use SVGZ files, remember to set the SVGZ MIME type (image/svg+xml) in your web server.*

chapter **4**

Creating SVG Images
with Adobe Illustrator

Adobe Systems, Inc., is a true juggernaut—the company's software dominates the world of graphic design and publishing, with Photoshop, Illustrator, GoLive, and more applications all backed up by the company's key technologies of PostScript and PDF. For several years, Adobe has worked to make its products the only ones any designer will need by incorporating more features and by streamlining and standardizing interfaces. This has resulted in a group of powerful and easy-to-use applications that includes Adobe Illustrator, the industry-standard drawing program.

Like other popular illustration programs—including Deneba Canvas, Macromedia FreeHand, and CorelDRAW—Illustrator has added multimedia and web publishing features in its last several versions, with the latest addition being support not only for the SVG format but also for SVG's interactive features. Using Illustrator, you can create vector images using standard shapes, Bézier curves, and type, then apply SVG filters to the objects. You can link a JavaScript to any object, animate the image using either frame-based or timeline-based animation, and then save it in normal or compressed SVG format with fonts and raster images embedded or linked. And, you can include variables within the image that enable it to be reworked on the fly with a database feeding it data. Illustrator does not include a source code view for SVG images, so all this takes place via the program's graphic interface.

This chapter gives a quick overview of how Illustrator works, touching on some of the program's features (but by no means all of them), and then goes on to look at the program's SVG-related features. If you want to learn more about this complex and powerful illustration software, refer to the program's printed documentation and online help, which are comprehensive and easy to use. You'll also find hundreds of third-party books about how to use Illustrator at your local bookstore or on the Web.

Illustrator Basics

If you're an Illustrator power user, you can skip right to the next section, "Working with SVG Images in Illustrator." If you're new to Illustrator, or if you haven't used the program in a few years, you'll find this section provides a useful tour of the program's workspace and some of its main functions. First we'll take a look at Illustrator's tools, palettes, and menus, and then we'll move on to create an example SVG image using Illustrator objects and effects.

The Illustrator Workspace

Illustrator's interface is built around a page metaphor—each document consists of a single "page," called the *artboard*, even if that document is destined to be used only on the Web and will never see print. Arranged around the page is a sometimes bewildering array of tools, palettes, and menus that in many cases offer more than one method of accomplishing the same thing. For example, you can use Transform menu commands or you can use Transform tools to apply transformations. The heart of Illustrator, however, is its Toolbox.

Illustrator's Tools

The Illustrator Toolbox holds 76 different tools, packing them into fly-out menus that appear when you click a visible tool and hold down the mouse button (see Figure 4-1). The tools can be loosely divided into the following groups:

- **Selection tools**   Use each of these tools to select objects within a document in a different way. For example, the Group Selection tool selects

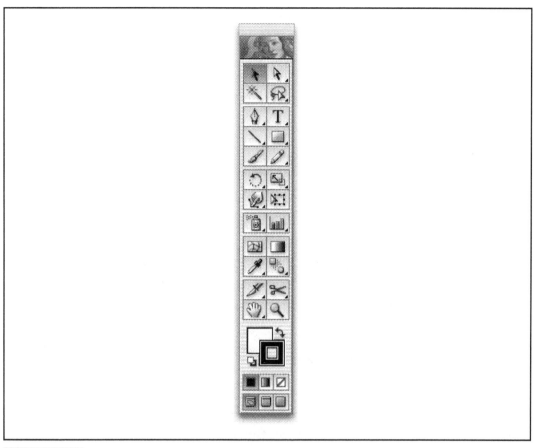

The Toolbox's different sections divide the tools into groups. ■

all the items in the selected object's group, while the Direct Selection tool selects only the object you click on. The selection tools are the Selection, Direct Selection, Group Selection, Magic Wand, Direct Select Lasso, and Lasso tools.

■ **Pen tools**   These are the heart and soul of Illustrator. Use these tools for drawing and editing Bézier curves. The pen tools include the Pen, Add Anchor Point, Delete Anchor Point, and Convert Anchor Point tools.

■ **Type tools**   As is apparent from their name, these tools enable you to set point type and type in text boxes both horizontally and vertically. They include the Type, Area Type, Path Type, Vertical Type, Vertical Area Type, and Vertical Path Type tools.

- **Shape tools**   When you're creating standard shapes such as rectangles, ellipses, or even spirals, use these tools rather than the pen tools. The group contains the Line Segment, Arc, Spiral, Rectangular Grid, Polar Grid, Rectangle, Rounded Rectangle, Ellipse, Polygon, Star, and Flare tools.

- **Drawing tools**   You have yet another method of drawing at your disposal with these four tools; use the Pencil tool for freehand drawing and the Paintbrush tool for creating wide, painterly freehand strokes. The Smooth and Erase tools enable you to edit existing curves.

- **Transform tools**   Using the transform tools, you can apply transformations freehand (by eye) or invoke the appropriate dialog box. Some of these apply traditional transformations such as shearing and resizing objects, and others modify objects in more unusual ways. The tools include the Rotate, Reflect, Twist, Scale, Shear, Reshape, Warp, Twirl, Pucker, Bloat, Scallop, Crystallize, Wrinkle, and Free Transform tools.

- **Symbolism tools**   Symbols enable you to draw an object once and refer to it throughout an image, reducing file size and ensuring consistency. With the symbolism tools, you can add symbols to your image and arrange or modify them in several ways; the tools include the Symbol Sprayer, Symbol Shifter, Symbol Scruncher, Symbol Sizer, Symbol Spinner, Symbol Stainer, Symbol Screener, and Symbol Styler tools.

- **Graph tools**   These tools invoke a miniature spreadsheet and turn the data you enter there into the specified kind of graph. The available graph tools include the Column Graph, Stacked Column Graph, Bar Graph, Stacked Bar Graph, Line Graph, Area Graph, Scatter Graph, Pie Graph, and Radar Graph tools.

- **Miscellaneous tools**   Within this mixed bag are the Mesh, Gradient, Eyedropper, Paint Bucket, Measure, Blend, and Auto Trace tools. The Eyedropper and Paint Bucket tools enable you to transfer attributes from one object to another, and the Mesh, Gradient, and Blend tools are used to apply different kinds of fills. You can measure distances with the Measure tool and create vector objects by tracing raster objects with the Auto Trace tool.

- **Slice tools**   By slicing an image into multiple sections, you can break it up into smaller images that are reassembled when the web page that contains them loads. The group consists of the Slice and Slice Select tools.

- **Cutting tools**   The Scissors and Knife tools are used for cutting shapes; for example, you can use the knife to turn an ellipse into multiple arcs.

■ **Navigation tools**   Designed to help you move around a document, the Hand and Zoom tools work as you might expect from their names. With the Page tool, you can determine where the image's content will fall within the margins of a printed page.

Each tool has a shortcut key (press R to switch to the Rotate tool, for example); you can see the shortcut in a ToolTip by holding the cursor over the tool for a second.

Illustrator's Palettes

The Toolbox is also known as the Tools palette, and there are several others that you'll be using almost constantly while you work in Illustrator. As you read through this chapter, you'll encounter a number of Illustrator's palettes, so this section will introduce you to some that you won't be seeing later on (see Figure 4-2).

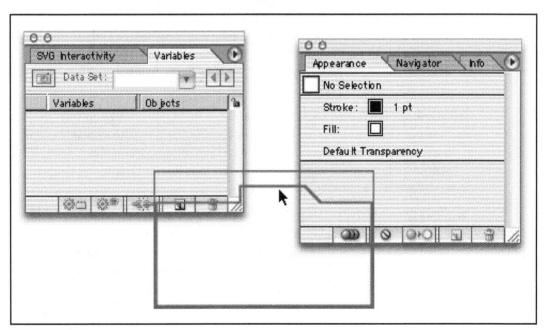

FIGURE 4-2   *Illustrator's palettes can be grouped and ungrouped to suit your taste; here, the Navigator palette is being dragged out of its default group into a palette of its own.* ■

- **Actions palette**   The Actions palette is the nerve center for Illustrator's built-in macro/scripting feature. You can record and replay a series of commands, called *Actions*, and you can apply Actions to batches of existing files as well as within the current document.

- **Attributes palette**   Use the Attributes palette to control lesser-known aspects of shapes (such as whether Illustrator displays the center point) and to apply URLs to image map sections.

- **Brushes palette**   This palette contains the various brushes available for use with the Paintbrush tool. You can edit them and also create your own.

- **Document Info palette**   If you want to monitor the colors, fonts, or other elements used in a document, or other global aspects of it, display the Document Info palette and click the triangle on its upper-right corner to display a palette menu of info categories.

- **Info palette**   This palette enables you to monitor what you're doing at any given time—the distance you've drawn or the amount you've resized an object, for example.

- **Links palette**   If you're using imported text or images (either raster or vector), the Links palette shows the status of the objects' links to their original files.

- **Magic Wand palette**   Here you can set options for the Magic Wand tool, which selects objects based on their similarity to the object you click on. The palette enables you to determine how similar an object must be and in what ways (fill color, stroke color, and so on) to be included in the selection.

- **Navigator palette**   Use this thumbnail to move around your image when you're zoomed way in; a rectangular outline indicates the portion of the image currently displayed in the document window.

- **Variables palette**   Variables are objects that can be modified using data sets you specify; files containing variables are templates. The Variables palette lists the variables used in your document and enables you to work with them.

Each of these palettes has a palette menu hiding under the triangle at the upper-right corner of the palette. You'll find palette preference settings, useful commands, and palette display alternatives (such as color modes) in palette menus.

Useful as they are, palettes do take up a lot of screen real estate, so it's worth taking the time to arrange them to maximize visibility. You can dock palettes to each other so that they can be moved as a block by dragging one palette over the bottom of another. You can also remove tabs from palettes by dragging them away from it; click a tab and drag it back over a palette's other tabs to put it back into that palette.

Tip *Useful as Illustrator's palettes are, sometimes they just get in the way. Press* TAB *to hide them all, or* SHIFT-TAB *to hide all but the Toolbox. Press the same key combination to bring them back.*

Illustrator's Menus

While we don't have room to go into a full-blown explanation of every menu command in Illustrator, we can give you a quick idea of what kind of commands each menu contains. Feel free to explore and to refer to some of the many good books on Illustrator if you need to know more. In the meantime, here are Illustrator's menus:

- **File** Here you'll find commands for opening, closing, and saving files, as well as commands to invoke Illustrator's setup dialog boxes for document size and color attributes.

- **Edit** Along with the standard Cut, Copy, Paste, and Undo commands, you'll find the Define Pattern command (for creating custom patterns) and the Keyboard Shortcuts command (for defining your preferred keyboard commands).

- **Object** Select an object and go to the Object menu to transform it, change its stacking order, lock or hide it, rasterize it, make it into a clipping mask, or any of several other object-related functions.

- **Type** This menu contains not only type options such as font and point size, but also text options such as spell checking and search and replace.

- **Select** Use the Select commands to select objects based on their stacking order or other attributes.

- **Filter**   Illustrator includes a wide selection of filters, some of which perform vector functions and others that work only on raster objects.

- **Effect**   Some effects have the same function as some of Illustrator's filters, while others are unique (including the SVG filters). See "Using Filters and Effects," later in this chapter, to learn about the difference between filters and effects in Illustrator.

- **View**   These commands control the zoom size as well as what interface elements—guides, grid, rulers, and so on—are visible.

- **Window**   All the palettes are listed alphabetically in this menu.

- **Help**   Turn here for Illustrator's online help or to go to the Adobe web site.

Drawing Objects

The basic functions of any illustration program are these: creating shapes and applying fills and strokes to them. In this section we'll look at how Illustrator handles these functions, and we'll start working on an example image that will reappear throughout this chapter.

Note   *All Illustrator shapes appear in an SVG document as paths rather than as SVG primitives such as "circle."*

Creating Shapes

Illustrator offers a multitude of ways to create objects: You can draw Bézier curves with the pen tools, use the Pencil or Paintbrush tool to draw freehand shapes, use the Pathfinder functions to combine objects into new shapes, or use the shape tools to create predefined shapes. No matter what tool or method you use, however, any shape you draw in Illustrator is composed of Bézier curves and can be edited with the pen tools.

The easiest way to create a new object is by using one of the shape tools. You can simply click and drag to draw a shape—choose Window | Info to keep track of the object's size as you draw it—or you can use it to invoke a dialog box in which you can enter the specs for the object you want to create. To begin creating our example, a navigation bar that will appear at the top of all the interior pages on a web site, follow these steps:

1. Choose File | New or press COMMAND-N to create a new document.

2. Make settings in the New Document dialog box as shown:

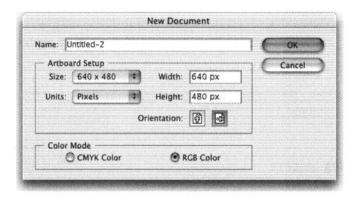

3. Click the Rectangle tool and hold down the mouse button to display a fly-out menu of tools, then move the cursor over to choose the Rounded Rectangle tool.

4. OPTION/ALT-click anywhere on the artboard to open the Rounded Rectangle dialog box and enter these settings:

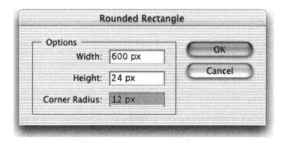

5. Click OK to create the rectangle.

6. If necessary, press COMMAND-MINUS a few times until you can see the entire shape in your document window. Position it within the artboard boundaries—the black edges—but don't worry about its position with respect to the page margins—the gray lines—which only affect printed documents.

7. Choose File | Save or press COMMAND-S to save the document; choose a name and location in the dialog box and click Save. Our file is named navbar.ai.

8. Finally, in the Illustrator Native Options dialog box, click OK again—the default settings are fine for this project.

This shape (see Figure 4-3) will form the basis for the navigation bar. We'll give it a gradient fill in the next section.

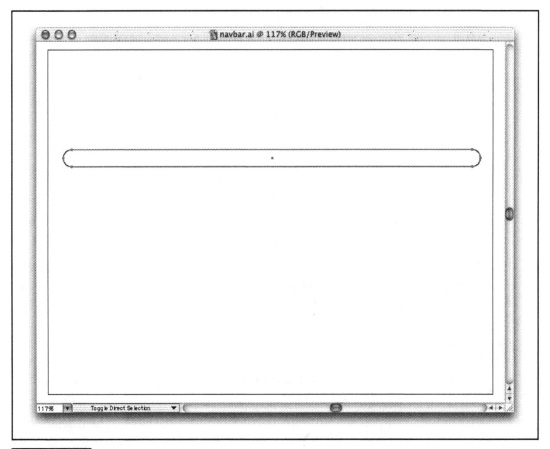

FIGURE 4-3 *The rounded rectangle's corner radius is exactly half the shape's height, making its ends completely round.* ∎

If you want to draw a nonstandard shape or edit an existing shape, you can use the pen tools to work directly with the Bézier curves that make up every vector object in Illustrator. The Pen tool itself creates line segments. To use it, click and then click again to create a straight segment, or click and drag to draw a curved segment with direction points (handles that you can use to adjust the curve). Click on the curve with the Add Anchor Point or Delete Anchor Point tool to create a new anchor point or remove an existing one. And if you want to change an anchor point's type—to give it direction points, to remove its direction points, or to change the respective angles of its direction points—click it with the Convert Direction Point tool.

Tip *Editing Bézier curves is an art all to itself. The best way to become proficient is to practice, and then practice some more. Try tracing scanned shapes to give you a better idea of how to shape curves.*

Sometimes a freehand shape is quicker to create using the Pencil or Paintbrush tool—just click and drag. You'll get the best results with these tools if you use them in conjunction with a graphics tablet and pressure-sensitive stylus.

To transform an existing object, choose Window | Transform to display the Transform palette. With the controls on this palette, you can resize, rotate, skew, and flip the selected object or objects. Finally, you can combine shapes to form more complex shapes using Illustrator's Pathfinder functions. Choose Window | Pathfinder to display the Pathfinder palette, then draw a few overlapping shapes and try each function. To see the name of each function in a ToolTip, poise the cursor over the button for a second.

Filling and Stroking Shapes

Illustrator supports three basic kinds of fills: gradients, patterns, and solid colors. You can apply multiple fills and strokes to a single object, and each fill or stroke can have its own transparency attributes—including blending mode, which determines how its color interacts with colors underneath it. When you save your image to SVG, each fill or stroke becomes a separate object but retains its transparency attributes.

To give an object a fill, first choose Window | Color or Window | Gradient to display, respectively, the Color or Gradient palette, as shown here:

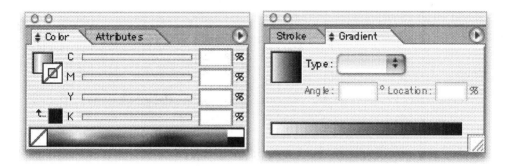

To create a color, first choose a color model from the Color palette menu, then use the sliders or the text entry fields to mix the color you want. As you work, the color is applied to the object's fill or stroke, depending on whether the fill proxy or the stroke proxy is to the front on the Color palette. Click the solid square in the upper-left corner of the palette to edit the fill; click the hollow square to edit the stroke.

Applying gradients works in much the same way. Follow these steps to apply a gradient to our navigation bar:

1. Select the rounded rectangle.

2. Choose Window | Gradient to display the Gradient palette.

3. Click the gradient swatch in the Gradient palette to apply a basic gradient to the object.

4. Choose Linear from the Type pop-up menu, then enter an angle value of 90 degrees. (Note that radial gradients don't have an angle value.)

5. To edit the default black-to-white gradient, double-click the black color stop at the right end of the gradient preview bar to open the Color palette.

6. Choose RGB Sliders from the palette menu and enter these values to turn the black color stop orange:

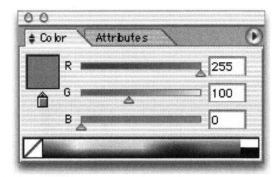

7. In the Gradient palette, click halfway between the orange stop and the white one to create a pale orange stop.

8. Click the white stop and drag it past the pale orange one toward the orange stop, then drag the pale orange stop all the way to the left end of the gradient preview bar and move the white one back to about the 25-percent location, as shown here:

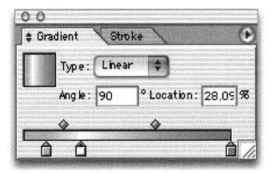

9. With the rounded rectangle still selected, click the stroke proxy in the Toolbox and click the None button below it (a white square with a red slash through it) to remove the object's stroke.

10. Save the file (File | Save or COMMAND-S).

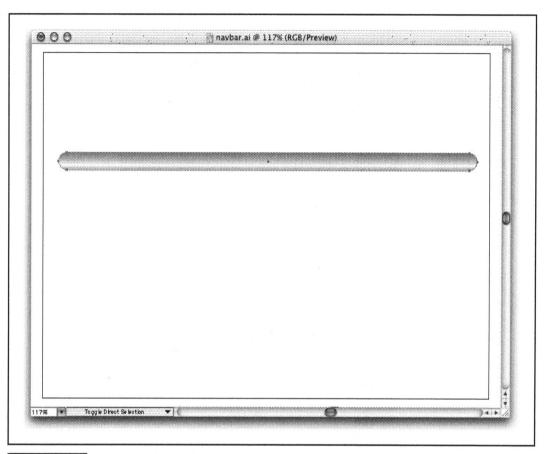

FIGURE   4-4   *It's easy to create a highlight effect using a gradient with just three color stops.* ∎

The rounded rectangle bar now has a colored fill with a highlight created by a gradient, as shown in Figure 4-4. We'll continue our work on this example image later in this chapter, in the "Working with Type" section. By the way, you can create gradients with as many stops as you want—you're not restricted to just three.

Note   *You can't apply a gradient to a stroke; strokes can only be solid colors or patterns.*

Applying patterns is even easier than filling with gradients. Illustrator's existing patterns are stored in the Swatches palette (see "Saving Time with Swatches,

Styles, and Symbols," later in this chapter). To define your own pattern, choose Windows | Swatches to show the Swatches palette, draw the elements you want to use, and drag them into the Swatches palette. To apply a pattern, select the object you want to color and click the fill or stroke proxy on the Toolbox—it works the same way as the one in the Color palette. Then click a pattern swatch in the Swatches palette.

Note *You can't create a pattern from objects colored with a gradient.*

All an object's fills and strokes—as well as other aspects of its appearance—are shown in the Appearance palette. To see and edit the transparency attributes of any stroke or fill, click its name in the Appearance palette and choose Window | Transparency. The Transparency palette, shown here, shows a number of options other than opacity:

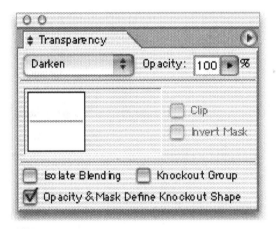

The Stroke palette enables you to specify three aspects of an object's stroke: its weight, whether it's solid or dashed, and the shape of its ends and corners. For dashed lines, you can specify the length of each dash and the space between dashes, as shown next:

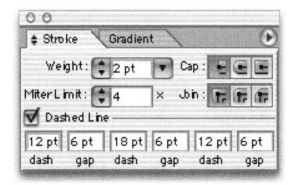

Using Filters and Effects

The terms *filter* and *effect* are often used interchangeably, but in Illustrator the two terms have distinct meanings. A filter is invoked from the Filter menu, and it's permanent—you can undo it, but you can't remove it later on without undoing everything that you did after you applied it. Effects, on the other hand, are invoked from the Effects menu and are portable, meaning that you can remove them or change their settings the entire time you're working on an illustration.

Note *You'll find the SVG filter set in the Effects menu, which means that you can modify the settings of an SVG filter at any time while you work on an image. Turn to "Using the SVG Filter Set," later in this chapter, for more information about the SVG filters.*

A few of Illustrator's filters and effects are the same, such as the Add Arrowheads, Drop Shadow, and Round Corners filters. You can choose to apply these from the Filter menu, in which case they're permanent, or you can use the Effects menu, in which case they can be changed or removed later on. This distinction is really only relevant for native Illustrator files, not SVG files; regardless of whether you use the filter or the effect, it won't be shown in an SVG file as such. For example, if you use the Add Arrowheads filter, the SVG file will simply contain paths shaped as arrowheads, not an arrowhead filter applied to another object.

Both the Filter and the Effect menus contain a wide selection of raster filters and effects in their bottom halves. These are similar to the plug-in filters that are part of Adobe Photoshop, and they can only be applied to an imported raster object or to a vector object that's been rasterized. In either case, these are generally filters you'll want to avoid using with SVG images, because raster images can't be resized well and because their inclusion within a file usually increases its file size astronomically.

Working with Type

You can work with three kinds of type in Illustrator: point type, area type, or type on a path. Special tools are provided for creating each variety of type, but you can use just the Type tool, as follows (see Figure 4-5):

■ To create point type, click in a blank area of the document and begin typing.

■ To create area type—text confined within a bounding box—click and drag, then release the mouse and begin typing. Or, click within an existing shape and begin typing. When you poise the cursor over an existing shape, it changes to a text cursor with a curved line on either side, rather than a square bracket, to indicate that clicking will create area type within the shape.

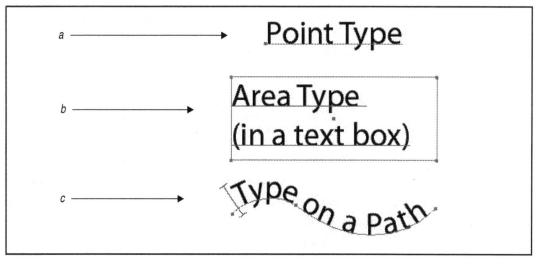

FIGURE 4-5 *Illustrator's three varieties of type are (a) point type, (b) area type, and (c) type on a path.* ■

■ To create type on a path, hold the cursor over an existing path so that it changes to a text cursor sitting on an angled line, then click and type. If you want to move the type along the path, or to the other side of the path, switch to the Direct Selection tool and drag the I-beam that appears at the beginning of the type to the desired location.

The type attributes that you can adjust, in addition to fill and stroke, include its font, size, leading, indents, tab stop locations, and more. Four palettes contain these controls, and they're grouped under the Type submenu in the Window menu (see Figure 4-6).

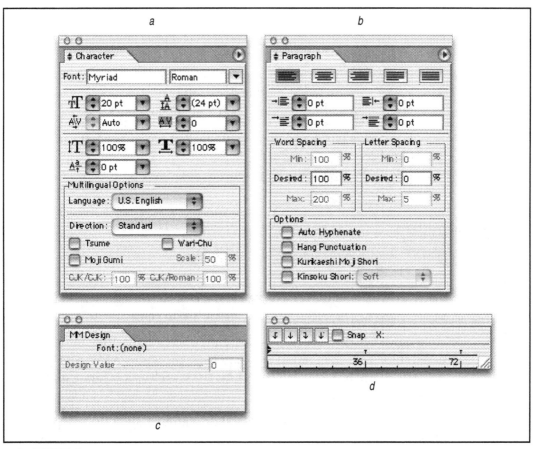

| **FIGURE 4-6** | The four Type palettes are (a) the Character palette, (b) the Paragraph palette, (c) the MM Design palette, and (d) the Tab Ruler palette. ■ |

The Character palette contains controls for font, size, character spacing, and leading, and the Paragraph palette has settings for indents and spacing above and below paragraphs. The Tab Ruler palette is just what it sounds like: a ruler on which you can set the locations of left, right, center, and decimal tabs. (Note that paragraph and tab settings only come into play with area type.) Finally, the MM Design palette enables you to create new instances of multiple master fonts, which can vary in their weight, width, and other attributes.

When you use type in an image, you can choose from three ways of making sure that it looks the same no matter what fonts are installed on the viewer's computer:

- Rasterize the type if you want to apply raster filters to it for special effects (such as making "flaming" type). Rasterized type isn't scalable—zoom in on it and you'll see pixels—and it isn't searchable, because it's not text any more.

- Convert the type to outlines if you want to retain its scalability but you don't care if it's searchable. Outlined text turns into vector objects that still look clean when you zoom in on them, but are no longer text.

- Keep the type as type and embed the fonts that you've used; turn to "Including Compact Embedded Fonts (CEFs)," later in this chapter, for more information on embedding fonts in SVG images.

Return to the navbar.ai example image you created earlier in this chapter and follow these steps to add text to it:

1. Switch to the Type tool.

2. Click anywhere on the artboard and type **HOME**; with the text cursor still active, press COMMAND-SHIFT-C/CTRL-SHIFT-C to center the text.

3. Hold down COMMAND/CTRL and click anywhere on the artboard to deselect the text, then repeat Step 2 to enter the words **NEW ARTICLES**, **ARCHIVE**, **ABOUT US**, and **CONTACT US**, each as a separate unit of point text.

4. Hold down COMMAND/CTRL again and drag around all of the five point text objects to select them.

5. Choose Window | Type | Character to display the Character palette and make the settings shown here (use a different font if you don't have Myriad):

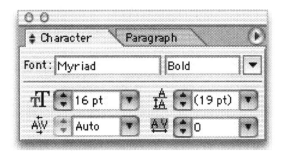

6. Choose Window | Color to display the Color palette and make the settings shown here to turn the type pink:

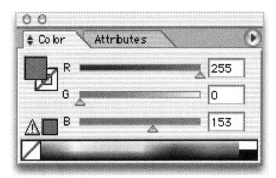

7. Move the text blocks to their approximate positions within the rounded rectangle (see Figure 4-7 for the final type positions).

8. Click the HOME text object and choose Window | Attributes.

9. In the Attributes palette, choose Rectangle from the Image Map pop-up menu, then type **index.html** in the URL field.

Note *Rather than creating an image map, this process actually creates text links within the SVG file.*

Warning *The original release of Adobe Illustrator 10 has a bug in the text link feature such that the closing quotation mark is omitted on export—in other words, an HTML link that should read* `<a xlink:href="index.html">` *will actually read* `<a xlink:href="index.html>`*. Until this bug is fixed (it's still present as this book is written), you'll need to enter that closing quotation mark yourself:* `index.html"`*.*

10. Repeat Step 9 for each text link, entering an appropriate HTML document name for each, and save the file.

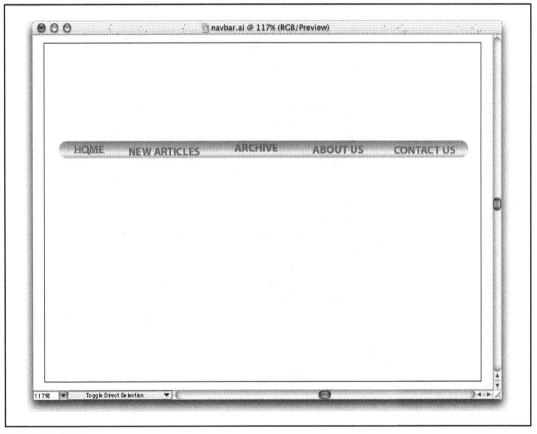

FIGURE 4-7 *The navigation bar now has text that's linked to the web site's various pages.* ∎

Arranging Objects

Although you use Illustrator to create two-dimensional art, the program actually works in three dimensions, in the sense that each element is stacked on top of other elements and below other elements. Choose Window | Layers to display the Layers palette, which lists every element and group in a document and enables you to segregate objects onto separate layers. Use the Layers palette, shown here, to hide objects, select objects, and change their stacking order:

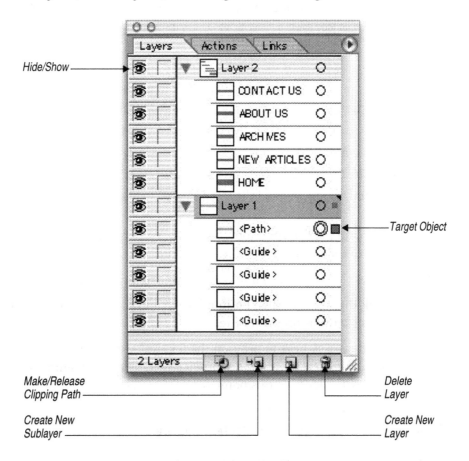

Tip　*If you want to apply attributes to a layer or group, be sure to use the Layers palette to target the layer or group, rather than selecting its individual components. This ensures that the attribute is added to the group tag within the SVG code, rather than repeated for each object.*

The Layers palette also enables you to assign XML IDs to objects and groups. Each layer is exported to SVG as a group, and that group is named with the layer's name. If you assign your own names to layers (such as "Background" or "Address text"), you'll find the SVG code easier to decipher and edit because the ID names will make sense to you.

Tip *XML IDs can't contain spaces, and they must begin with a letter, an underscore, or a colon. No two objects within a document can have the same ID. To be sure that your layer and object names conform to these rules, choose Edit | Preferences | Units & Undo and click XML ID in the Names section. In the Layers palette, "Layer 1" is immediately changed to "Layer_1."*

To arrange objects in the other two planes—vertically and horizontally on the artboard—you can use the Align palette. It contains both alignment and distribution functions so that you can align objects with respect to other objects and distribute objects across a space. To set the *key* object—the one that won't move when the other objects are aligned to it—click or drag to select all the objects you want to align or distribute, then click once more on the key object. Return to the navbar.ai image we've been working on and follow these steps to align the text links:

1. Switch to the Selection tool or hold down COMMAND/CTRL and SHIFT-click each of the five text objects to select them.

2. Choose Window | Align to display the Alignment palette.

3. Click the Vertical Align Bottom button and then the Horizontal Distribute Center buttons on the palette.

4. Use the arrow keys to position the text links vertically so that they're visually centered within the rounded rectangle (see Figure 4-8 to see how the nav bar looks at this point).

Saving Time with Swatches, Styles, and Symbols

Swatches, styles, and symbols are all ways of using the same elements or attributes throughout a document. By using styles and swatches, you can ensure consistency and update colors and other attributes quickly, and symbols offer the additional advantage of reducing file size because, like patterns and gradients, each symbol is defined only once in the document, regardless of the number of times it appears.

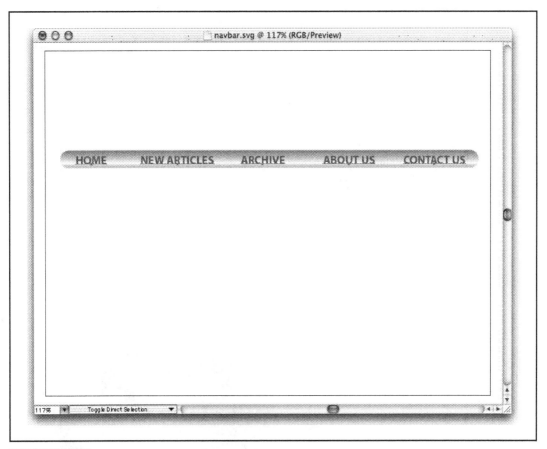

navbar.svg @ 117% (RGB/Preview)

HOME   NEW ARTICLES   ARCHIVE   ABOUT US   CONTACT US

117%   Toggle Direct Selection

FIGURE   4-8   *The text links are now positioned correctly within the navigation bar; the image is almost complete.* ■

Using Swatches

The Swatches palette stores swatches, or samples, of colors, gradients, and patterns. You can add a swatch by dragging an object into the palette; that object's fill, whatever it is, is turned into a swatch.

To make a color swatch a global definition, so that changes to it are reflected in any items to which it's been applied, double-click the swatch and click the Global check box. Then make any changes using the sliders in the dialog box. Pattern and gradient swatches can't be global; if you edit these swatches, objects colored with them won't be updated.

Similar to the Swatches palette are the standard swatch libraries, each within its own palette, that come with Illustrator. To display any of these, choose Window | Swatch Libraries and select the desired library from the submenu. You can use these libraries on their own, applying colors from them as desired, or you can drag swatches from a library palette into the Swatches palette.

Using Styles

Styles, listed in the Styles palette, are the next step up in sophistication from swatches. A style can encompass all the aspects of an object's appearance, including multiple strokes and fills, opacity, and effects (see Figure 4-9).

Note *Don't be misled by the name; Illustrator's styles have no relationship to Cascading Style Sheets (CSS).*

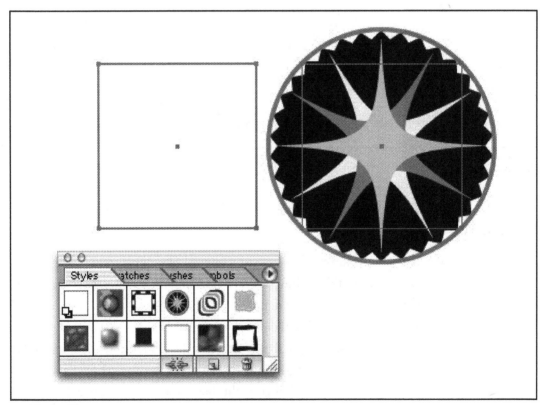

FIGURE 4-9 *The object on the left has the default appearance (1-pt. black stroke, white fill); the right-hand object is a duplicate to which the Star Burst style has been applied.* ■

Like global swatches, styles are linked to the objects to which they're applied. If you modify a style, all the objects within a document that use that style are automatically updated to the new appearance of the style. Styles are easy to modify—make the desired changes to an object that uses the style, then choose Window | Appearance and choose Redefine Style from the Appearance palette menu.

Using Symbols

Symbols are a handy way to use an object more than once within an illustration, yet only define it once in the file. You can use the symbols provided in Illustrator's Symbols palette, and you can create your own by dragging any object or objects right into the palette. Several special tools are provided for placing and arranging symbols within an image. (See "Illustrator's Tools," earlier in this chapter, for a description of the program's wide variety of tools.)

You can distribute single symbols around the artboard by dragging them out of the palette to the desired location. If you want to place multiple symbols randomly along a path, select a symbol in the Symbols palette and switch to the Symbol Sprayer tool, then click and drag.

Tip   *Double-click the Symbol Sprayer tool or any of the symbol tools) in the Toolbox to change its settings, including the radius of the path along which the sprayer distributes symbols.*

Any changes made to the "master" for that symbol are reflected in each instance of it. To update a symbol, follow these steps:

1. Click an instance of the symbol; its original is selected in the Symbols palette.

2. Click the Break Link to Symbol button at the bottom of the Symbols palette; the instance turns back into regular Illustrator paths.

3. Edit the objects that make up the unlinked symbol.

4. Select the edited objects, hold down OPTION/ALT, and drag the objects on top of the original symbol in the Symbols palette. The symbol and all its instances are updated.

If you want to make a new symbol based on an old one, you can drag the modified objects into a blank area of the palette instead. The other instances of the existing symbol will stay the same.

Working with SVG Images in Illustrator

SVG is just one of the many formats Illustrator supports, so for the most part you work on SVG images in the same way you'd work on any artwork in Illustrator. Although you can use all of Illustrator's tools and features to create SVG images, there are some that you'll be better off avoiding (see "Illustrator's SVG Do's and Don'ts," later in this chapter). This section outlines the ways Illustrator supports SVG's unique features.

Note *Unlike Jasc WebDraw, which is designed specifically for creating SVG images, Illustrator doesn't have a source code view; it's entirely WYSIWYG. If you want to edit an SVG image's source code, you'll need to save it and then open it in a text editor.*

Opening SVG Images

You can open an SVG file the same way you'd open any file in Illustrator: drag and drop it onto the program icon, or choose File | Open from within Illustrator. If you're reopening an image that was created in Illustrator, you may find that its layers, effects, and other elements of the file aren't as you left them; this happens when a file is saved with the Preserve Illustrator Editing Capabilities option in the SVG Options dialog box unchecked. (Turn to "Saving SVG Images," later in this chapter, for more information about saving SVG files from Illustrator.)

Adding SVG Features

SVG images are more than just pictures—they can contain animated elements and programmatically controlled data, and they can carry their own fonts along with them. They also use a special set of vector filter effects that are defined in the SVG specification. Illustrator provides ways to access most of these special SVG features.

Using the SVG Filter Set

The SVG filters included in Illustrator use combinations of the mathematical filter effects built into the SVG language to create more sophisticated effects that are still vector data, rather than being rasterized. Many of the native Illustrator effects result in the creation of raster objects (such as soft drop shadows) when the image is saved to SVG format, so it's important to use the SVG filters as much as possible to preserve the vector nature of your artwork.

Note *A few of these included effects have animated elements (such as AI_PixelPlay, AI_Static, and AI_CoolBreeze). The animations don't appear on Illustrator's artboard, but you can edit their attributes in the Edit SVG Filter dialog box.*

You can use the default settings for the SVG filters, or you can edit them to produce your own variations. You can also create your own combinations of effects to produce new filters. Follow these steps to add a drop shadow to the navigation bar in the example image we've been working on:

1. Select the rounded rectangle.
2. Choose Effect | SVG Filters | Apply SVG Filter; in this dialog box you can preview the filter you're applying, modify its settings, or create a new filter.
3. Check the Preview button so you can see the results your choices, then select the AI_Shadow_2 filter from the list.
4. To edit the filter's default settings, click the Edit SVG Filter button and change the dy and dx values in the feOffset line to 5 instead of 8 to shrink the shadow a bit.

Note *You may see some "clipping" around the edges of the object to which you're applying the filter. You can modify the "x," "y," "width," and "height" attributes of the filter element (as in AI_BevelShadow_1) to fix this problem. These attributes determine the area in which the filter effect is calculated with respect to the object.*

Tip *Chapter 15 of the SVG specification (www.w3.org/TR/SVG/) lists all the filters and explains their properties. Be warned—you'll need some serious math to understand everything about these filters, but you can glean enough information from the specification to experiment even if you're not a* *math whiz. If you're not familiar with SVG codes, you can still experiment with modifying filters by changing their numerical values and seeing what effect your changes have on the image.*

5. If you prefer, you can create a new filter (click the New SVG Filter button) or duplicate an existing filter and then modify it (drag and drop the filter on the New SVG Filter button).

6. If you're making a new filter, enter a new name for the filter in the ID attribute in the first line of the SVG code. This is the name you'll see in the Apply SVG Filter dialog box and on the SVG Filters submenu.

7. Apply the filter by clicking OK, then save the final image (see Figure 4-10).

Because Illustrator doesn't display SVG directly, you'll see a rasterized version of the SVG effect on the artboard. To modify the resolution at which this preview is

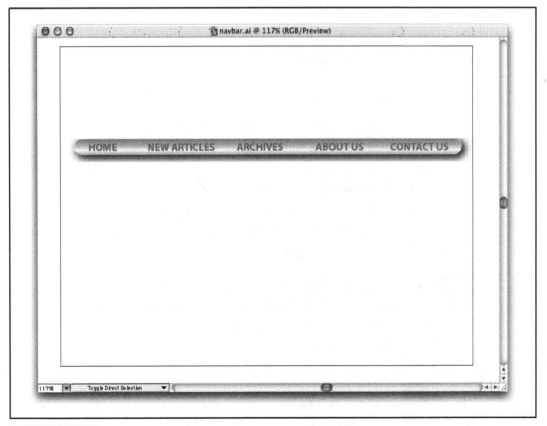

FIGURE 4-10 *The navigation bar artwork is complete; now you only need to save it as SVG.* ∎

created, choose Effect | Document Raster Effect Settings. The rasterization resolution setting doesn't affect the final SVG image, just the Illustrator preview of it.

Tip   *If you've created your own SVG filters, you can import them into another document by choosing Effect | SVG Filter | Import SVG Filter from within the new document. You can also import filter effects from any SVG document using this command.*

Including Compact Embedded Fonts (CEFs)

When you choose to embed fonts while saving an SVG image (any embedding option other than None), they're converted to CEF (Compact Embedded Font) format. Font files saved in this format are usually very small (only a few kilobytes), but they contain both shape and hinting information for each glyph (character). Hinting enables characters to be displayed slightly differently at lower and higher resolutions for optimum clarity.

You can choose to store CEF fonts right in an SVG image (try this and then take a look at the file's source code to see what CEF looks like), or externally in a file that can be referred to by the current SVG image and others. External files are a good option if you're creating multiple files for a single project; for example, if you're working on a company web site, the corporate fonts can be stored in CEF format on the server and don't have to be stored in every single graphic that uses them.

Subsetting enables you to include only some of the characters that exist in the fonts in question. How you choose to subset depends on how you'll use the file later on. If you don't want to embed any fonts—in other words, you expect the user's system to have the image's fonts installed—choose None. If you want to embed the fonts but don't expect to edit the text in the SVG file, choose Only Glyphs Used. And if you do expect to edit the text, choose the option that reflects the kind of characters you are most likely to use, as follows:

- **Common English**   The basic characters used in the English language.

- **Common English and Glyphs Used**   Additional special characters used in English, such as accented characters or alternate glyphs.

- **Common Roman** Common English plus characters with accents used in other languages.

- **Common Roman and Glyphs Used** Common English, accented characters from other languages, and alternate glyphs.

- **All Glyphs** The complete font set. This option yields a significantly larger CEF file, so you should only choose All Glyphs if you absolutely must have every glyph available within the file.

Creating Animated Images

SVG supports three kinds of animation:

- Traditional frame-based animation, in which a series of images is displayed to give the impression of movement. This kind of animation requires you to create a separate image for each change you want to make in the overall image, and the animation's timing depends on the user's computer system.

- Declarative SVG animation, in which an object's properties, such as its color, size, or location, are modified over time. This kind of animation is built into SVG and requires only that you specify the changes you want to make to an animated object and when those changes should take effect. It uses SMIL (Synchronized Multimedia Integration Language), an open standard.

- JavaScript animation, in which JavaScript is used to create more complex effects.

With SVG's advanced animation capabilities, there's no reason to rely on traditional frame-based animation, which is inefficient and time-consuming to create. Unfortunately, Illustrator doesn't provide an interface or any tools to create declarative animation. If you're authoring SVG images in Illustrator, you'll need to add animation in a separate application, such as Jasc WebDraw, or work directly with the SVG code. (Remember, however, that some of Illustrator's SVG filter effects include simple animation.) See "Adding Animation" in Chapter 3 to learn about the simple and efficient way that Jasc WebDraw handles this native form of SVG animation.

To learn more about how Illustrator enables you to add JavaScript functionality to SVG images, see the next section, "Adding Interactivity."

Adding Interactivity

In this context, *interactivity* refers to the use of JavaScript to add dynamic effects to your SVG images. Triggered by common user actions such as clicking or moving the mouse cursor over an image, JavaScripts can create effects such as highlighting, ToolTips, pop-up windows, and animation. Like SVG animation, JavaScript rollovers in SVG don't need to swap images. Normally, to create an image that changes when the mouse cursor moves over it, the designer must supply two images: the original and the changed image. With SVG, you can just specify a change in the object's properties that takes effect when the specified trigger (such as a mouseover) happens. To learn more about Javascript, check out *JavaScript: A Beginner's Guide* by John Pollock (Osborne/McGraw-Hill, 2001).

The SVG Interactivity palette (choose Window | SVG Interactivity) is the control center for using JavaScript within SVG. It displays all the events and JavaScript files used in your document, and it contains the controls for creating links between scripts and their triggers. Here's a look at the SVG Interactivity palette and its controls:

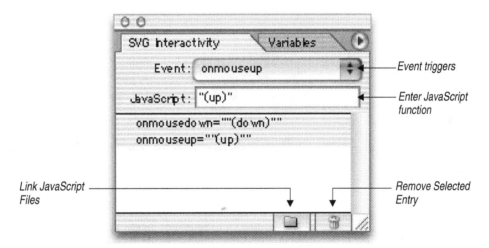

To attach a JavaScript function to an object, follow these steps:

1. Select the object or target a group or layer.

2. Choose Window | SVG Interactivity to display the SVG Interactivity palette.

3. Choose an event trigger from the pop-up menu. In the SVG code, this event will become an attribute of the object or group. See Table 4-1 for an explanation of each trigger.

Note *In earlier versions of the Adobe SVG Viewer, JavaScript-driven SVG doesn't work with current versions of Internet Explorer for Macintosh, including the Mac OS X version. Version 3.0 has solved this problem, so if you're having trouble viewing SVG images with JavaScript, try upgrading to the latest SVG Viewer.*

Command	Trigger
onfocusin	The object is selected.
onfocusout	The object is deselected.
onactivate	A click or key press, depending upon the SVG object.
onmousedown	The mouse is held down on an object.
onmouseup	The mouse is released over an object.
onclick	The mouse is clicked over an object.
onmouseover	The cursor is moved onto an object.
onmousemove	The cursor is over an object.
onmouseout	The cursor is moved away from an object.
onkeydown	A key is pressed.
onkeypress	A key continues to be pressed.
onkeyup	A key is released.
onload	The entire SVG document has been read.
onerror	An error occurs, such as an object not loading properly.
onabort	Page loading is canceled before the object is completely loaded.
onunload	The SVG document is removed from a window or frame.
onzoom	The zoom level is changed.

TABLE 4-1 *Triggers for Activating JavaScripts* ■

4. Enter a JavaScript function in the JavaScript text entry field. In the SVG code, this function will become the value of the event attribute.

5. Click the Link JavaScript Files button to add an external JavaScript file that contains the source for the function you've added.

Note *If you want to learn more about creating and using JavaScript, a good place to start is JavaScript: A Beginner's Guide, by John Pollack. If you're in too much of a hurry to wait for the book to arrive, you can also try some of the many tutorials listed in directory.google.com/Top/Computers/Programming/Languages/JavaScript/Tutorials/.*

Saving SVG Images

Like most processes in Illustrator, saving SVG images can be as simple or as complex as you want to make it. The program offers a wide selection of options, but you can click past those, accepting the default settings, and be fine in most cases. Here's a look at all the steps that *can* be involved in saving files in SVG format; remember that not all these steps are required every time you save an image.

To save the example navigation bar image in SVG format, open it and follow these steps:

1. Choose Window | Appearance to display the Appearance palette.

2. Select the rounded rectangle and drag the Appearance palette entry for its SVG filter to the bottom of the palette, just above the transparency entry. If there are any other effects following the SVG filter in the Appearance palette, the SVG filter will be turned into a raster object.

3. Choose File | Save and set the Format to SVG in the pop-up menu.

4. Enter a filename (**navbar.svg**) and navigate to the location where you want to save the file.

5. In the SVG Options dialog box, set these options:

   ■ Choose which font glyphs (characters) you want embedded in the file, or choose None. In this case, choose Only Glyphs Used since we don't expect to need to edit this file.

- Choose whether you want the fonts to be embedded directly in the image or stored separately from the file. (This option isn't available if you've chosen Only Glyphs Used, in which case the fonts will automatically be embedded.)

- If you had used raster images in the file, you'd need to make the same choice about raster images. They can be embedded within the SVG file or stored externally.

- Check Preserve Illustrator Editing Capabilities if you plan to edit the file in Illustrator later on; this will make sure that Illustrator-only features are retained.

6. Click Advanced to set more options:

- Choose a method of including style attributes within the SVG code. Presentation Attributes is the default; switch to Style Attributes if you plan to apply transformations using Extensible Stylesheet Language Transformation (XSLT). Use Style Elements if you want the SVG document to share a style sheet file with HTML documents. For the best performance, use Style Attributes.

- Choose a number of decimal places between 1 and 7 to be used for measurements in the vector data. The higher the number, the larger your file—but the more precise the object measurements within the file. If users may zoom in on the file, use a higher value to make sure that the image looks right at higher magnification.

- Choose a character encoding method. UTF-8 is the most compatible method, including Roman characters and common Asian characters. ISO 8859-1 works only for Roman characters, while UTF-16 is used to include all Roman and Asian characters.

- Check Optimize for Adobe SVG Viewer to decrease rendering time for images that you know will be viewed using Adobe's SVG viewing plug-in. Either way, images will always be viewable with both Adobe's viewer and other viewers.

- Check Include Extended Syntax for Variable Data if you are creating a template. This enables you to fill in text from a database by designating objects as variables using the Variables palette; see the Illustrator documention for more information.

- Check Include Slicing Data if you've sliced the image into smaller images, each of which will be saved as a separate file.

Check Include File Info if you want to include Illustrator's File Info data as metadata within the file. This only works if you choose UTF-8 encoding.

7. Click OK to save your file.

Note   *When you save an SVG file, each Illustrator layer is changed into a group element (<g>) within the SVG code. Hidden layers remain hidden with their display property set to "none."*

Illustrator's SVG Do's and Don'ts

All SVG artwork is not created equal. To produce the smallest, best-looking SVG images, follow these general guidelines:

- Don't use raster images within an Illustrator image, and don't rasterize vector elements so that you can apply filters to them. As a vector format, SVG isn't at its best when used to convey raster data, because raster images can't be scaled infinitely as vector images can. Remember that some built-in Illustrator styles incorporate filters that result in rasterized data, and avoid other special effects that require the image to be rasterized, including gradient meshes.

- Take advantage of symbols and patterns wherever possible to maximize performance and reduce file size.

- Simplify paths—manually or using the Simplify command—whenever possible, and avoid using brush strokes that yield a lot of small, complex paths if possible. More complex paths increase file size and reduce redrawing speed.

- To make sure that objects on different layers (that is, within different SVG groups) appear transparent, make sure you apply transparency effects to the objects instead of to their layers. SVG doesn't handle group transparency the same way Illustrator handles layer transparency.

chapter 5

Creating SVG Images with CorelDRAW

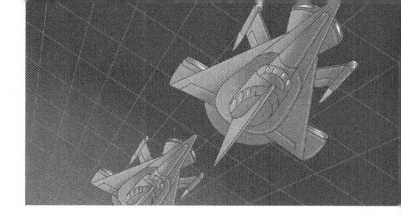

Corel was one of the first software developers to embrace the SVG standard and released a beta SVG import/export filter for version 9 of its flagship product, CorelDRAW, in 1999. Unfortunately, the developer's attention has been focused elsewhere since that time. Although SVG import and export capabilities are now native to CorelDRAW 10, the program has no support for SVG's special features, including SVG filters and animation. For this reason, CorelDRAW as it now exists probably won't be most people's choice for authoring SVG graphics.

However, you can use CorelDRAW to translate legacy graphics into SVG or to create images that will be enhanced with SVG features using another application. This chapter briefly reviews CorelDRAW's basic features and then covers its SVG import and export options. Throughout the chapter we'll show the step-by-step creation of an example graphic drawn in CorelDRAW.

CorelDRAW Basics

CorelDRAW is a full-fledged illustration program with a long history, mostly on the Windows side of the aisle. Some versions have been available for both Mac OS and Windows, while others have been Windows-only. The current version of CorelDRAW, version 10, runs on Windows, Mac OS 9, and Mac OS X, but you can still see the program's Windows heritage in its interface.

The CorelDRAW Workspace

Like Illustrator, CorelDRAW uses a page metaphor, displaying a "drawing page" that defines the printable area in the middle of a blank workspace within each document window (see Figure 5-1). Unlike Illustrator, CorelDRAW supports multipage documents, although this feature is unlikely to be of use to SVG designers. The lower-left corner of the document window contains navigation controls that enable you to move from page to page and add pages. Clicking the blank square at the bottom left-hand corner of the window opens a thumbnail display that you can use to navigate through an image.

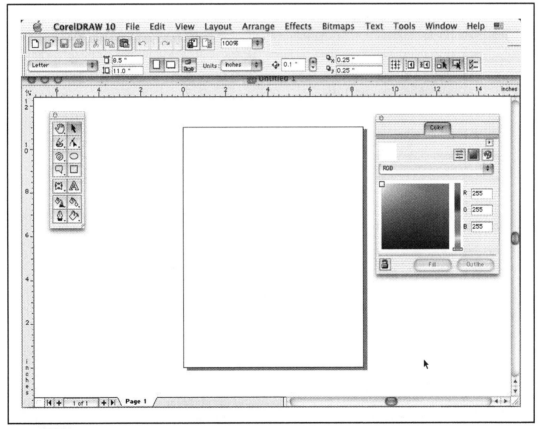

FIGURE   5-1   *CorelDRAW's interface makes use of standard toolbars and floating palettes, all surrounding a document window containing a drawing page.* ∎

An amenity that other programs would do well to copy, the Status Bar, appears at the bottom of the screen and displays information about selected objects and the current tool, as well as the cursor's coordinates. It offers helpful reminders about tool behavior and lets you know the size and type of each object you select.

CorelDRAW's Tools

CorelDRAW's Toolbox is quite similar to Adobe Illustrator's (see Figure 5-2). Most of its tools are segregated into flyouts, as follows:

■ **Zoom**   The Zoom and Hand tools control the view percentage and the drawing page's position in the document window, respectively.

■ **Curve**   Here you'll find tools for creating paths. The Freehand and Bézier tools are self-explanatory. The Artistic Media tool adds elaborate brushstrokes, the Dimension tool adds dimension lines complete with numeric measurements, and the Interactive Connector tool creates flowchart connectors.

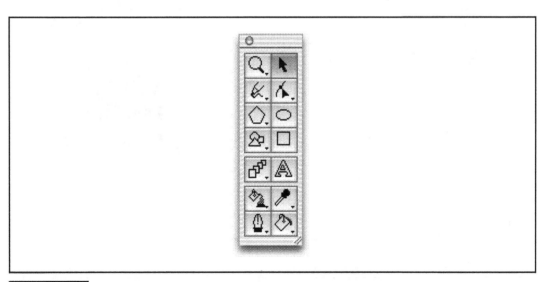

FIGURE   5-2   *Click and hold to display the extra tools that are hidden under the visible tools in the Toolbox.* ■

- **Shape Edit**   These are the Shape, Knife, Eraser, and Free Transform tools, for editing existing paths.

- **Object**   Use the Polygon, Spiral, and Graph tools to create these kinds of objects.

- **Perfect Shapes**   You can create a selection of prefab shapes using the Basic Shapes, Arrow Shapes, Flowchart Shapes, Star Shapes, and Callout Shapes tools.

- **Interactive Tools**   Similar to the Free Transform tool, these tools enable you to alter the shape or other characteristics of an object by clicking and dragging its anchor points: these include Interactive Blend, Interactive Contour, Interactive Distortion, Interactive Envelope, Interactive Extrude, Interactive Drop Shadow, and Interactive Transparency tools.

- **Interactive Fill**   The Interactive Fill and Interactive Mesh Fill tools enable you to add fountain fills (CorelDRAW's term for gradient fills) or mesh gradient fills to objects by clicking and dragging (as opposed to through a dialog box).

- **Eyedropper**   You can duplicate fills and strokes from other objects using the Eyedropper and Paintbucket tools.

- **Outline**   These "tools" actually provide quick access to the Outline Pen and Outline Color dialog boxes, the Color palette, and various widths of outlines.

- **Fill**   Here you'll be able to access the Fill Color, Fountain Fill, Pattern Fill, PostScript Fill, and Texture Fill dialog boxes and the Color palette.

In addition to these tools, you'll find the Pick tool (for selecting objects), the Ellipse and Rectangular tools, and the Text tool.

CorelDRAW's Toolbars

CorelDRAW has several toolbars that provide quick access to the program's functions (see Figure 5-3), and you can customize them to contain only the buttons you need. The included toolbars are these:

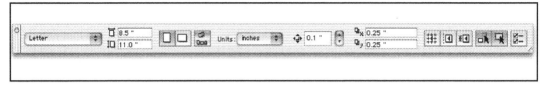

FIGURE 5-3   *Like several of CorelDRAW's toolbars, the Property Bar is context-sensitive; its settings change depending on the situation.* ■

- **Standard**   Commands common to most modern computer programs appear here, including Save, Print, Copy, Undo, and the like.

- **Property Bar**   Here you'll find information about the selected object or the active tool.

- **Text**   Use the Text toolbar to quickly change font or point size or apply a style to the selected text.

- **Zoom**   The buttons on this toolbar enable you to zoom in on specific objects or the page itself, as well as enter arbitrary view percentages.

- **Internet**   A variety of functions for web graphics are accessible via this toolbar, including rollovers, image maps, and HTML export. These features are only preserved if you use SWF (Flash) or HTML export, so they aren't available to SVG images in CorelDRAW.

- **Print Merge**   You can use these controls to create customized documents such as mass mailings.

- **Transform**   You can use these buttons to apply standard transformations such as scaling, skewing, flipping, or rotating an object or a copy of an object.

- **Status Bar**   The selected object's position and hints about the current tool's behavior appear on this toolbar.

Any toolbar, including the Toolbox, can float or be docked to the top or bottom of your screen, and you can resize a toolbar by dragging its lower right-hand corner.

CorelDRAW's Palettes

Twenty different floating palettes offer easy access to most of CorelDRAW's features (see Figure 5-4). To display a palette, choose Window | Palettes and then choose its name from the submenu. Here's a list of CorelDRAW's palettes:

- **Artistic Media palette**   The brushstrokes shown on this palette can be applied to shapes.

- **Bitmap Color Mask palette**   Masks applied to bitmap (raster) images can either hide the specified color or display only that color.

- **Blend palette**   Use this palette to control a blend between two or more shapes; blends consist of a specified number of shapes that morph in shape and color from one original shape to another as they get closer to it.

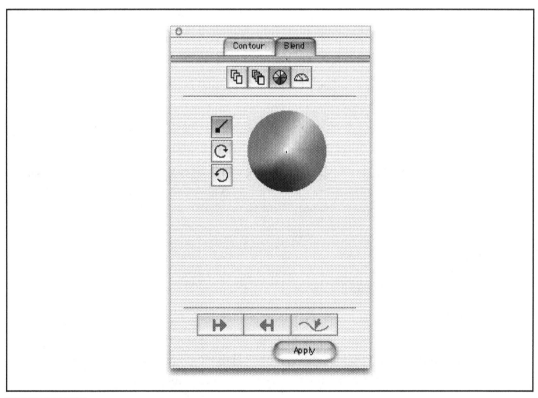

FIGURE   5-4   *Several palettes have Apply buttons, enabling you to make all your settings before applying them to the selected object.* ■

- **Color Palette Browser**   Here you can access the predefined color libraries that are built into CorelDRAW.

- **Color palette**   On this palette you can define colors using swatches, sliders, or a color wheel.

- **Color Styles palette**   Here you can store swatches of frequently used colors.

- **Contour palette**   This palette enables you to add contour lines within or outside of shapes, as you'd see on a map.

- **Envelope palette**   By applying an envelope to text or other shapes, you can force those objects to take on the shape of the envelope.

- **Extrude palette**   This palette enables you to apply and control three-dimensional effects created by "extruding" shapes.

- **Graphic and Text Styles palette**   Styles enable you to change an object's attributes with a single click to match those defined in the style.

- **Internet Bookmark Manager**   You can create and delete hyperlinks using this palette.

- **Lens palette**   Use the Lens palette to turn an object into a lens that distorts the color or shape of objects under it.

- **Link Manager**   You can use this list of links to external documents to update links and open linked files in their originating applications.

- **Object Manager**   This is CorelDRAW's equivalent of Illustrator's Layers palette, listing both the different layers and pages within the document and all the objects contained on those layers and pages.

- **Properties palette**   Containing panes for Fill, Outline, Page, and Form, this palette enables you to specify both the basic appearance of objects and the basic info to be included in a HTML page or a web form generated from the current document.

- **Shaping palette**   The functions on the Shaping palette enable you to combine multiple shapes in different ways to form new shapes.

- **Symbols and Special Characters palette**   You can insert punctuation and other special type characters by clicking on this palette.

- **Transformations palette**   Change an object's location or other attributes using the Position, Rotate, Scale, Size, and Skew functions on the Transformations palette.

- **Undo palette**   Here you'll see a history of the changes you've made to the current file; click a step to return to that point in the document's development.

- **View Manager**   Using this palette, you can control your view of the document, including the zoom percentage, and save views for future use.

Tip   *You can combine palettes by clicking the name tab of a palette and dragging it on top of another palette. The two will appear in a single floating window with two tabs.*

CorelDRAW's Menus

CorelDRAW's menus are more modular than those of many illustration programs, breaking out functions for text and raster images into separate menus. Other than that, the commands included in each menu are fairly standard both in function and location. Here's a rundown of the program's menus:

- **File**   Here you'll find commands to open, save, and print files, and to send them to other venues such as a commercial printer, PDF, or the Web.

- **Edit**   This menu contains Undo and Redo commands, along with the usual Cut, Copy, and Paste, as well as search and replace functions and functions for customizing CorelDRAW's color management and other behaviors.

- **View**   In this menu there are five commands to display different levels of detail, as well as the options of displaying guides, gridlines, and other interface elements.

- **Layout**   The Layout menu includes commands for managing pages within a document.

- **Arrange**   These commands enable you to transform, align and distribute, group, and lock objects.

- **Effects**   Listed here are special effects commands relating to vector objects.

- **Bitmaps**   The commands found in the Bitmap menu are mostly special effects for raster images.

- **Text**   The Text commands control both type (size, font, and so on) and text (spell checking and the like).

- **Tools**   Included in the Tools menu are commands to view the palettes that affect entire documents, such as the Links palette.

- **Window**   Window-related commands include access to all of the program's toolbars and palettes and give you the ability to create a new window (with a different view) for an open document.

- **Help**   This is a standard Help menu containing commands for the online help, as well as links to the CorelTUTOR tutorial and information about Corel's technical support.

Drawing Objects

CorelDRAW provides a wide array of drawing tools and gives you the ability to create both freehand and prefab shapes and edit them in several ways.

Creating Shapes

Like most illustration programs, CorelDRAW builds all its shapes from Bézier curves—but that doesn't mean you have to deal with them. You can draw curves using the Bézier tool, or you can use the Freehand tool to sketch curved shapes. Finally, you can use the Shape tools to create prefab shapes such as rectangles, ellipses, spirals, arrows, and more.

To draw shapes with the Bézier tool, you need to understand how the tool's movement affects the curves it's creating—and practicing the tool's use is the best path to understanding how it works. Follow these steps to create a simple Bézier shape:

1. Switch to the Bézier tool.

2. Click anywhere on the drawing page and hold the mouse button down as you drag to the right; then release the button.

3. Click below and to the right of the first point you created—if the first point was at noon on an imaginary clock face, click at three o'clock—and drag straight down.

4. Click again at six o'clock and drag to the left before releasing the mouse button.

5. Click and drag at nine o'clock; this time, drag upward.

6. Click on the first point to close the shape and drag to the right again. Here's what you should end up with:

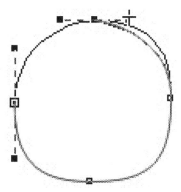

Depending on how much you dragged at each point, your shape looks more or less like a circle. The idea is to drag in the opposite direction from the way you want the "belly" of the curve to extend.

Of course, if you're actually trying to draw a circle, it's usually more efficient just to use CorelDRAW's Ellipse tool. The same is true if you want to create a rectangle, which is the first step in the example graphic for this chapter. Follow these steps:

1. Choose File | New or press COMMAND-N to create a new, blank file.

2. Switch to the Rectangle tool.

3. Click and drag diagonally to draw a rectangle that's about three times as wide as it is tall, as shown here:

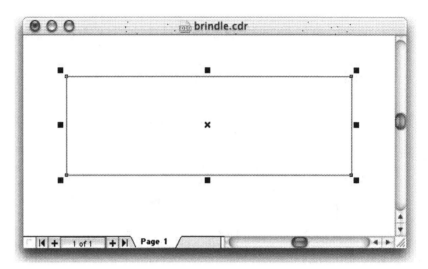

4. Press COMMAND-S to save the file in CorelDRAW format temporarily as you work on it. Our file is called brindle.cdr.

To make a shape symmetrical—circular or square, in the case of the Ellipse and Rectangle tools, respectively—hold down SHIFT as you drag. The Properties Bar contains settings for each tool so that you can customize shapes as you draw them.

To construct complex shapes by combining simpler ones, use the Shaping commands: Weld, Trim, and Intersect. Weld combines two shapes into one, Trim removes the part of a shape that's covered by another shape, and Intersect creates a new shape from the intersection of two shapes. With each operation, you have the option of preserving either or both of the original shapes as you create a new shape.

Filling and Stroking Shapes

The basic method for adding fills and strokes—or *outlines*, as they're called in CorelDRAW—to objects is to use the Color palette. Just select the object, mix the color you want, and click the Fill or Outline button to apply it to the object. Store colors that you use throughout a document in the Color Styles palette by dragging objects directly onto the palette.

Now for the more interesting fills: patterns and fountain fills, as CorelDRAW calls gradients. You can apply patterns using the appropriate Fill tools: Pattern Fill, Texture Fill, and PostScript Fill. Pattern fills are composed of repeating vector objects. Texture fills are similar, but are designed to simulate three-dimensional textures. PostScript fills are simple patterns with editable attributes such as line width and shade. To apply any of these, choose the appropriate tool, set the color or pattern options in the dialog box, and click OK (see Figure 5-5).

Fountain fills can be two-color or multicolor gradients, and you can choose linear, radial, conical, or square shapes for them as well as choosing the colors used. In the Fountain Fill dialog box, you'll need to specify colors and other settings, such as angle (for linear gradients), and the location of the midpoint between the colors.

Tip   *CorelDRAW 10 doesn't handle linear gradients in quite standard fashion, which may cause display problems for some images. If you feel up to a little text editing, however, you can fix the gradients by inserting the text* **gradientUnits="userSpaceOnUse"** *in each linearGradient or radialGradient element. See Appendix A for more information about the SVG gradient spec.*

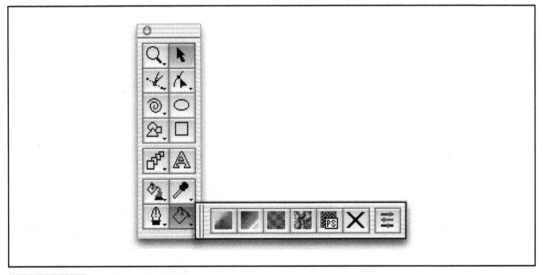

FIGURE   5-5   *Fill dialog boxes can be accessed via the Toolbox.* ∎

You can also create a variation on a fountain fill, called a *mesh gradient,* which applies multiple radial gradients to an object at points specified on an invisible grid (a *mesh*) within the object. Mesh gradients are fun to experiment with and can be used to create complex effects, both fantastical and photorealistic. However, SVG doesn't support mesh gradients, so you may wish to avoid using them in SVG images. If you do use a mesh gradient, it will be converted to a raster object when the image is exported to SVG format.

The same is true of conical and square gradients, which are converted to multiple objects, each with a slightly different shade of color fill from the one preceding it. The idea is to simulate the gradient effect while still using vector objects, rather than rasterizing the objects.

Tip *To transfer outlines and fills from one object to another, use the Eyedropper tool to "pick up" a color by clicking on an object that uses it; then switch to the Paintbucket tool and click another object to fill or outline it with the selected color.*

To adjust an object's outline width, enter a new value in the Outline Width field on the Property Bar. Also located in the Outline flyout are several preset outline widths that you can apply to selected objects by just clicking them. And if you want to change an outline's style to something other than a standard rule, choose Effects | Artistic Media, or just switch to the Artistic Media tool and choose a brush stroke effect from the pop-up menu in the Property Bar.

Note *Shapes that use these complex outlines are converted into separate vector objects on export to SVG, losing their identity as individual paths.*

Working with Type

CorelDRAW is equipped with a nice set of text layout features, including automatic and bulleted lists, multicolumn text boxes, and comprehensive hyphenation and justification controls comparable to those found in page layout programs.

You can create two kinds of text in CorelDRAW: artistic text and paragraph text. Artistic text is sometimes called *point text,* and it's not confined by a box, while paragraph text flows within a box and can use paragraph settings such as indents and space above and below. The same tool works to create either kind of text: the Text tool. Click and begin typing to create artistic text, or click and drag out a box shape, then begin typing to create paragraph text.

Note   *CorelDRAW 10 exports paragraph text to SVG as individual text lines, which means that users won't be able to select an entire paragraph in the final image.*

To format either kind of text, use the Format Text dialog box; choose Text | Format Text or press COMMAND-T/CONTROL-T (see Figure 5-6).

- **Character**   You can set font, size, style, and script (Latin or Asian), and use incremental positioning and kerning controls.

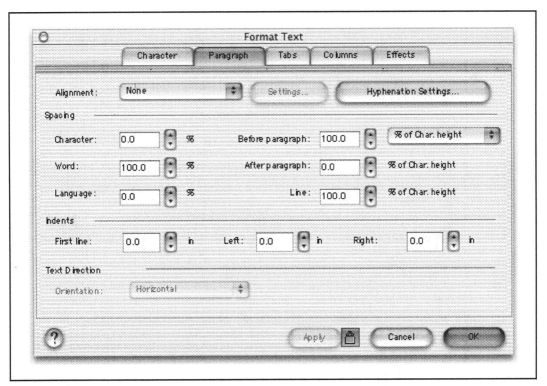

FIGURE   5-6   *The five tabs in the Format Text dialog box contain all the text controls you'll need.* ∎

- **Paragraph**   Here you'll find settings for character and word spacing, indents, and text orientation (vertical or horizontal).

- **Tabs**   The tab controls enable you to set one or more tabs with left, right, center, or decimal alignment. You can also add tab leaders.

- **Columns**   You can have up to eight columns in a single text box, and you can set both the gutter widths and the column widths individually if you wish.

- **Effects**   This tab enables you to turn the selected paragraphs into a bulleted list, or format the first letter as a drop cap.

A third kind of text is artistic text that's anchored to a path. To create path type, create the artistic text and the path, then select both and choose Text | Fit Text to Path.

Note   *CorelDRAW 10 exports artistic text to SVG as individual words, which means that users won't be able to select an entire line in the final image. It also means that if the SVG file is modified to use a different font, the words may not be spaced correctly.*

Most of the time, you'll use point text in illustrations. Follow these steps to add the text to our example illustration:

1. Open the brindle.cdr file.
2. Switch to the Text tool and click inside the rectangle.
3. Enter the text **BRINDLEDOG** and press COMMAND-A to select the entire text line.
4. Press COMMAND-T to open the Format Text dialog box.
5. Change the font and size to fill the width of the box, leaving a little space at the top and bottom. In the example, the type is 24-point Futura Bold Condensed.
6. Switch to the Pick tool and position the text inside the box, with room below it for another, smaller line of text.

7. Choose Window | Palettes | Color to display the Color palette.

8. With the text line still selected, choose a bright red and click the Fill button to turn the type red.

9. Switch to the Text tool.

10. Click outside the box to create another line of text, and type **SUPPLIES FOR YOUR GREYHOUND**.

11. Press COMMAND-A to select the entire text line.

12. Change the font and size of the second text line so that it fits nicely under the first line, and increase the range kerning setting so that the text is spaced out to the same line length as "BRINDLEDOG."

13. Switch back to the Pick tool and position the second line of type under the first one inside the box.

14. Use the Color palette to turn the second line of text bright blue.

15. Press COMMAND-S to save the file.

Figure 5-7 shows the box and text that you've created so far.

FIGURE 5-7 *The box and two lines of text will be enhanced with special effects to create a logo.* ∎

> **Tip** *As you know, type used in an SVG illustration program remains type, rather than being converted to pixels as it would be in a GIF or JPEG image. However, the thing to remember about type is that if it stays editable, it's subject to being changed in a way that may not be compatible with your design. Changing the font changes the size and shape of the text such that it might stick out of a box or no longer align with another object correctly. When you're creating images that may be modified in this way, consider testing them with all available fonts and other attributes to make sure that your design looks as intended no matter what.*

Using Filters and Effects

CorelDRAW's special effects for vector objects are found in the Effects menu, although many of them are accessible via the Toolbox or in other ways. They include

- **Adjust**   This submenu contains commands for adjusting the brightness, contrast, and other color attributes of an object.

- **Transform**   Using these commands, you can change the shape, size, and position of an object.

- **Artistic Media**   This command calls up the Artistic Media palette, which you can use to apply a wide variety of special strokes to objects.

- **Blend**   Morph one object into another with any number of intermediate steps.

- **Contour**   This command adds concentric shapes inside or outside the selected object.

- **Envelope**   Using an envelope, you can reshape an object to match the envelope's shape without changing the contents of the object.

- **Extrude**   Create three-dimensional objects by drawing flat shapes and using the Extrude command to extend them into the third dimension at any angle.

- **Lens**   You can turn any vector shape into a lens that affects the appearance of the objects below it in any of a variety of ways.

- **Add Perspective**   By skewing an object in one or two directions, you can make it appear to be placed at an angle to the viewer.

- **PowerClip**   This is a cute name for an important basic feature: clipping paths, by which an object can be visible only within the bounds determined by another object.

- **Rollover**   Use this command to add rollover effects to Web graphics.

To apply any effect, select the object or objects you want to modify, and choose the command you want to use from the menu. Your selection may vary depending on the effect you're using. For example, if you want to create a lens effect, make sure you create and select an object to become the lens, rather than applying the lens effect to the object you want to view through the lens.

Tip   *Once you've applied a vector effect to an object, you can copy it to another object by creating the object and then choosing Effect | Copy Effect. Select the effect you want to copy from the submenu, and click the object from which you want to copy. The same effect settings are applied to the new object.*

Effects for use on bitmap (raster) objects are on the Bitmap menu and are similar to those available in Adobe Photoshop or other image editors—you can blur, add noise, apply a variety of textures, and so on.

The best effects to use for SVG images are those that simply modify the shape of a path or add additional vector objects. Two of these filters will finish off the example graphic we've been working on:

1. Open the brindle.cdr file.

2. With the Pick tool, click the box to select it.

3. Choose Effects | Contour and enter the settings shown here in the Contour palette:

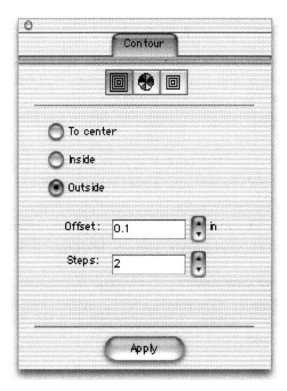

4. Click Apply to add two extra rules to the outside of the box.

5. Switch to the Interactive Envelope tool and click to select the "BRINDLEDOG" text.

6. Click the top-middle handle of the text's bounding box and drag it upward to reshape the text, as shown in Figure 5-8

7. Save the file.

Arranging Objects

Once you've created an object, you need to switch back to the Pick tool to move it or resize it. You can switch temporarily by holding down the COMMAND/CTRL key. Click and drag to move an object, or click and drag a corner handle to resize it. If

FIGURE 5-8 *The BRINDLEDOG logo is now complete and ready to be exported to SVG format.* ∎

you hold down SHIFT as you move or resize, you'll restrict your motion to straight lines or preserve the object's proportions, respectively.

For more complex arrangements, you'll need to transform objects. Technically, moving and resizing qualify as transformations, but you can execute the more interesting transformations by choosing Arrange | Transformations. Choose the transformation you want, then click and drag. The Transformation palette appears, and you can use it to switch transformations without returning to the menu, to make transformations numerically rather than by dragging, and to determine the point from which the transformation is calculated.

Another important aspect of an object is its position in the third dimension with respect to other objects in the drawing; is it in front of or behind them? You can change the stacking order of objects, as well as review all the objects used in the current document, by choosing Window | Palettes | Object Manager to display the Object Manager palette. This palette shows all the pages in the document and all the objects on those pages; you can drag an object to position it above or below other objects, or you can click it and then click the Trash button to delete it.

Two commands in CorelDRAW's Arrange menu have similar, but quite distinct, functions: Group and Combine. Choose Arrange | Group to associate the selected objects with each other so that they can be moved and resized as one. Clicking on one object in a group selects the entire group. Choose Arrange | Combine, on the other hand, if you want CorelDRAW to treat the shapes as two or more parts of one large, fragmented shape. Combined objects have the same fill—for example, a linear gradient goes across all the combined objects, not across each one separately—and if they intersect, those intersections are "holes" in the combined object. Choose Arrange | Ungroup to return a group to its constituent parts, or Arrange | Break Apart to do the same thing for combined objects.

Getting SVG Images Into and Out of CorelDRAW

While CorelDRAW doesn't yet have features to support SVG filters, animation, or other effects, it does have a simple and streamlined import/export process. When creating SVG files, remember that you have a choice of methods. You can use the Save command or the Export command. Either method creates a new SVG file; the difference lies in which file remains open on your screen. If you use Save, the current file is turned into an SVG file, so any changes made to it after saving in SVG format are part of the SVG document. With Export, on the other hand, a new file is created that's separate from the open document on your screen. If you make any changes in the current document after you export an SVG file, you'll need to export again; the Save command won't update the SVG file.

Opening SVG Images

CorelDRAW can open SVG files consisting purely of the basic SVG elements—vector shapes, raster images, and text. However, because CorelDRAW doesn't support other SVG features, it converts elements such as SVG filters into objects that it can understand. This limits the SVG files that you'll be able to edit in

CorelDRAW. When in doubt as to whether a file contains unsupported elements, always keep an archive copy, and check the SVG code carefully after exporting the image from CorelDRAW to make sure that all the original elements are still there.

To bring an SVG image into CorelDRAW, you have two choices:

- Choose File | Open to open the image file itself.

- Choose File | Import to place the image within the document you're currently editing.

You don't have any options to choose when you're opening an SVG image.

Exporting SVG Images

CorelDRAW makes exporting SVG images very simple, with all the settings you'll need to consider collected into one dialog box. Before saving images, CorelDRAW automatically checks for potential problems within the file, a process known as *preflighting*. Five issues are included in the preflight checklist for SVG files:

- **Conical/Square fountain fills**   Fountain fills are what CorelDRAW calls gradients, and SVG doesn't support square or conical gradients, so objects colored using these options are converted to multiple objects when exported to SVG. This results in either a very complex file, or, if you reduce the number of steps in the fill, a banded appearance.

- **2-color pattern fills**   CorelDRAW rasterizes two-color pattern fills on export to SVG.

- **Mesh fills**   These are also converted to raster images on export to SVG format.

- **Bitmap images**   Bitmap, or raster, images can dramatically increase file size, so CorelDRAW wants to make sure that you realize you're including them in your images.

■ **Sound files**   Sound files can't be directly embedded in an SVG document, so CorelDRAW warns you if you've used one.

When you export to SVG format, you'll be alerted to any of these situations that exist in your file. Follow these steps to preflight the example image we've been working on and save it in SVG format:

1. Open the brindle.cdr file.

2. Choose File | Export, or press COMMAND-E/CONTROL-E.

3. Enter a name for the file and navigate to the location where you want to save it.

4. Choose W3C SVG (Mac) or SVG – Scalable Vector Graphics (Windows) from the Format pop-up menu.

Note   *"W3C" stands for the World Wide Web Consortium, the international body that governs web standards, including the standard for SVG.*

5. Click Export.

6. Click the Issues tab of the SVG Export dialog box to see if there are any problems you need to deal with before saving the image. If so, click Cancel to return to the image and make changes. Then start over at Step 1.

Note   *If no problems are encountered, the Issues tab of the SVG Export dialog box is labeled "No Issues." If problems are found, the tab is labeled with the number of issues found.*

7. Make the following settings in the SVG Export dialog box, shown here:

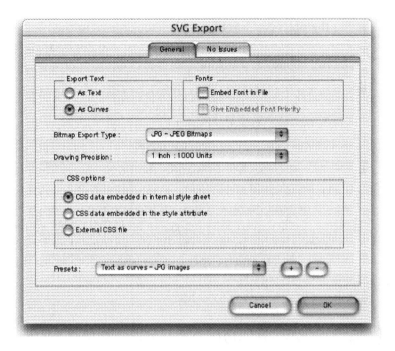

- Choose to export text as text or as curves (in other words, converted to outlines). Text converted to curves isn't editable or searchable. In this case, we don't need the text to be searchable, so it saves space to convert the text to curves.

- Choose whether you want to embed fonts in your SVG file. If you check Embed Font in File, make sure you also check Give Embedded Font Priority to make sure that the font included in the file is used rather than the user's default web browser font. In the case of the example file, we are converting the text to curves, so there's no need to include the fonts we used in the SVG file.

Note   *Because of anomalies in CorelDRAW 10's font embedding feature, unusual fonts aren't property embedded and may not be displayed correctly on the end-user's system. You can play it safe by converting text to paths, although you will lose the ability to select, edit, and search for text in the final SVG image.*

- Set the precision level for the vector objects in the file; this determines how exactly each path must be drawn, and affects the file size. The default setting is fine for our example.

- Choose a file format—PNG, JPEG, or GIF—for any raster images that you've used in the file (or any special effects that will be converted to raster images). We don't need to worry about this in this case, because the document contains no raster images.

- Choose where style information should be saved—in an external style sheet, an internal style sheet, or within each style attribute. This choice would depend on how styles are used on the rest of your web site. If you plan to embed your SVG images in an HTML page, you may be able to use the same CSS file for both the HTML document and the SVG document, which makes it much easier to keep things consistent throughout a site.

8. Click OK to save the SVG file.

Tip *If you find yourself using the same settings over and over, click the plus button at the bottom of the SVG Export dialog box to save the settings in a named group of presets that will appear in the Presets pop-up menu.*

chapter **6**

Creating SVG Images
with Other Drawing Apps

The three preceding chapters have looked at traditional illustration applications—one new program purpose-built to generate SVG, and two "old" programs that have been titans in the design software field for years. But when it comes to creating SVG images, these three programs are far from your only choices. Products from small developers, offerings from shareware programmers, and open source programs are getting more press and gaining more fans. The range of operating systems available to designers and programmers has grown, too, with many turning to various implementations of UNIX as well as the various flavors of Windows and both old (Mac OS 9 and earlier) and new (Mac OS X) versions of the Macintosh operating system.

In this chapter, we investigate several more tools available to designers who want to create SVG images. Each takes a different approach and offers users a different feature set—and a different price tag. Just as savvy designers may use a variety of page layout programs—choosing Adobe InDesign, QuarkXPress, or Corel Ventura, depending on a project's requirements—so too can illustrators benefit from keeping a variety of programs in their tool sets and choosing the most appropriate tool for each project.

Designing with Mayura Draw

You can think of this compact $25 shareware program, which at one time was called PageDraw, as the MacDraw of SVG—which is not a bad thing at all. Mayura Draw is fast, it's uncomplicated in comparison to the more expensive programs we've looked at, and it offers a quick way of creating simple diagrams and line art. Its uncluttered interface is shown in Figure 6-1.

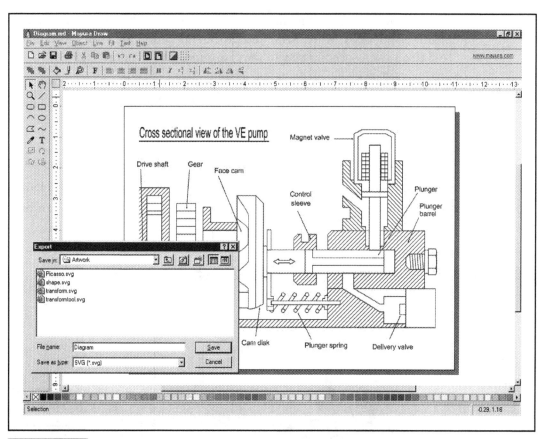

FIGURE 6-1 *Mayura Draw focuses strictly on drawing, rather than animation or interactivity, and thus is an efficient little drawing machine.* ■

Of course, Mayura Draw has the basic drawing tools, including the Rectangle, Ellipse, Rounded Rectangle, Line, Arc, Polygon, and Curve tools, and it offers four transform tools, a Text tool, and an Eyedropper tool for picking up the fill color from other objects and applying it to the selected object. In addition, you'll find these more sophisticated features in Mayura Draw:

- The ability to set the point (origin) from which transformations are calculated—you aren't stuck with the object's center, but can place the origin anywhere you want when you use the Scale, Rotate, Skew, or Reflect tool. This enables the creation of much more complex transformed objects than would otherwise be possible.

- A wireframe view (Outline mode) that shows objects but not their strokes or fills; even today, when RAM and processing power are cheap, you may find this view a speedier way to move around within a drawing.

- True Bézier curves (via the Curve tool) that you can edit by adjusting curve handles, just the way you would in CorelDRAW or Illustrator.

- The ability to apply URLs to paths and other objects.

Mayura Draw fully supports such SVG features as transforms and compound paths, and it automatically creates a style for each combination of fill and stroke that it finds in a document (see Figure 6-2). Its implementation of pattern fills,

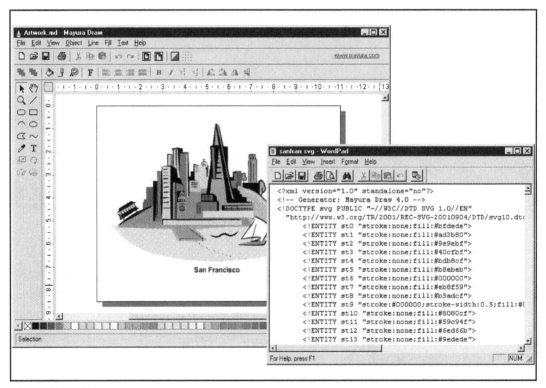

FIGURE   6-2   *A total of 20 styles are automatically created and applied to the elements of this drawing.* ■

however, is definitely reminiscent of MacDraw and similar programs—the Pattern menu includes nine primitive pattern fills that can only appear in black and white. Gradient fills are not supported.

Designed to enable scientists and engineers to create technical diagrams, Mayura Draw is clearly a quite competent sketch program for anyone who doesn't always need the bells and whistles of larger, more expensive applications. For a better idea of what it's capable of doing, take a look at Figure 6-3.

FIGURE   6-3   *This image created in Mayura Draw is a copy of Picasso's **Girl Before a Mirror.*** ■

Designing with Virtual Mechanics' IMS Web Engine

IMS Web Engine is a much more complex program than Mayura Draw, with a wide variety of features. It's a web design application, rather than strictly a drawing program, but you can choose to publish your designs in DHTML (with bitmap graphics) or SVG. Web Engine is one of three related products: Web Engine at the high end, Web Spinner in the middle, and Web Dwarf at the low end—it's free for personal use. All three programs can output SVG, but only Web Engine supports animation.

The program's features center around animation, and it approaches drawing from that standpoint, using animation terminology rather than illustration terminology. This means that you'll encounter such features as the Vector Editor, Open Geometry, and the Vertex Editor when using Web Engine. However, all this takes place within a WYSIWYG interface that looks very much like that of a page layout program (see Figure 6-4).

Web Engine documents can contain multiple pages, with each page producing a separate file when the project is published to HTML or SVG format. You can preview the code for your document in either HTML or SVG, and you can switch back and forth as you work. When publishing or previewing code in either of these formats, you can choose from seven variations:

- **Auto HTML**   Determines whether animation features are needed for each page, and saves files accordingly.
- **Static HTML**   Uses HTML only.
- **HTML + JavaScript**   Includes JavaScript animations.
- **Dynamic HTML**   Includes a full range of DHTML features.
- **Auto SVG**   Determines whether animation features are needed for each page, and saves files accordingly.
- **Static SVG**   Creates static images, leaving out any animated features.
- **Animated SVG**   Creates an animated SVG file.

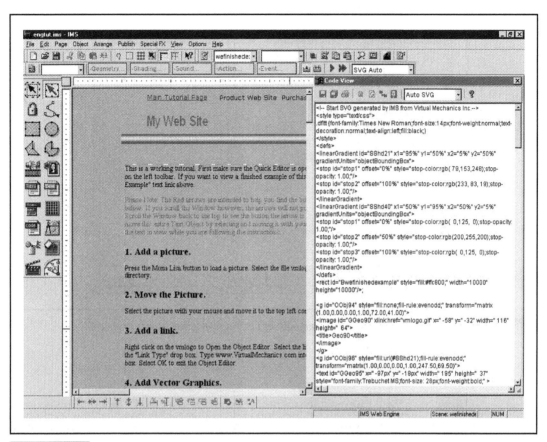

FIGURE   6-4   *Drawing tools, alignment buttons, and a page view bounded on two sides with rulers exist next to a code view window in Web Engine.* ■

This means you can simply create your projects using Web Engine's tools and commands without worrying about how they'll be implemented. The software can create final files that work in HTML, SVG, or JavaScript, and you don't need to decide which of those you'll use until you're ready to publish the project. When you do publish, by the way, Web Engine can send your files directly to your Web server via a built-in FTP client (see Figure 6-5).

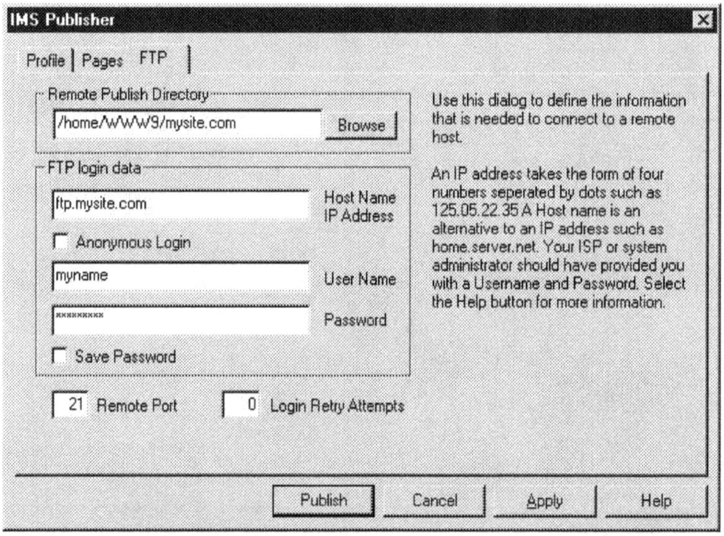

IMS Publisher

Profile | Pages | FTP

Remote Publish Directory
/home/WWW9/mysite.com   Browse

Use this dialog to define the information that is needed to connect to a remote host.

FTP login data

ftp.mysite.com   Host Name IP Address

☐ Anonymous Login

myname   User Name

*********   Password

☐ Save Password

21 Remote Port   0 Login Retry Attempts

An IP address takes the form of four numbers seperated by dots such as 125.05.22.35 A Host name is an alternative to an IP address such as home.server.net. Your ISP or system administrator should have provided you with a Username and Password. Select the Help button for more information.

Publish   Cancel   Apply   Help

FIGURE   6-5   *You can publish directly to your web site just by entering your server, username, and password.* ■

In creating Web Engine documents, you can choose from a bewildering variety of tools and other features to create text, images, animations, and more. There's a fairly standard array of drawing tools and features, such as transformation and compound path tools, as well as align commands, a grid, guides, and a ruler. The Geometry Editor is used for modifying objects' size, shape, and stroke attributes.

With Web Engine, you can include multimedia elements, including sounds, raster images, and animations, and you can add interactivity by creating what Web Engine calls *behaviors*. Each behavior has a specified trigger event (such as a mouseover) and can include links, motion, and sounds that are activated when the trigger event takes place. You can also create math formulas that give objects values based on trigger events and the status of other objects; this feature enables you to create complex logical processes to control interactivity. The Metamorph feature can be used to modify objects' shapes and actions based on trigger events (see Figure 6-6).

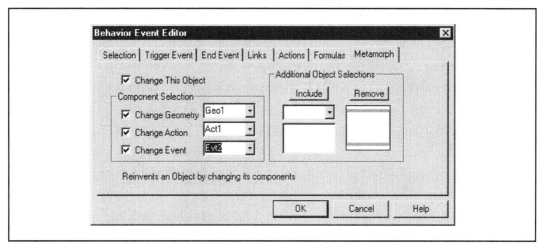

FIGURE   6-6   *Attaching Metamorph settings to an object enables you to modify the object's attributes or animation settings based on a trigger event.* ■

Animation in Web Engine is accomplished by modifying the values in a "transformation matrix" attached to each object. This matrix lists the object's position, scale, and rotation, and each of these values can be controlled over time. In addition, animations can control shading and transparency, and they can involve combinations of objects and groups of objects. The Action Editor enables you to program animations, controlling their speed and timing, orientation, and the like.

Special-purpose tools include a Navigation Bar tool specifically for creating web navigation elements, and a full-featured table editor. A Link Library can store frequently used URLs for quick access.

Not all of Web Engine's interface is WYSIWYG. You enter text in a text editor, a separate window that works like a miniature word processor, with font, point size, alignment and style controls, as well as buttons that create automatic bulleted and numbered lists. There's a ruler for measuring line length and tabs, and there are controls for creating HTML links.

Designing with XML Spy

If you're the hands-on, tweak-it-till-it-screams type, you'll undoubtedly end up working directly with the SVG code in your images. SVG is human-readable and, for the most part, very easy to understand, so it's easy to modify directly. While you can use any text editor, such as Wordpad in Windows or TextEdit in Mac OS X, if you're planning to do serious manipulation of SVG code you'll probably want to try out an XML editor that's designed for working with XML code. (Remember, SVG is an instance of XML.)

XML Spy (see Figure 6-7), from Altova, is a suite of XML editing components for Windows 95 through XP. You can buy the whole suite or just the XML Spy Document Editor, which offers syntax highlighting, automatic completion of elements and attributes, and validation against the SVG DTD. A browser view enables you to preview your images within XML Spy, and you can also choose between source view (with syntax coloring) and a grid view that shows the structure of your document. Extensive find and replace commands enable you to make global changes easily.

The XML Spy Document Editor comes in three forms: as a stand-alone application, as a browser plug-in for Internet Explorer or as an additional view of the XML Spy suite. As this chapter is written, the suite costs $399, and the stand-alone application and plug-in each cost $199.

Other Tools to Keep an Eye On

So far we've looked at three full-fledged illustration applications, a more compact and streamlined draw program, a web design application, and a code-oriented text editor. A variety of other tools exist to help you create and edit SVG, some of them commercial and others shareware or open source.

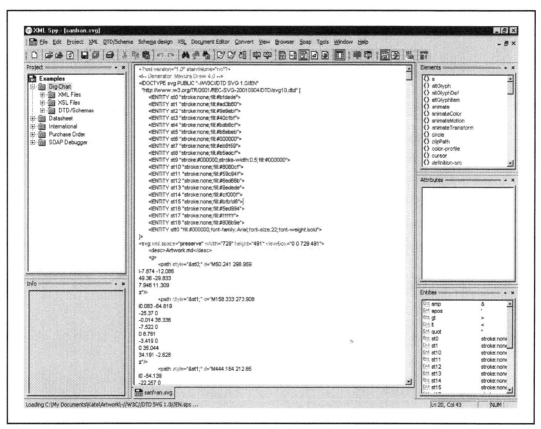

FIGURE 6-7 *XML Spy reads the SVG DTD and lists all the available elements, attributes, and entities so that you can insert them simply by double-clicking.* ■

SVG Studio

This graphical web design application from PCX Software can create entire web sites and presentations; you can use it to create vector graphics, apply effects, and animate your content. SVG Studio has three components, focusing on design, animation, and script writing. That third component, the script editor, is what makes this application (which is still in development as this chapter was written) so intriguing. The script editor enables you to work with JavaScript, VB script, and Perl.

SVG Studio will run on Windows 95, Windows 98, Windows Me, Windows 2000, and Windows XP. A future version will run on Linux, and developers hope to release a Mac OS version eventually.

GraPL

If you're interested in producing charts and graphs in SVG, take a look at GraPL from Causeway Graphical Systems, a graphing and charting program for Windows that can format data from into a wide range of charts with features such as moving averages, smoothing, and sorting. The program supports several output formats, including SVG.

GraPL imports data from spreadsheets, and you can copy and paste from most Windows applications. It can create the following types of charts and graphs:

- Bar charts
- Line charts
- Scatter plots
- Pie charts
- Polar charts
- Min/max charts
- Frequency plots
- Box and whisker plots
- Gantt charts
- Step charts
- Trace charts
- Kite charts
- Tower charts
- Cloud charts
- Response surfaces
- Trellis charts

Oak Draw

Designed for kids but powerful enough to be used for real work, Oak Draw (from Dial Solutions) is a vector drawing program for Windows that can output SVG. Unlike most low-end illustration applications, Oak Draw has some fairly sophisticated features:

- Paths can have any weight.
- Path ends can have three types: butt, round, or triangular.
- Path corners can be rounded, mitred, or beveled.
- A full range of colors is available.
- Multiple objects can be grouped.
- You can use English, metric, or publishing (points) measurement systems.
- You can zoom up to 800 percent.

Curved paths are edited using Bézier control points, and you can even create compound paths (called, inexplicably, *moves*).

IsoDraw

Technical illustrations—used to illustration instruction manuals and catalogs—are a special category of illustration, with their own requirements. IsoDraw, from ITEDO, is a Windows drawing package created specifically for technical illustration. It includes special tools, such as the Shaft tool for drawing gearing, as well as a library of standard manufacturing components, and it applies perspective automatically.

IsoDraw can import and export a wide variety of formats besides SVG, including WebCGM, CGM, PNG, JPEG, DWG, IGES, DXF, HPGL, Adobe Illustrator, WMF, EPS, TIFF, Macintosh PICT, PCX, BMP, CALS Raster, Interleaf ASCII, and FrameMaker MIF. The program can also produce illustrations from 3D and 2D wireframe data, and its native format stores object attributes so that you can associate information such as part numbers with objects.

SVGmaker

You can generate SVG files from many standard Windows applications using this Windows print driver. It works like the Adobe Acrobat print driver that creates a PDF file from any document you can print. SVGmaker can also create a user interface to navigate through documents such a PowerPoint presentations. The company's web site (www.svgmaker.com) features a gallery of SVG images created from a wide variety of applications: AutoCAD, PowerPoint, Family Tree Maker, Visio, and many more.

Batik SVG Toolkit

While this open source SVG Java toolkit is geared toward developers who want to include SVG input and output in their applications, some of its modules can be helpful to designers as well. For example, the SVG Font Converter can convert TrueType fonts directly into SVG fonts; this tool would be useful any time a font isn't embedding properly. Other included components are the SVG Browser, which enables you to view SVG files, zoom, pan, and rotate them, and select text items within them; SVG Rasterizer, which converts SVG files into JPEG or PNG images; and SVG Pretty Printer, which "neatens" the SVG code's alignment and indention so that it's easier to read.

Plazmic Workshop Start

If you're intrigued at the idea of creating SVG content for cell phones and other handheld mobile devices, check out Plazmic Workshop Start, a development application for interactive and animated graphics. Content created using Workshop Start runs on Plazmic Media Engine, an interactive media player for mobile devices. You can use a simulator to see how your content will look on the small screen and test your interfaces. For content definition, Plazmic Workshop Start uses SVG, and it runs on Java so you can use it on any platform.

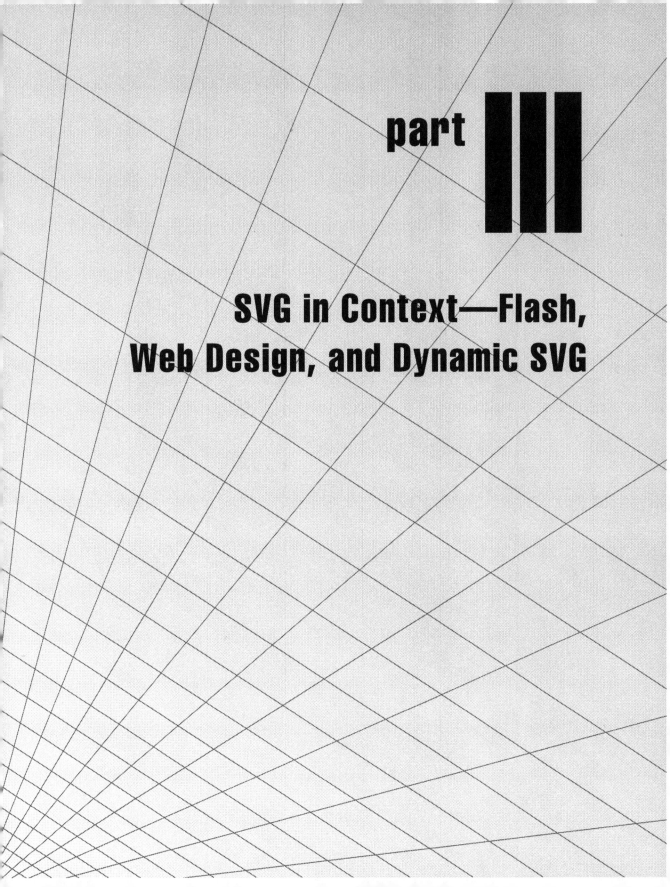

part III

SVG in Context—Flash, Web Design, and Dynamic SVG

chapter **7**

SVG for Flash Designers

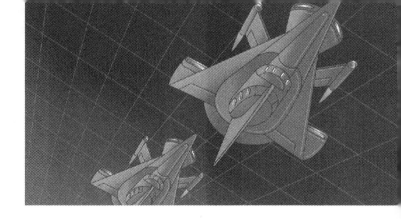

If you want to produce multimedia web content that almost every web user can view right now, today, with no additional software needed, your choice of format is clear: SWF, often referred to as Flash. That may seem a strange statement to read in a book about SVG, but there's no denying that right now Flash has a big lead over SVG in terms of market penetration. A March 2002 study by NPD Research showed that that 98.3 percent of web users are using computers on which the Flash player is already installed. Meanwhile, Adobe is shipping the Adobe SVG Viewer with all its software, but the company hasn't yet achieved anywhere near the saturation level that competitor Macromedia has with the Flash format.

But market penetration isn't the only factor to take into account when deciding how to present web content. SVG shares many characteristics of Flash, but it has some unique capabilities of its own. And the fact is that you don't have to stick to one or the other—you can use both in one site or use different formats for different projects. This chapter looks at reasons to use SVG over SWF or vice versa, without regard to the various authoring applications available for each format. Indeed, it's fairly common for multimedia development programs to output to both SVG and SWF, so in many cases the choice need not be made until a final file is being created.

Before going any further, let's define a few terms. Macromedia Flash is actually an authoring application that produces files in the Flash file format, or SWF. SWF stands for "Shockwave Flash" and is pronounced "swiff." It's a compact vector format designed specifically for efficient delivery of multimedia content over the Internet's limited bandwidth. So "Flash file format" and "SWF" are synonyms and can be used interchangeably.

What's the Difference?

Just as PNG (Portable Network Graphic) format was conceived as a royalty-free alternative to GIF (Graphics Interchange Format), SVG can be seen as a publicly owned, open alternative to Macromedia's proprietary Flash format. Both are vector formats that can convey multimedia content over the Web. They're designed to be compact, and thus bandwidth-conserving, and because they are based on vectors rather than pixels (although both SWF and SVG documents can contain raster data), their quality is high no matter what the viewing conditions.

However, the XML-based SVG format was designed from the ground up to be more flexible and more accessible than SWF. That objective has resulted in a number of major differences between the two technologies.

Ownership

The first and most obvious difference between SVG and SWF is in the two technologies' ownership. SVG is an open standard governed by the World Wide Web Consortium (W3C), the international standards body for the Web. SWF, on the other hand, is a proprietary format owned by Macromedia, Inc.

This attribute of the two formats can really be seen as three separate issues:

- **Is the format open or closed?** How accessible is it to developers who want to support it in their software and to users who want to take advantage of its features?

- **Is the format proprietary or public?** Who owns it and who can change it?

- **Is the format a standard?** Is it widely used or even dominant in its field? Is it compatible with other standards?

Although the Flash file format is often described by open standards advocates as a "closed" format, in fact its specification has been released to the public and is available free of charge to any application developer who's willing to agree to Macromedia's fairly liberal terms. Macromedia also distributes a free software development kit (SDK) so that any developer can create software that outputs SWF files. As a result, more and more applications are being created than can export to SWF, in addition to Macromedia's applications designed explicitly to use the format, such as the Flash authoring environment. However, to gain access to *all* the features of the Flash format, you *must* use Macromedia's authoring tools—obviously not the case with SVG, which can be created in any text editor.

For viewers, both SVG and SWF are eminently accessible—even if the appropriate viewer isn't installed on your computer, it's a trivial task to obtain it and install it. Web designers are looking at a different task: creating SVG or SWF content. In this area, SVG is much more accessible, because it's a text-based format that can be created using not only proprietary design tools, such as Illustrator, but also text editors and XML generators that can interact with databases and other software. You can write SVG in the dirt with a stick—not so the binary Flash format.

And even though it's open, SWF is still a proprietary format, meaning that it's owned by Macromedia and the company is free to change the format or stop distributing specifications and developer tools if it desires. With each new version of the product, there is a new specification and a new Player, forcing Flash designers to scramble to make sure their work is still compatible (as well as learning how to use new features).

According to the license agreement, "Macromedia may amend, modify, change, and cease distribution or production of the SDK at any time." So while SWF is technically an open format, its status as such is subject to the actions of its owner.

SVG is both open and public. It was created by the W3C, and its specification is available to anyone who wants to read it. It's owned by the public instead of being owned by a private company, which means that its current status is safe and not subject to change—no one's going to start charging developers to use the SVG format in their software, and no one's going to change the format without a long public comment period first. Working drafts are published on the W3C's web site (www.w3.org/Graphics/SVG/) so that everyone can see what's in the works.

Finally, the question of standards comes down to a conflict between legislated standards and de facto standards that end up dominating the market despite a lack of official sanction. SVG falls into the former category, while SWF falls into the latter. Flash has nearly become a de facto standard, one that is considered standard simply because everyone uses it. The question for designers contemplating adding

SVG to their tool sets is whether SVG really has the potential to compete with SWF and even overtake it when everyone's already using SWF and many people have never even heard of SVG. The answer is yes—the potential is definitely there, for the reasons outlined throughout this book. SVG is a competitive vector multimedia format that is already being adopted by applications developers throughout the design world. And it has the potential to be much, much more. All that remains is for designers to recognize that potential and start taking advantage of it.

Accessibility

In most cases, web designers want to open up their work to as many viewers as possible, which means ensuring both that people can find it on the Web and that they can read it once they get there. Making sites accessible both to search engines and to a variety of users—including those with impaired vision, for example—therefore becomes important.

The innards of Flash format files are essentially invisible to search engines, and it's harder to grab links from a Flash page than from an HTML page. Both of these problems are especially annoying when entire sites are built using Flash, as Macromedia is pushing designers to do. Creating entire pages and sites in the Flash format, rather than combining HTML with bits and pieces of embedded SWF, enables selective updating of page images as the data behind them changes, rather than having to redraw entire pages every time a user enters new data. One application of this concept is in online commerce, in which users' shopping carts and the attributes of the objects they're buying can be updated immediately without having to send a whole new HTML page each time something about the transaction changes.

Web experts offer solutions ranging from making extensive use of meta tags and page titles to creating an entire alternate HTML version of an all-Flash site. However, others point out that search engines aren't the only way to gain exposure and draw viewers to a site—advertising, reciprocal links, and the kind of sheer coolness that gets a site talked about are all ways to increase viewership.

On the other hand, if search engine accessibility is important to you, then SVG is more attractive than SWF. Because it's a human-readable, text-based format,

SVG can be read and indexed by any search engine, both online and locally on your own computer or intranet.

Similarly, it's much easier to build accessibility into SVG than into SWF files. This doesn't mean that every SVG designer will take the necessary steps to do so—just that it can be done. SVG was designed with this issue in mind, and the W3C has published some very useful information on making SVG content accessible to all comers (for example, see www.w3.org/TR/SVG-access/). SVG features that contribute to accessibility include

- **Scalability** Literally, the ability to zoom in on content helps ensure that visually impaired users, or those who are situated further than usual from their monitors, can see everything there is to see.

- **Structured images** By its very nature, SVG includes information about the structure of each component in an image, which makes it easier for assistive technologies to reproduce images in a way that is comprehensible to their users. SVG's use of the Document Object Model, or DOM, to define every element makes certain that each element can be manipulated as necessary to ensure that it and the image as a whole are accessible to users.

- **Alternative equivalents** Each logical component of an SVG image can include alternate ways of describing that component, including a title, again making it easier for people with a wide range of disabilities to understand an image.

- **Plaintext** Because SVG is plaintext, any SVG file's contents can be output as Braille, read by a screen reader, or rendered in other ways that make it easier both to understand and to author.

- **Style sheets** The rendering of SVG images can be controlled using style sheets, enabling styles to be created that maximize accessibility for various categories of users.

- **Extended styling features** SVG properties other than those included in CSS can be used to further increase accessibility for people with visual impairment and people who use assistive technologies. By changing fonts and filters, designers can easily adapt content for use by people with low vision, those with color deficiencies, or users of assistive technologies.

Interoperability

For both users and designers, a perfect world is one in which technology never impedes the flow of information. For that to happen, different technologies have to work together seamlessly; they must be able to share data and pass it back and forth, as well as present the results to the user without unsightly bugs, errors, or other problems. And this kind of interoperability is what the W3C is all about, as expressed in its "Seven Points":

Twenty years ago, people bought software that only worked with other software from the same vendor. Today, people have more freedom to choose, and they rightly expect software components to be interchangeable. They also expect to be able to view Web content with their preferred software (graphical desktop browser, speech synthesizer, Braille display, car phone . . .). W3C, a vendor-neutral organization, promotes interoperability by designing and promoting open (non-proprietary) computer languages and protocols that avoid the market fragmentation of the past. This is achieved through *industry consensus* and encouraging an *open forum* for discussion.

SVG provides a means of describing vectors while enabling extension via other XML instances, scripting languages, CSS, and the DOM, whereas SWF is a web-based multimedia format that has limited application outside that milieu. Unlike SVG, the Flash format is not XML-based, which narrows its range of display and interactivity options to what's built in by Macromedia. By basing SVG on XML, the W3C has made it possible to combine SVG with other XML instances, such as MathML (for math) and CML (for chemical equations), embedding them all within the same document and using whichever is most appropriate for the type of content that appears in each section of the document.

All this is not to say that the Flash format is incompatible with the most current technology, or that users currently have problems making it work—just that users who want access to SWF content are limited to using only the technology that Macromedia enables them to use. Text-only browsers, for example, are not well supported by Flash, and likely won't be in the future.

Scalability

Providing content to a variety of platforms and devices is another requirement often placed on designers these days. You're supposed to be able to create one file that will work anywhere—on a desktop PC, a PDA, or a cell phone. Of course, that's rarely possible. But today's authoring applications are increasingly enabling users to specify the target display device so that content can be customized to the device. This means that you can have one source file from which you can generate the specialized versions needed to publish to many devices. Migrating documents to less capable platforms, such as cell phones and other handheld devices, still requires a certain level of user intervention, however, and is likely to do so for quite some time.

Macromedia has released the Flash Player for Pocket PC, for the Nokia 9200 Communicator Series, a high-end cell phone with a high-resolution color display, and for other devices. Developers are rushing to create Flash content for mobile devices, and Flash MX (the latest version of Macromedia's primary Flash authoring application) includes a module that enables designers to optimize content for smaller devices. All this is part of an effort by Macromedia to bring Flash content to all kinds of devices, including set-top boxes and gaming systems.

Meanwhile, developers have realized that an SVG interpreter can be added to just about any application, even embedded software like that found in cell phones and handheld organizers. In the spring of 2002, the W3C released a candidate recommendation for two new SVG profiles: SVG Tiny for use in cell phones, and SVG Basic for use in PDAs. These two subsets of SVG enable designers to know in advance exactly what parts of SVG will work on a mobile device, and to design accordingly. Meanwhile, work continues on eSVG, a version of SVG intended for use in embedded systems, and developers are creating all kinds of fascinating implementations of SVG, such as Nokia's GoLive plug-in for 3G Multimedia Messaging Service (MMS).

SVG and SWF are entering the world of content for mobile and embedded systems, and it's just too early to tell which will end up on top.

Workflow

Possibly the biggest difference between Flash and SVG—and the most important reason that Web content developers are turning to SVG—is workflow. With SVG, designers design and developers develop, in parallel, using their favorite tools in media they already know. Developers can use any of a number of standard scripting languages because SVG uses the DOM, and it therefore takes developers just minutes to start scripting dynamic SVG. Meanwhile, designers familiar with CorelDRAW and Adobe Illustrator can simply save their artwork as SVG. Of course, they should learn some SVG basics in order to optimize their content—hence this book—because neither of these programs is really designed for SVG. And that's where programs like Jasc WebDraw come in—to allow designers to access all SVG's features when necessary.

With Flash, on the other hand, you need to use Macromedia Flash (the program) to access all of SWF's features, but the program has a stiff learning curve, and Flash (the format) is fairly inflexible.

Which Should You Use?

Obviously, this book is based on the premise that SVG should be your first choice for providing what Flash designers like to call "rich media" or "rich content." It's open, it's interoperable, and it can do almost everything Flash can do. That's right, *almost* everything. SVG's biggest handicap is the fact that it's a relatively new player—Flash content hit the Web in 1997, while SVG 1.0 was only finalized in 2001. Until that point, SVG was little more than a novelty that interested primarily techies—not a viable option for designers.

Today, designers have the power to choose either SVG or SWF for any given project. This section presents a few reasons why you might choose one format over the other.

When to Choose SVG

The first reason to choose SVG over SWF is its textual nature. If you want to tweak code manually or generate it from a database publishing system, you're going to need to use a text format rather than a binary format. When you're concerned about accessibility issues, too, SVG will be a better choice for the reasons already (see "Accessibility," earlier in this chapter). Whether you want to ensure search engine access or optimize accessibility for people with disabilities, SVG clearly beats SWF.

Similarly, dynamic publishing is much easier with SVG than with SWF because of the number of systems already available to generate XML dynamically, ranging from high-end XML publishing systems to CGI scripts. Any method of creating textual content on-the-fly will enable you to publish to SVG. A limited set of tools is available to do dynamic publishing of Flash format content, but the wide range of XML tools is much more versatile.

Modifying SVG content using style sheets enables you to revise the presentation of your content to suit different audiences without reworking the content itself. SWF doesn't support alternate content or multiple style sheets, while SVG supports both internal and external style sheets. In fact, if you want to use your content for anything other than a web site, SVG may be a better answer than SWF. SVG doesn't have to live in a browser. It can work with any other software application for onscreen display, and it can be printed—in other words, it can exist outside the World Wide Web. Like the raster format JPEG—which in addition to being used on the Web has also become the de facto standard for use with digital cameras and in stock photography—SVG can be used for any kind of image display, not just for displaying images on the Web.

When you want to integrate other XML-based data sources with images and multimedia, SVG is obviously the best choice. As a part of XML, SVG has great potential to interact with other data types that can also be described in XML. An XML document can contain SVG fragments, along with sections in other grammars derived from XML. While SWF supports rudimentary XML tagging, it has nothing to compare with SVG's interoperability with the entire XML universe.

A related advantage of SVG is its use of the Document Object Model (DOM), which means that every object within an SVG document is accessible to a script. This enables you to use a variety of scripting languages with SVG that Flash doesn't support.

Finally, SVG is beginning to look like a universal vector graphics language, in the same way that RTF was supposed to be a universal text language. Of course, since SVG is not owned by Microsoft, its prospects for staying universal are much brighter. So SVG can be used when you want to move vector images from one application to another.

When to Choose SWF

Opting for the Flash format is most likely to be the best decision—at least for the moment—when you want to be relatively sure that a heterogeneous audience already has the viewer. It's impossible to predict how the installed base of SVG will change over the next few years, but Microsoft and Netscape have both committed to including SVG support in future releases of their Web browsers. When that happens, Flash will immediately lose its greatest advantage over SVG.

Another reason you might choose SWF over SVG is that you know your audience doesn't already have either viewer, and bandwidth or disk space is limited. The Flash Player plug-in is about 200K, while the SVG Viewer plug-in is about 3MB, so some users may be less willing to download and install the SVG Viewer. However, it's worth remembering that this discrepancy in file size is partly due to the fact that SVG content is rendered when it's viewed, rather than being prerendered when it's created. This means that there's more processing happening within the SVG Viewer than within the Flash Player. It also means that SVG files are considerably smaller than are SWF files with identical functionality.

Finally, it's sad but true that there's currently no way to stream SVG content. SVG isn't displayed until the entire document has been downloaded, which means that viewers will spend more time waiting around than they'd like.

Moving from SVG to Flash and Back

The good news: SVG and SWF are vector formats with similar capabilities, so it should be eminently possible to transfer documents from one format to the other.

The bad news: It isn't possible, not really, not yet. Macromedia's stance is that SVG is primarily useful as a graphics interchange format, rather than as an online content delivery technology, so it seems unlikely that the company will provide SVG import and export in its Flash development tools anytime soon. Independent programmers have been experimenting with converters; for instance, one Python scripter has written a script to convert an SVG file into a Flash file (www.es-kimo.com/~robla/svg2swf/), while another programmer at the UK's University of Nottingham has put up an experimental SWF to SVG converter that will convert the first 100 frames in an SWF document (http://broadway.cs.nott.ac.uk/projects/SVG/flash2svg/). But there is no full-fledged converter available, commercial or otherwise, for either direction. It's likely that a program will come along before too long that can handle both formats, since both are open and accessible to developers.

If developers see a movement toward SVG, then they will rush to provide a migration tool. In the meantime, it's possible to convert static images by exporting them in an intermediate format such as Illustrator's native format, and then opening them in an SVG-capable or Flash-enabled application and exporting to the other format. And in some cases you can actually copy and paste elements from Flash to Illustrator; your results may be unpredictable, but doing this and then fixing glitches may still be faster than exporting.

chapter **8**

Incorporating SVG in Web Sites

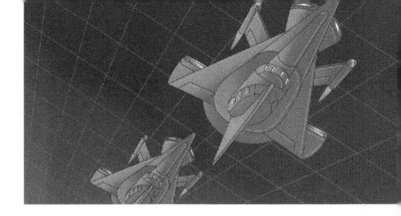

This chapter addresses how you can work SVG images into your larger web site designs, what support you will find in web authoring and development tools, and what experience your users may have with your SVG images—depending on their browsing environment.

As with many emerging web technologies, support for SVG is going to be uneven across commercial and shareware products. Some development and browsing environments will offer complete support for SVG, some will offer little or none, and there will be many, many variants in between. This will also change very quickly, as both commercial and open source products add SVG support. Moreover, SVG itself will continue to change; at this writing, the W3C is developing the next version of the specification.

As a result, we do not attempt to exhaustively document every tool out there. Instead, we take a close look at a few tools, and provide some example code that will work with certain tools. We begin with a walk-through of some example HTML code that incorporates SVG graphics, and explain how it works with certain browsing environments.

SVG and Browser Basics

As we have seen in previous chapters, SVG files will display in a browser such as Internet Explorer when you have downloaded the Adobe SVG Viewer (http://www.adobe.com/svg/viewer/install/main.html). If you have installed the SVG Viewer, you can point your browser to any valid and properly named SVG file, and it will appear in the browser window precisely as the SVG file specifies, as shown in Figure 8-1. The viewer installs in both major browsers—Microsoft Internet Explorer and Netscape. If you have both browsers on your system, it will actually install to both upon download.

In such a simple example, only two things can go wrong: The SVG file itself could be invalid, or the file could be incorrectly named. You don't want to pass either of these problems on to your end user, though. As we have seen in Chapter 2, and as shown in Figure 8-2, the feedback that comes with invalid SVG files can be opaque, to say the least!

Unlike HTML, which can be very forgiving of some kinds of errors, the SVG file will simply fail to display, and will instead likely display some vague, inscrutable error message. Such an outright failure to display is one important difference between SVG files and HTML files.

This differs, even, from a corrupted or somehow invalid JPG or GIF file, which will also fail to display but will at least give a familiar symbol (a red boxed "x" in Internet Explorer, as in Figure 8-3) to indicate the file is present and unable to display, or the file is not found.

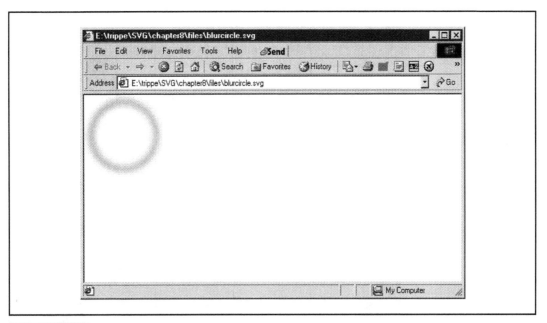

FIGURE 8-1   *Once you have downloaded the SVG Viewer, Internet Explorer will use it to display your SVG files.* ∎

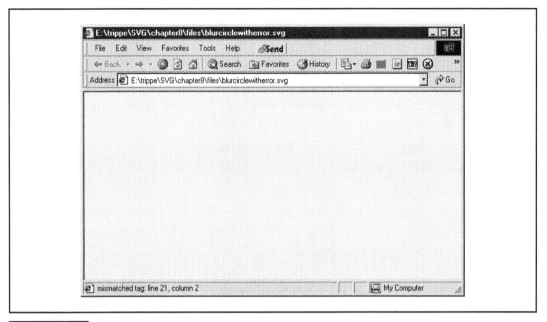

FIGURE 8-2 *In this example, an invalid SVG file produces the cryptic error messages in the status bar (lower left) of the browser window: "line 21, column 2."* ■

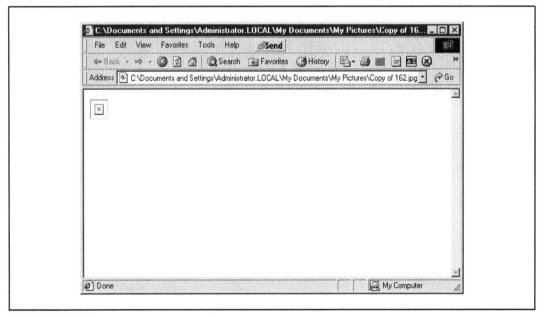

FIGURE 8-3 *This corrupted JPG also fails to display, but at least the user sees a symbol to indicate that something has failed.* ■

All this detail aside, the clear solution is to test all your files before deploying them on a web server. The additional caution with SVG, at least for now, is that the error conditions produced by invalid SVG files may be even more cryptic, and more frustrating, than other kinds of errors your users have heretofore encountered.

Simple Case: Embedding SVG In an HTML Page

The simplest method for including an SVG image within an HTML page is to use the <EMBED> tag. The following example works:

```
<html>
   <head>
      <title>Simple HTML, with embedded SVG</title>
   </head>
   <body>
      <p>This shows a simple HTML document,
         with an SVG document included by reference.</p>
      <embed src="textboxline.svg">
   </body>
   </html>
```

That code produces the workable, but mundane result shown in Figure 8-4.

Experienced web developers will know that the <EMBED> tag is not an "official" tag; that is, it is not part of the formal HTML DTDs published by the W3C. But the major browsers recognize it, though with some differences in the supported attributes. You can generally count on the following attributes being supported:

Attribute	Comments
SRC="*url*"	Indicates the URL of the SVG file.
WIDTH="*n*"	Indicates the width of the area the SVG file will occupy.
HEIGHT="*n*"	Indicates the height of the area the SVG file will occupy.
ALIGN="*value*"	Commonly used options are *top, bottom, center, left, right*.
HIDDEN="(true|false)"	Defaults to false.

There is one caveat on using the height and width attributes with the <EMBED> element: If you set the height and width in the HTML to be smaller than the declared

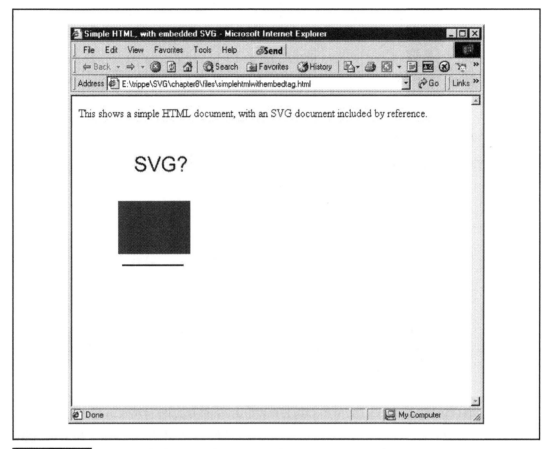

FIGURE   8-4   *The <EMBED> tag can be used as a simple, generic method for including an SVG image in your HTML.* ■

height and width of the SVG image, you will likely get some surprising and unintended results. In the example shown in Figure 8-5, the HTML <EMBED> is first set to equal the SVG file, then set smaller than the SVG's height and width. The resulting image is cropped, and not reduced in size.

Compare this result with the GIF file in Figure 8-6, which is reduced in size by adjusting the height and width attributes of the <IMG> tag. In this case, the bitmap is reduced in size—not partially cropped.

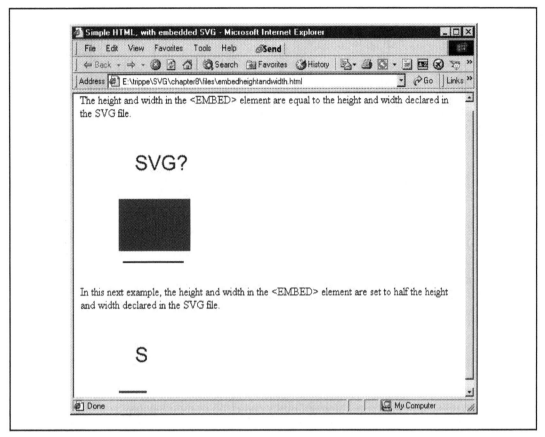

FIGURE   8-5   *The height and width attributes in the <EMBED> tag can produce unintended results if they conflict with the height and width established in the SVG.* ∎

As a simple workaround, if you want the SVG to behave like a GIF, simply remove the fixed height and width and height attributes in the SVG, or set them to 100%. The SVG will then scale to the <EMBED> size.

Using the Object Element

If you know your readers will include people using older browsers, especially older versions of browsers besides Microsoft Internet Explorer, the <EMBED> element will be your safest lowest-common-denominator choice. If you are certain

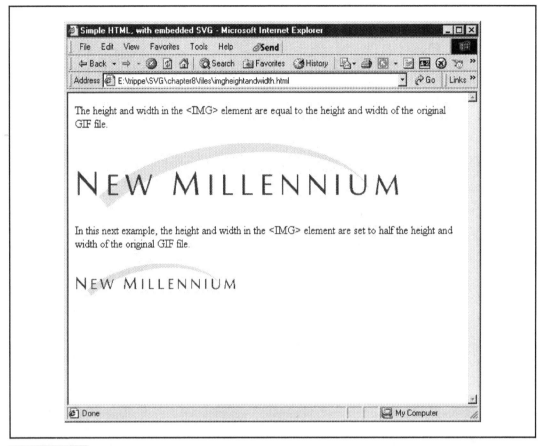

FIGURE 8-6 *Designers may be more accustomed to the proportional sizing they can get with the height and width attributes in the <IMG> tag.* ■

that your users will be mainly using Internet Explorer, you should probably use the <OBJECT> element instead.

The <OBJECT> element works similarly to the <EMBED> element, though the simplest case has you using slightly different attributes to reference the SVG image. Note the following sample HTML code:

```
<html>
   <head>
      <title>Simple HTML, with embedded SVG</title>
```

```
    </head>
    <body>
       <p>This shows a simple HTML document,
          with an SVG document included by reference.</p>
       <object type="image/svg+xml"  data="textboxline.svg">
       </object>
    </body>
    </html>
```

Instead of the SRC attribute used above, the <OBJECT> tag relies on a type attribute to indicate the mime type, and a data attribute to indicate the source of the SVG data. That code produces the results shown in Figure 8-7.

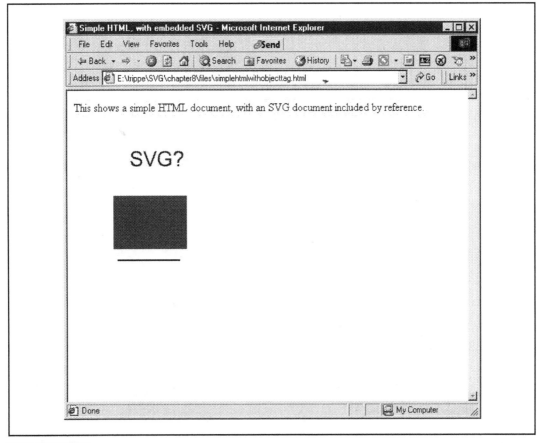

FIGURE 8-7 *The <OBJECT> tag can also be used as a simple method for including an SVG image in your HTML, especially in an Internet Explorer environment.* ∎

A distinct advantage to the <OBJECT> tag is that it can take text, other HTML tags, or even graphical elements between the start and end tags. In the event that the browser cannot process and display the SVG image, it will display the contents of the <OBJECT> tag instead. Thus, the file above could include at least some explanatory text, or even an alternative image to display instead of the SVG.

In the following example, the <OBJECT> tag references an SVG document, but then also includes some alternative text and links, directing the user to download the Adobe viewer:

```
<html>
<head>
<title>Simple HTML, with embedded SVG</title>
</head>
<body>
<p>This shows a simple HTML document, with an SVG document included by
    reference.</p>
<object type="image/svg+xml"  data="textboxline.svg">
<b>Your browser is currently unable to display SVG images.<br>
We recommend you download the Adobe SVG viewer from the
<a href="http://www.adobe.com/svg/viewer/install/main.html">Adobe Web
    site.</a>
<br>
<br>
<a href="http://www.adobe.com/svg/viewer/install/main.html">
<img src="svgdownload.gif" height="31" width="88"></a>
</object>
</body>
</html>
```

If the SVG Viewer is installed, the resulting page displays exactly as shown in Figure 8-7. However, if the SVG Viewer is not installed, the HTML tags and text inside of the <OBJECT> tag will be displayed instead, resulting in the page shown in Figure 8-8.

If you do rely on the <OBJECT> element, the following attributes are typically supported:

Attribute	Comments
DATA="*url*"	Indicates the URL of the SVG data.
TYPE="*mimetype*"	Indicates the mime type of the data.
WIDTH="*n*"	Indicates the width of the area the SVG file will occupy.
HEIGHT="*n*"	Indicates the height of the area the SVG file will occupy.
ALIGN="*value*"	Commonly used options are *top, bottom, center, left, right*.

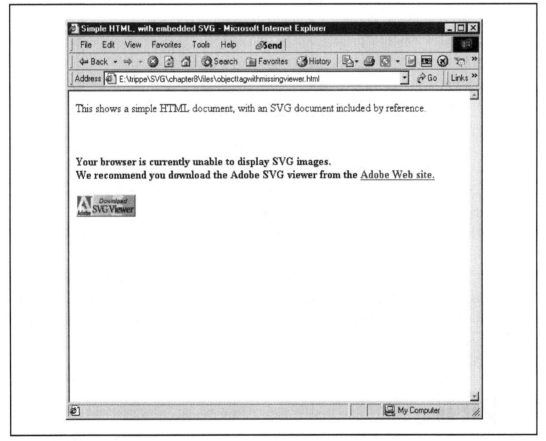

FIGURE 8-8 *The HTML tags and text inside of the <OBJECT> tag will be rendered when the <OBJECT> tag references an SVG image and a viewer is not available.* ■

Some Practical Considerations

The <EMBED> and <OBJECT> tags are just two ways of getting HTML pages to include SVG images. Another straightforward method is to have the HTML page link to the SVG file. The SVG specification on the W3C site does exactly this. The pages describe the SVG elements, provide sample code, and include a PNG version of the sample SVG so you can view what it looks like, even without the SVG Viewer. The actual SVG examples are then linked to separately. See http://www.w3.org/TR/SVG/shapes.html#RectElement for a good example of this approach.

You could also develop a script to programmatically deal with the problem of whether a viewer is present. Adobe's official SVG site, for example, runs a script prior to downloading the page. It checks for the presence of the SVG Viewer, and if it is not there, it prompts the user to download the viewer. If you have a computer without an installed SVG Viewer, point it at the http://www.adobe.com/svg/demos/main.html page and see the result.

Finally, Adobe provides scripts for autoinstalling the viewer. We experimented with the version provided at http://www.adobe.com/svg/basics/intro.html. The script is provided in both Visual Basic and JavaScript, and the Adobe site provides the script as well as the HTML snippets you will need to include in your web page. The scripts can be freely distributed, with the caveat that they are not warranted and cannot be modified.

At the time we were writing this book, the majority of web pages we visited were using the <EMBED> tag to include SVG images in their pages. This will likely be the best lowest-common-denominator choice until the browsers themselves support SVG viewing.

W3C Amaya

Amaya might be the best-kept secret on the Web. In a web-browsing world increasingly dominated by Microsoft Internet Explorer, Amaya is a combination browser and web page editor. Developed by the W3C and available as binaries or source code, Amaya is an open source program that runs on most flavors of Windows,

Linux, and Solaris. It allows you to create, edit, and view web pages, and it has native support for newer, W3C-backed technologies such as MathML and, yes, SVG.

As a result, Amaya could a significant tool for web developers and designers, especially those who want to be able to easily deal with pages that include vector graphics and math. The Amaya editing tool provides graphical user interfaces for creating SVG drawings and for complex math equations.

At the time we were writing this chapter, the Amaya binary was in version 6.1 (released April 29, 2002), and could be downloaded from http://www.w3.org/Amaya/User/BinDist.html. Macintosh versions are not currently available, though the source code can be downloaded and compiled (see http://www.w3.org/Amaya/User/SourceDist.html for instructions for downloading and compiling).

Amaya is a full-featured browser and web page editor, with substantial features that have been documented online (http://www.w3.org/Amaya/User/Overview.html), as well as having an update FAQ (http://www.w3.org/Amaya/User/FAQ.html) and mailing list (http://www.w3.org/Amaya/User/Mailing.html). This section will not attempt to exhaustively document Amaya's features; instead, it will highlight some of Amaya's features for creating, editing, and viewing SVG images.

Browsing SVG Images with Amaya

Keep in mind that Amaya is both a browser and editor; assuming that you have not changed any of the default settings, Amaya will actually launch in editor mode. If you are new to the tool, this isn't wholly obvious. The browser opens to an installed web page on your local drive (as shown in Figure 8-9), and you will be tempted to just start surfing.

Once you switch out of editor mode, you can browse web sites as you normally would. You will notice some differences from Internet Explorer and Netscape defaults for browsing. To begin with, the default color for links in Amaya is red, and links are enabled with a double-click and not a single-click. You can play with the settings by choosing the Preferences selection under the Special menu.

Amaya has its own, built in SVG Viewer, so you can point it at any valid SVG file and it will display, as shown in Figure 8-10.

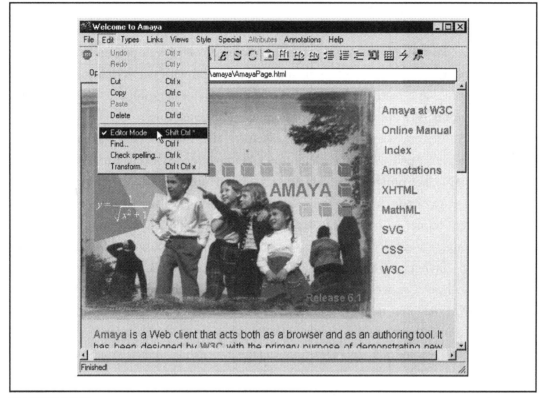

The Amaya tool opens onto a downloaded web page, and seems ready for browsing. You need to switch out of editor mode, though, to just browse HTML pages and SVG images. ■

Amaya SVG Viewer vs. Adobe SVG Viewer

There are two important differences with viewing SVG files in Amaya vs. the Adobe Viewer. First, the Amaya Viewer falls short of supporting the whole W3C specification, and there are many instances where the viewer will not display the SVG properly. These limitations include animated elements, interactive elements with mouse events, and filter effects. Second, the Amaya Viewer only supports the SVG specification as published by the W3C (though, at this writing, it stops short of supporting the entire standard). The Adobe Viewer also supports the SVG specification (it also stops slightly short of supporting the entire standard), but it also supports Adobe's own additional SVG namespaces. These namespaces have been

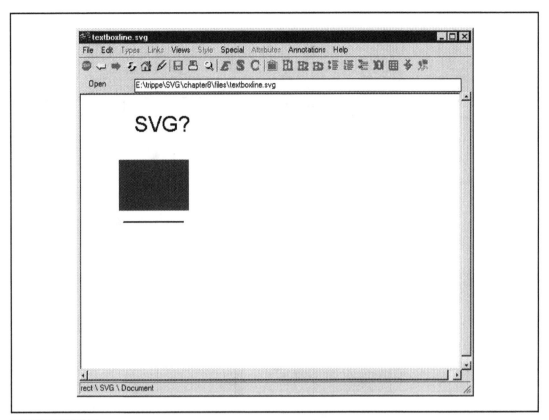

FIGURE   8-10   *The Amaya browser can view most valid SVG files* ■

created by Adobe to work with particular rendering effects that you can get using Adobe authoring tools. As a result, some SVG images may display differently in Amaya vs. Adobe, especially if the images use the Adobe namespaces. In the example shown in Figure 8-11, the blurcircle.svg image we have shown previously displays differently in the two viewers.

When the SVG image is first opened in the Amaya browser, you are presented with a warning message (see Figure 8-12), and a chance to view the errors. In the case of this SVG image, the highlighted "errors" are actually valid SVG elements that that Amaya does not yet support, notably the <FILTER> element and the <feGaussianBlur> element.

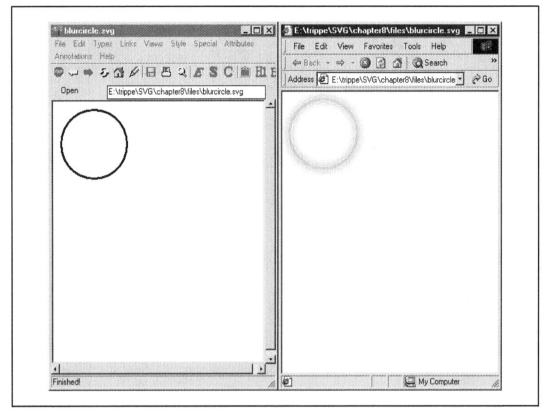

FIGURE 8-11   *The two viewers show the same SVG image with markedly different results. The image on the right is rendered with the Adobe Viewer, which at this writing supports some SVG elements that the Amaya Viewer does not.* ■

You can then agree to view the errors, and Amaya brings up a fairly helpful editing window, showing the SVG code (with line numbers) and a separate window that keys the error messages to the line numbers in the code (see Figure 8-13).

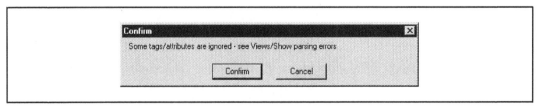

FIGURE 8-12   *The SVG Viewer in Amaya will produce warning messages when it encounters SVG tagging that is not part of the core SVG specification.* ■

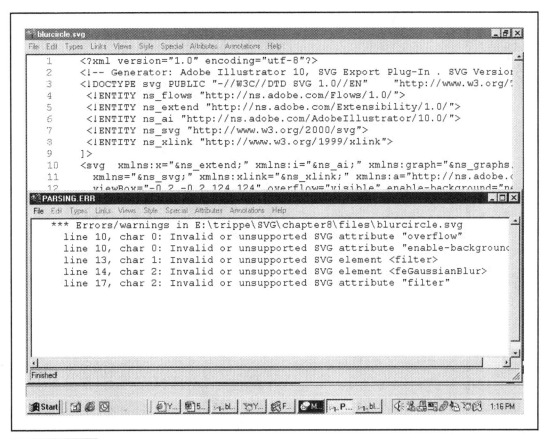

```
blurcircle.svg                                                    _ | 8 | X |
File  Edit  Types  Links  Views  Style  Special  Attributes  Annotations  Help
    1      <?xml version="1.0" encoding="utf-8"?>
    2      <!-- Generator: Adobe Illustrator 10, SVG Export Plug-In . SVG Versior
    3      <!DOCTYPE svg PUBLIC "-//W3C//DTD SVG 1.0//EN"      "http://www.w3.org/!
    4      <!ENTITY ns_flows "http://ns.adobe.com/Flows/1.0/">
    5      <!ENTITY ns_extend "http://ns.adobe.com/Extensibility/1.0/">
    6      <!ENTITY ns_ai "http://ns.adobe.com/AdobeIllustrator/10.0/">
    7      <!ENTITY ns_svg "http://www.w3.org/2000/svg">
    8      <!ENTITY ns_xlink "http://www.w3.org/1999/xlink">
    9      ]>
   10      <svg  xmlns:x="&ns_extend;" xmlns:i="&ns_ai;" xmlns:graph="&ns_graphs.
   11         xmlns="&ns_svg;" xmlns:xlink="&ns_xlink;" xmlns:a="http://ns.adobe.(
   12         viewBox="-0.2 -0.2 124 124" overflow="visible" enable-background="n(
```

```
PARSING.ERR                                                       _ | □ | X |
File  Edit  Types  Links  Views  Style  Special  Attributes  Annotations  Help
  *** Errors/warnings in E:\trippe\SVG\chapter8\files\blurcircle.svg
     line 10, char 0: Invalid or unsupported SVG attribute "overflow"
     line 10, char 0: Invalid or unsupported SVG attribute "enable-backgrounc
     line 13, char 1: Invalid or unsupported SVG element <filter>
     line 14, char 2: Invalid or unsupported SVG element <feGaussianBlur>
     line 17, char 2: Invalid or unsupported SVG attribute "filter"
```

```
Finished!
```

```
Start  | □ @ □  | | @ Y... | ₪ 5... | .,, bl. | ₩ Y... | @ F. | @ M. | .,. P... | .,, bl. | ⟨ ⅗ ⬚ ⬚ ⬚ ⬚ ⬚ ⬚ ⬚  1:16 PM
```

FIGURE 8-13 *The Amaya Viewer allows you to edit the source SVG code, with a separate window providing error messages.* ∎

Having this more stringent parsing of the SVG might suggest a workflow for web developers and designers. One could imagine developing SVG images in a variety of ways, then testing them for viewing with the Amaya Viewer as a lowest common denominator. We are still too early in the life of SVG to know what kind of accommodations you will have to make to various browsers and viewers. If you were to deploy today, you could probably safely assume that most of your users would have the Adobe Viewer, and you likely wouldn't have to worry about a large audience of Amaya users out there.

However, Amaya is not the only reason you will likely require a workflow to support simpler SVG images than those supported in the Adobe Viewer. Keep in mind that the W3C is already working on other versions of SVG (besides up-grades), including two "mobile" profiles of SVG called SVG Tiny and SVG Basic. These are intended for mobile phones (SVG Tiny) and personal digital assistants (SVG Basic), and both will be subsets of the full SVG standard. A complex illustration created in, say, Adobe Illustrator, will likely need to somehow be filtered down to SVG Tiny and SVG Basic.

In the long run, the best solution will be for you to work collaboratively with a web developer. The web developer can help script viewer and platform detection to serve up either alternate content or alternate styles for the your SVG. That is, in the long run, you will want to have a lot of platforms to support, and you should not feel restricted to creating content that has to work on all platforms or versions of SVG. That is part of the beauty of SVG—it can be dynamic and is customizable to as many purposes as you need it to be. Chapter 9 will deal with this question of dynamic SVG in more detail.

Using the Amaya Editor

The Amaya editor works much like any other WYSIWYG HTML editor. The default editing window is WYSIWYG, but there is a source code editor and a structure view that also allow you to select, delete, and move major elements. Because Amaya is open source and faithful to the W3C specifications for HTML and SVG, it has a kind of "bare bones" appearance, as shown in Figure 8-14, but don't let that fool you. It is a full-featured editor, and is the only tool that provides WYSIWYG editing of HTML, SVG, and MathML, all in one interface. The following is a quick run through of the menus:

- **File**   The File menu provides all the standard file-handling functions such as Open, Save, Close, and Exit. It also has reload document feature, which is a nice way of abandoning an edit session and starting from scratch. Finally, it also allows you to modify the kind of HTML you are producing through a Modify doctype function.

- **Edit**   The Edit menu provides Cut, Copy, Paste, and Delete, as well as spell checking. You will also find the menu selection to toggle between the editor mode and browser mode. It also has a nice (though, from what we can see, buggy) capability to "transform" structural elements, allowing you to, for example, turn a bulleted list into a table.

- **Types**   The Types menu is essentially a tag insert menu, allowing you to quickly access and insert the major HTML elements.

- **Links**   The Links menu provides a WYSIWYG interface for creating links, and has commands for creating links and targets.

- **Views**   The Views menu combines functions for changing the way the application displays (button bars, address window, and so forth) with some powerful features such as the structural viewer/editor and source code editor.

- **Style**   The Style menu provides menus-based style markup, as well as tools for inserting and linking to Cascading Style Sheets.

- **Special**   The Special menu is a bit of a grab bag. Amaya has some publishing features, including section numbering, and also a direct interface to creating IDs for whole documents or single HTML elements. You also access preferences here.

- **Attributes**   The Attributes menu allows you to apply attributes to the overall document or to the current HTML element.

- **Annotations**   This menu accesses some developing tools for allowing users to annotate documents for collaboration. Amaya supports what is called the WEBDAV protocol (Web-based Distributed Authoring and Versioning), which is an extension to HTTP that allows authors to collaborate over remote web servers.

- **Help**   Amaya provides excellent online (HTML) help.

Creating an original SVG image in Amaya is analogous to working in a word processor that has a drawing tool. The rightmost button on the toolbar launches a tool palette that provides a GUI for creating basic SVG shapes, as shown in Figure 8-15.

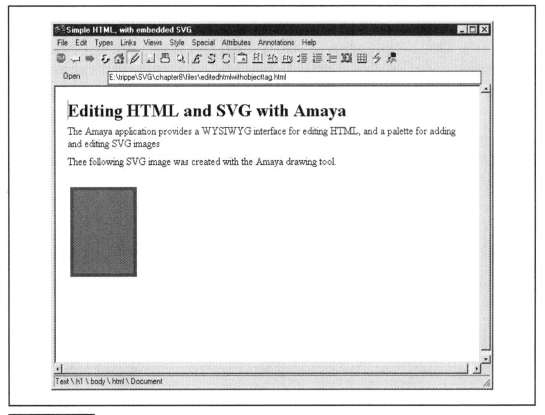

FIGURE 8-14 *Amaya may have a bare-bones look and feel, but it has a unique combination of features for editing HTML, SVG, and MathML.* ■

If you were so inclined, you could use Amaya to create and edit HTML pages and to create and edit SVG files. You could create these SVG images in separate files, or inline with the HTML pages you are creating. However, if you decide to use Amaya to create the SVG images in line with HTML pages, you will likely have trouble displaying the HTML pages in browsers—except for Amaya itself. At this writing, Internet Explorer and Netscape do not support inline SVG; instead, you must write the SVG images to a separate file, and use either the <EMBED> element or <OBJECT> element to reference the SVG.

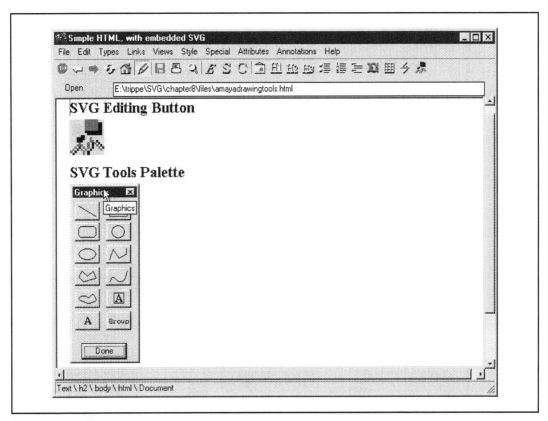

FIGURE 8-15 *Amaya's SVG Editing palette can be launched from a toolbar button.* ∎

It's important to note, though, that the future direction of SVG and HTML (as well as SVG and XHTML, and SVG and XML) is toward allowing the SVG to appear inline. This is specifically why SVG takes advantage of namespaces. It makes all the sense in the world for developers to be able to create, in an editor as well as on the fly, a single text stream that will include HTML and SVG. Until the commercial browsers catch up to Amaya in this regard, you will need to create and manage the SVG files separately from the HTML.

Adobe GoLive

Adobe GoLive, now in version 6.0, is a full-featured HTML editor and web publishing application. It also bills itself as a workflow and site management tool, and does in fact have some good facilities for managing small- to medium-sized web sites. Because of this, GoLive is a large and complex application, and a complete treatment of it is well beyond the scope of this chapter, or even of this book.

As a result, this section will focus on the facilities within GoLive for working with SVG files, and in particular for managing SVG and web pages. Because GoLive is tightly integrated with Adobe applications, and because GoLive is oriented to the development of graphically rich web sites, it has some interesting features for working with SVG files.

Adobe GoLive and "Smart Objects"

GoLive 6.0 provides a visual editing environment for creating HTML pages, including ones that have SVG images. As shown in Figure 8-16, it allows you to toggle easily between a WYSIWYG layout editor, a source editor, and a preview pane. You can also easily launch browsers on the page you are currently editing through a Preview In function available from the File menu.

GoLive has a number of graphical features for editing web pages. For example, it is pretty straightforward to drag and drop image files onto the layout editor, and then move them into place. GoLive has a further capability for images that is called "Smart Objects." The idea behind Smart Objects is that you may well want to have one or more web versions of an image, while maintaining its source in, say, Adobe Illustrator or SVG. This will allow you to reuse a graphical object many times, with minor changes such as colors, sizes, and so forth. In the event the source image changes, you can propagate the changes to all the instances of the file on your web site. This can be very useful for sites that contain many graphical objects, and where the developers want some help effectively managing them.

When you require an image file that is not ready for web delivery, such as a TIFF file, GoLive allows you to first import it into the web site you are developing, and

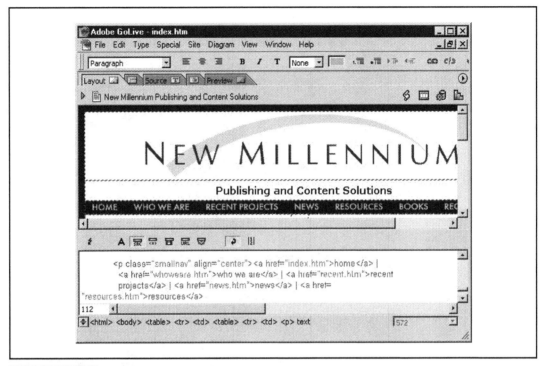

FIGURE   8-16   *Adobe GoLive offers several means to create and edit web pages.* ■

then move it onto the target page. When you drag and drop the image file onto the page layout editor, GoLive provides you with a Save for Web tool, as seen in Figure 8-17, that combines the process for converting the TIFF file to, say, JPG, along with some tools for touching up and optimizing the image.

This same process of Save for Web can be applied to SVG files as well. If you drag and drop an SVG file onto the page layout editor, GoLive provides you with the same Save for Web tool Given the lack of uniform support for SVG, it may make sense for some images and web pages to simply save the SVG as a GIF, JPG, or PNG and deploy the GIF to the server. There may also good reasons to use both; the example SVG images on the W3C site use both the SVG file itself and a PNG version of it.

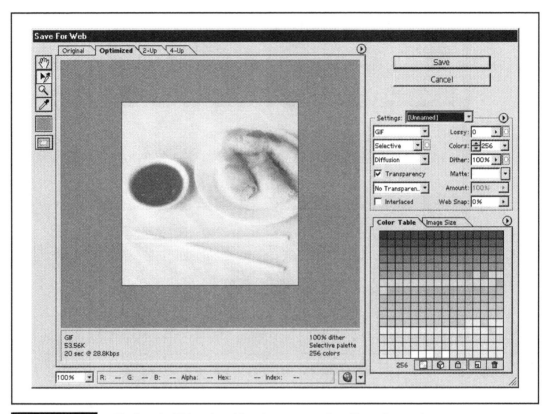

FIGURE 8-17   *The Save for Web tool combines image conversion with touch-up tools.* ∎

If you want the Smart Object to end up as an SVG file on the web site, GoLive actually requires you to start with a Native Illustrator file, add it as a Smart Object, and then save it as SVG. It also presumes that you have Adobe Illustrator running on the same computer that is running GoLive. If you don't have Adobe Illustrator installed on the same computer, you are limited to the Save as Web options that save the SVG or Adobe Illustrator file in a bitmap format, or adding the SVG itself to the web page with the <EMBED> or <OBJECT> elements.

If you do have Adobe Illustrator installed on the computer, you have a number of further options for including your images as SVG Smart Objects, and optimizing these images. These optimization options include

- **Font subsetting**   This is for choosing which glyphs are stored with the SVG file.

- **Font location**   Use this for choosing whether to embed or link to the fonts.

- **Image location**   This is for choosing whether to embed or link bitmaps.

- **Optimize for Adobe Viewer**   This saves the SVG in a way that will have the best performance with the Adobe Viewer.

Finally, you can use some tools within GoLive to revise and fine-tune your SVG. GoLive allows you to open the SVG files as text and edit them, and you can use the syntax checking tools within GoLive to validate the SVG syntax.

Web Browser Support for SVG

As you can see, the current state of browser support for SVG is a mixed bag. Unless they are using Amaya (not a high likelihood), your users will need to download and install the Adobe Viewer. To accommodate the varying support for HTML's <OBJECT> element, you likely want to use the <EMBED> element for now. If you wanted very much to always include SVG files but also include an alternate (for example, GIF), you could use the <OBJECT> element, but then you would need to count on your users having Microsoft Internet Explorer.

If you are especially conservative, you could use an approach such as that available through GoLive, and maintain the SVG files as a source, but instead deploy bitmaps. Ultimately, each developer must decide for himself or herself what the user base requires and will tolerate. If you are confident that your users will see the value in downloading the Adobe Viewer, deploy the SVG and tell them where to download the viewer. Many people already have, especially when you consider that the Adobe SVG Viewer has been shipping with Acrobat Reader 5.0 and higher, as well as Adobe Illustrator 9 and higher.

Of course, if your site is dynamically generated, or you have some scripting capabilities, you can devise code that will test which browser type each user has and whether they have the viewer installed, and generate the appropriate version of the page.

We are confident that, in the long run, the major browsers will support SVG viewing without requiring the separate download and installation of the Adobe Viewer. We are also confident that the browsers will support *inline* SVG, where the SVG text appears in the same text stream as the HTML, XHTML, or XML. There are many good reasons why this should happen, and precious few why it shouldn't.

chapter 9

Generating SVG
on the Fly

The Web has been around a long time, and we are perhaps well into at least the third generation of web sites. If this first generation of web sites were "brochureware" sites, and the second generation began to bring a level of dynamic serving of data, then the third generation of web sites has been an attempt to bring more integration of structured and unstructured data. There is a great deal of focus in the recent year on "enterprise" content management and digital asset management, and more serious attempts to merge the technologies of web serving with the complex back-office processes that have not yet made it to the Web.

What has lagged, of course, in this new automation is any attempt to include graphics serving in this new generation of web sites. This has mainly been because web graphics have long been dominated by heavy, static, bitmap images. What has been needed all along has been a way to dynamically store, aggregate, and serve graphical information.

SVG has given us exactly this opportunity, and exactly these capabilities. This kind of approach makes all the sense in the world, and is possible with SVG for a number of reasons:

- SVG is *a textual format*, thus easily generated with a variety of processes and programming languages.

- As you have seen from the example code throughout the book, SVG can also be designed to be *modular and hierarchical*. Thus, the SVG can be combined, split, and recombined. Programmers can take advantage of an application programming interface (API) such as the Document Object

Model (DOM) to traverse an SVG document structure, and select and process individual or multiple nodes.

- Because SVG is based on XML, and both SVG and XML can exist in their own namespaces, XML, SVG, and XHTML data can be *liberally combined into a single text flow* to create whole pages on the fly.

- Also, because SVG is textual, it can be *easily extracted from a single or multiple data source.* Thus, cartographic applications could be drawn from a GIS database, with supporting data taken from another data source or derived on the fly.

The combination of these characteristics makes SVG ideal for dynamic serving. With the right up-front planning, the SVG source materials could be designed for high-performance, flexible serving.

This chapter looks at three commercial technologies for SVG image serving—Adobe Altercast, Causeway Graphical Systems' GraPL.net, and Savage Software's DataSlinger. The strong verbs in the product names alone are impressive, and we found the products to be very useful, full-featured systems. Since this is a very early market, this bodes well for the future of this kind of software.

While this is far from an exhaustive look at these products in particular or this technology in general, we do think it provides a useful introduction to the topic, to these particular technologies, and to the major issues of image conversion, manipulation, and serving.

Adobe AlterCast

Adobe AlterCast is multipurpose image-serving software. It allows web developers to automatically create and update images, convert them to different formats, and serve them over the Web. It can operate as a stand-alone server or in conjunction with other web servers, and it can be integrated with complementary technology such as content management and e-commerce systems.

Adobe's tagline for AlterCast is "deliver dynamic, data-driven images to any audience." Despite the unfortunate alliteration, this is a reasonable claim for the product, though perhaps they could add, "Especially if you are using Adobe's graphic creation and editing tools such as Illustrator and PhotoShop." We were able to install the AlterCast, get it running, do the canned demos that come with the product, and then extend it some ourselves. We were impressed with the comprehensiveness of the product, the ease of installation, and the ability to quickly modify a few simple commands.

Product Requirements

AlterCast is a server-side product that runs on Windows (2000 and NT) and Sun Solaris. While your specific environment will require more analysis to determine exactly what sort of hardware and software will best support it, Adobe offers the following general guidelines:

- In a Windows environment, Adobe recommends a 500-MHz Intel Pentium III processor or higher, with a minimum of 256MB of RAM and 120MB of disk space for the installation itself. The software is delivered on CD-ROM. AlterCast runs on Windows 2000 Server or NT 4.0 with Service Pack 6a.

- On Sun Solaris, Adobe recommends a 167-MHz Sun UltraSPARC processor, with a minimum of 128MB of RAM per CPU (512MB per CPU recommended), 120MB of disk space for the installation itself, and swap disk space totaling the RAM size plus 128MB. The software is delivered on CD-ROM. AlterCast runs on Sun Solaris 7 or 8.

We installed AlterCast on a machine running Windows 2000 Server. Prior to installing AlterCast, we followed Adobe's recommendation of ensuring Internet Information Server (IIS) and the Java Software Development Kit (JDK) were both installed. If you don't already have the JDK for Windows installed, or if it is version 1.2.1 or below, you can download the latest version from http://java.sun.com.

Finally, because we knew that we would be creating and working with a number of illustrations, we made sure we had plenty of disk space available for working files and the document root.

By default, AlterCast runs from the 8008 port, so accessing the default home page for AlterCast is done through the following URL: http://localhost:8008.

AlterCast in Action

Once we had installed AlterCast on a local server, we then accessed the default home page and demo sites through another Windows machine on the same network, running Windows 2000 Client and Internet Explorer. AlterCast is delivered with several sample web sites, as shown in Figure 9-1, and reference code that can be implemented in Java or COM APIs. The sample code can be used as a starting point for creating new sites.

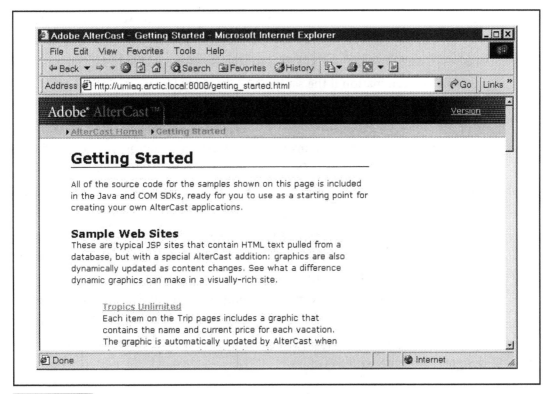

FIGURE   9-1   *The default home page for AlterCast includes sample web sites that show a variety of the software's capabilities.* ■

To Adobe's credit, the example web sites are well done, and do a good job of highlighting the various functions available with AlterCast. The delivered web sites provide a ready means of doing the following:

- Updating all or many of the images on a graphic-intensive web site
- Automatically resizing one or many images in different formats
- Automatically creating a banner ad or image
- Creating a dynamic graph with SVG

We should point out that we did not test the AlterCast sample code in a production environment, so we cannot comment if it is production worthy or not. However, we did exercise each of the example sites over several days of testing, with no crashes or error messages. Experienced web developers should be able to make their own determination if the sample code is ready for use.

We should also point out that AlterCast has many capabilities beyond working with SVG files. In fact, AlterCast works with GIF, animated GIF, JPEG, PNG, WBMP, SVG, and PSD files. Many of its core features—such as updating, resizing, and converting images on the fly, shown in Figure 9-2—cut across all of the file types. Moreover, AlterCast comes with a comprehensive, XML-based command language for scripting these functions into workflows and into processes that would enhance a web site. As you will see later in this section, the XML-based command language can also be used across file types, but it has some particularly useful hooks for working with SVG.

We mention these broader capabilities only to point out that we did not attempt to evaluate every one of AlterCast's features. Instead, while we did focus on a few of the general-purpose features, our primary focus was the feature set of most use to designers working with SVG files.

Improved Panning and Zooming

As we have discussed elsewhere in the book, one of the key benefits of SVG over bitmaps is the improved zooming of detailed illustrations, such as maps. As you know, bitmap graphics are typically optimized for one size and one resolution. So,

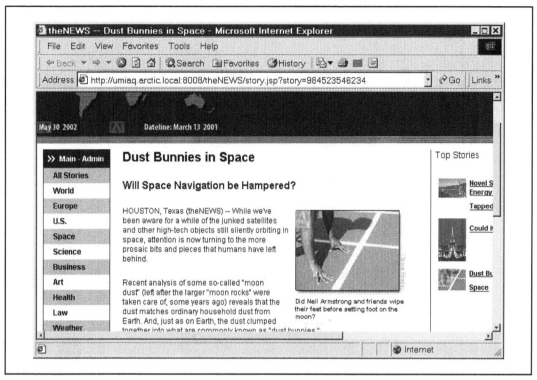

FIGURE 9-2 *AlterCast has a number of general-purpose tools for resizing images. This shows an image that was dynamically resized to fit into an existing web page layout.* ∎

with a detailed illustration, there will always be tradeoffs between providing enough detail and making the bitmap file unnecessarily large. Cartography is a particularly challenging application, because if the user is looking to zoom to a highly detailed level (streets or individual properties, for example) the files can be enormous—even in a relatively compact format such as SVG.

One solution is to dynamically serve the SVG files as they are requested. In the example shown in Figure 9-3, AlterCast first serves a wider view of the mapped area. A request to zoom in actually results in different SVG data being served, as shown in Figure 9-4. For example, a closer view may require additional data to be served, such as street names that were not appropriate for the wider view.

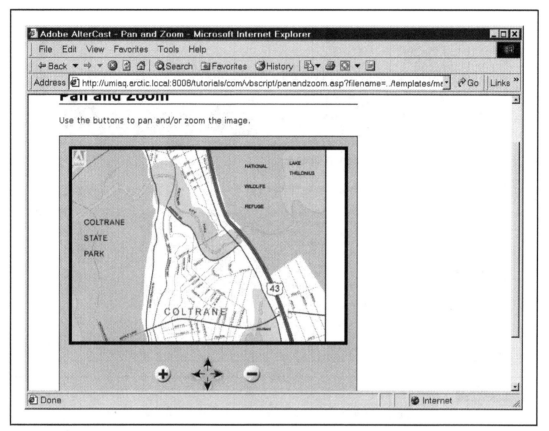

FIGURE 9-3 *AlterCast first serves a wider view of the mapped area.* ∎

Interacting with Dynamic Charts

AlterCast is delivered with a dynamic charting application that takes user input and creates and modifies various charts, such as pie charts, bar charts, and scatter diagrams. In a way, this is analogous to the kind of charting one can do in a spreadsheet application such as Microsoft Excel. But the AlterCast application is more comprehensive, as it can take user input through a forms interface, for example, and regenerate the graphic.

Of course, the real advantage to this kind of application is that it is browser based, and will require no special software for the end user aside from an SVG

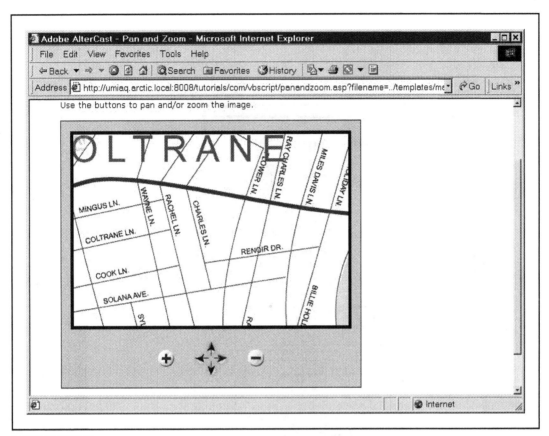

FIGURE   9-4   *When the user requests to either zoom or pan, AlterCast dynamically serves the appropriate SVG data for the mapped area.* ■

Viewer. Once again, this is one of the real advantages of SVG—to bring this kind of interactivity and graphical rendering to the Web.

One of the AlterCast applications shows a bar chart accompanied by a forms-based interface for modifying the data. The user is presented with a rendered drawing and preset values, as shown in Figure 9-5. In particular, this demonstration shows an Illustrator template being dynamically modified. If you are accustomed to working in Adobe Illustrator, you can use the charts and graphs features of Illustrator, along with the Variables palette, to create templates for AlterCast.

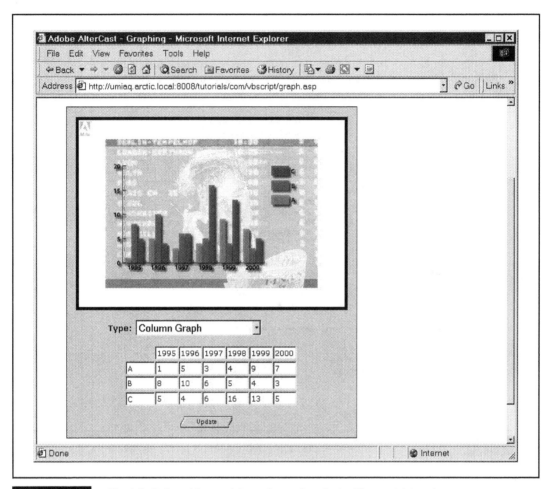

The user can then modify the data, and regenerate the drawing, as shown in Figure 9-6 or choose a different graph type, as shown in Figure 9-7.

One can imagine a number of even more sophisticated uses for this kind of application. A financial services site could present users with what-if scenarios for retirement, prompting them for current holdings and future savings rate. Formulae

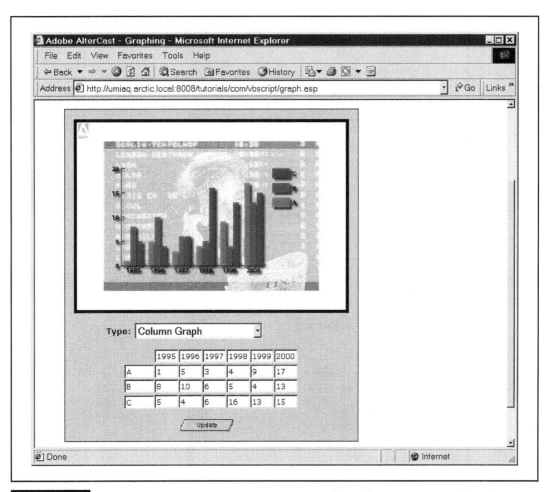

FIGURE 9-6 *The user can first modify the values, and then regenerate the same kind of graph. In this example, we modified the year 2000 values.* ■

could be applied to the input data and graphs could be created projecting future income. A group of scientists could share gene sequence data, and generate graphical views of sequences on demand, based on certain search criteria. Indeed, the potential applications are endless when you combine the kinds of data sources that are available with the rendering capabilities of SVG.

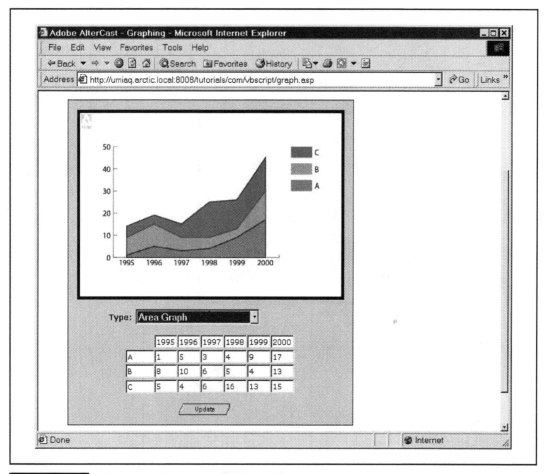

FIGURE   9-7   *The user can then choose a different chart type. In this example, we've switched from a columnar bar chart to an area graph.* ■

Using AlterCast's Command Language

The "canned" demos and applications are useful for understanding AlterCast's feature set, but we were especially impressed with the XML-based command language for manipulating graphics. In essence, the command language allows you to use an XML-like syntax for manipulating graphics. For example, the following command loads an SVG file for processing:

```
<loadContent source=file:///New Millennium/Program Files
/AlterCast 1.5/samples/images/svg/logo.svg/>
```

And then this next command changes the existing width of the SVG element to 222 pixels:

```
<set target=/svg/@width" value="222">
```

While this is a simple example, the underlying power and flexibility of this kind of command language is significant. Recall that the opening syntax of an SVG file typically includes the SVG element itself, with the width and height declared as attributes, as shown here:

```
<svg height="100" width="100">
```

The set command then tells AlterCast to traverse the SVG file, find the width attribute within the svg element, and set the value to 222. The command language is, in essence, using the DOM to traverse the tree structure of the SVG and manipulate this particular node. Thus, it could be used to do a variety of specific manipulations to SVG data, making it a powerful and flexible means to transform SVG files.

AlterCast is delivered with several command language examples, sample input and output, and a simple forms-based editing shell for experimenting with the language, as shown in Figure 9-8. This first example shows an Adobe logo, rendered in an SVG file. The original logo is shown in the left; the resulting output logo is shown on the right. The command set, displayed in the lower window, does basically two things to the source image: It changes the overall height and width, and it changes the rendered path from red to blue.

We spent several hours writing very simple commands to change source files. By no means did we become proficient in the language, but we did experiment with isolating and manipulating elements and attributes, and with creating varied output of source SVG files. A simple example is shown in Figure 9-9, where we've taken the same source Adobe logo and changed the dimensions and color again—this time using different values.

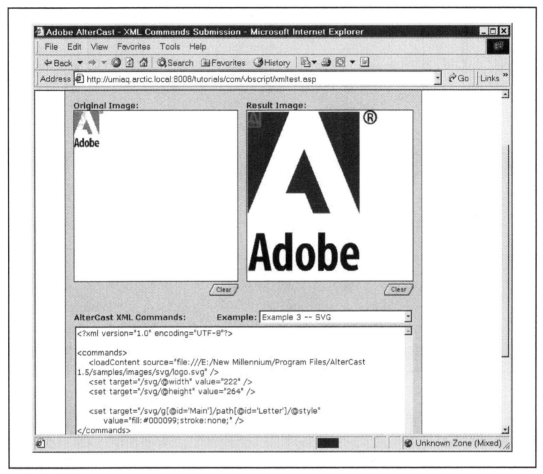

FIGURE 9-8 *This simple editing interface is provided with AlterCast for experimenting with the XML-based command language.* ■

Summing Up AlterCast

AlterCast seems to be an impressive, multipurpose image-serving product. Sitting on top of a core of Adobe image processing functionality, it is well suited to automate the time-consuming, repetitive tasks of converting, modifying, and serving images in many formats. We were also impressed with the specific SVG capabilities shown, such as dynamic serving to support applications such as cartography. Finally, we are intrigued with the XML-based command language and its potential as a flexible tool for SVG image manipulation.

We offer a caveat here that we will have to make with each of these server products. Our testing and evaluation was limited to nonproduction environments. We installed and tested each of these products on a small network of three Windows machines, and had a maximum of two users accessing server functionality at any one time. As a result, we have to stop short of declaring these products production ready, but we are confident that your analysis, and discussions with both the vendor and current users of the software, will help you determine whether AlterCast and the other products can meet your production needs.

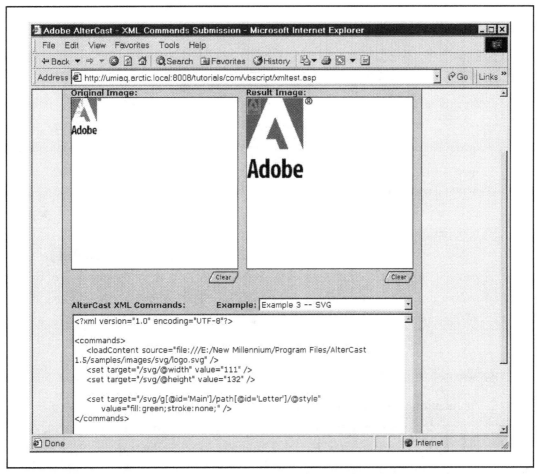

FIGURE   9-9   *A similar example to Figure 9-8, this time providing slightly different values for the output.* ■

GraPL.net

GraPL.net is a moderately priced server-side product for dynamically generating SVG and other graphic formats on the fly. It allows developers to develop server-side Visual Basic scripts that then make calls to the GraPL charting engine to create data-driven graphics on the fly.

Unlike AlterCast, which is a general-purpose tool for image serving and manipulation, GraPL.net is specifically a scripting platform for web developers. It comes delivered with a generous set of example code, showing sample output for SVG, PDF, and other formats. You can view all of the sample code and output online at http://titan.causeway.co.uk/graplnet.

Product Requirements

GraPL.net is a server-side product that runs on any version of Windows that can run Internet Information Server (IIS). (We ran it on Windows 2000 Server.) It requires Windows Scripting Host, which comes with IIS, and client machines need to be running Internet Explorer 4.0 or higher. According to the company, Causeway Graphical Systems, GraPL.net can run on any processor, though a Pentium-class machine is recommended, and requires 20MB of hard disk space for installation.

We installed GraPL.net on the same server as AlterCast. It included an AMD Athlon 1400-MHz processor and 512MB of RAM. We then exercised all of the installed example scripts in a small network of three Windows machines, with a maximum of two users accessing the server at any one time.

GraPL.net in Action

As mentioned above, GraPL.net installs with a large suite of example code. The scripts demonstrate dynamic serving of data into various graphical formats, including bar charts, scatter diagrams, and a variety of other formats. The example scripts produce output in SVG, VML, PDF, and PNG.

Along with the example scripts, which are all spelled out in detail, the GraPL.net documentation (available as Windows help) provides excellent walk-throughs of the code. For example, they include their equivalent of a "Hello, World" script, with a set of fairly obvious commands for rendering a bar chart showing sales for the months January to May.

```
.FrameStyle = "Wiped,Boxed"
.Margins    = array(42,48,36,18)
.Heading    = "My First Chart"
.XLabels    = array("Jan","Feb","Mar","Apr","May")
.Style      = "Forcezero,Values,Redraw"
.Axes       = "Black,1,Solid"
.XCaption   = "Months"
.YCaption   = "Sales in £"
.YStyle     = "Atend"
.Barchart array(23,12,34,19,7)
```

The actual values of the bars are listed in the array .Barchart array; thus, this code would result in bars of 23, 12, 34, 19, and 7 for the months Jan, Feb, Mar, Apr, and May.

The commands shown here could then be included in an ASP script that would output the chart, in this case as a PNG file:

```
<%@ LANGUAGE=VBScript %>
<%
Set grapl = Server.CreateObject("grapl.engine")  ' Connect
With grapl
 .New 0,0,432,324
 .FrameStyle = "Wiped,Boxed"
 .Margins    = array(42,48,36,18)
 .Heading    = "My First Chart"
 .XLabels    = array("Jan","Feb","Mar","Apr","May")
 .Style      = "Forcezero,Values,Redraw"
 .Axes       = "Black,1,Solid"
 .XCaption   = "Months"
 .YCaption   = "Sales in £"
 .YStyle     = "Atend"
 .Barchart array(23,12,34,19,7)
End with
With Response
```

```
 .Expires = 0
 .Buffer   = TRUE
 .Clear
 .ContentType = "image/png"
 .BinaryWrite grapl.RenderPNG(72,true)
 .End
End with
%>
```

Such a script could then be embedded in a simple HTML page as follows:

```
<html><head><title>GraPL.NET - Example</title></head>
<body>
<h2>Simple chart</h2>
 <img src="Checkout.asp" height=324 width=432 border=0 >
</body>
</html>
```

Let's look at a couple of examples charts, and then one in depth, to understand how the dynamic generation and serving happens, and how it then results in viewable SVG files.

Some Examples

The GraPL.net illustrations are effective, subtle, intelligently rendered examples of data-driven graphics. One of the first charts combines a time series illustration with small pie charts at each data point, as shown in Figure 9-10.

The script to generate this graph is actually quite short and fairly readable. It once again uses small arrays of data as the values for the graphics—in this case, both the line itself and the individual pie charts.

```
Set grapl = Server.CreateObject("grapl.engine")  ' Connect
' An easy (and rather silly) test piece.
'
' This just draws a small piechart at each
  datapoint in the timeseri ...
  With grapl
  .New 0,0,432,324
  .FrameStyle   = "Wiped,Boxed"
  .Margins      = array(60,64,36,36)
```

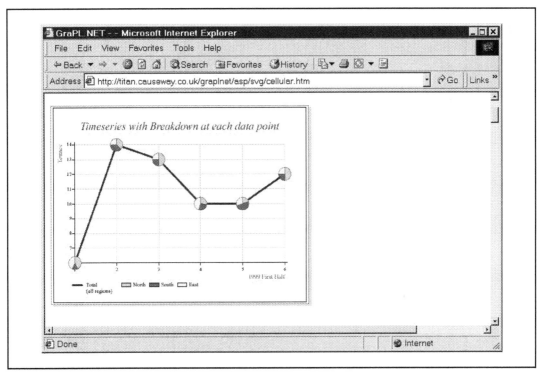

FIGURE 9-10 *While the Causeway web site refers to this as "an easy (and rather silly)" test piece, it shows how SVG can efficiently bring a great deal of information to a single graphic.* ∎

```
.Heading      = "Timeseries with Breakdown at each data point"
.HeadingStyle = "Centre,Top"
.HeadingFont  = "TII,18,Navy"
.Nibs         = "3"
.Style        = "Lines,grid,cells"
.CellSize     = array(32,32)
.Axes         = "Black,1,Solid"
.XCaption     = "1999 First Half"
.YCaption     = "Tonnes"
.Linegraph array(6,14,13,10,10,12)
.ResetOptions = "Keys"
.Reset
.NewCell
.Margins      = array(0)
.Pie array(3,1,3)
.NewCell
```

```
.Pie array(3,3,2)
.NewCell
.Pie array(4,2,2)
.NewCell
.Pie array(3,3,5)
.NewCell
.Pie array(2,5,3)
.NewCell
.Pie array(2,1,1)
.New 0,0,432,324
.Margins    = array(42,64,36,18)
.Key        = array("Total;(all regions)","North","South","East")
End with
Response.ContentType = "image/svg+xml"
Response.Write grap1.RenderSVG
```

This is too much code to walk through line by line, but it is worth highlighting a few key lines to see how the data is interpreted and eventually output as SVG.

The first few lines establish the size and boundaries of the illustration, together with the heading and how it is to be styled:

```
.FrameStyle   = "Wiped,Boxed"
.Margins      = array(60,64,36,36)
.Heading      = "Timeseries with Breakdown at each data point"
.HeadingStyle = "Centre,Top"
```

A few lines later, the script establishes the style of the chart, the axes, the captions for the axes, and the array of data that will render the chart itself:

```
.Style      = "Lines,grid,cells"
.CellSize   = array(32,32)
.Axes       = "Black,1,Solid"
.XCaption   = "1999 First Half"
.YCaption   = "Tonnes"
.Linegraph array(6,14,13,10,10,12)
```

The individual pie charts are then created with a series of commands that render the pie charts and how they should be segmented, the brief array in each .Pie statement providing the division points for the pieces of the pie:

```
.NewCell
.Margins = array(0)
.Pie array(3,1,3)
.NewCell
.Pie array(3,3,2)
```

The script then concludes with the GraPL charting engine commands required to create SVG on output, as shown in Figure 9-11.

```
    End with
Response.ContentType = "image/svg+xml"
Response.Write grapl.RenderSVG
```

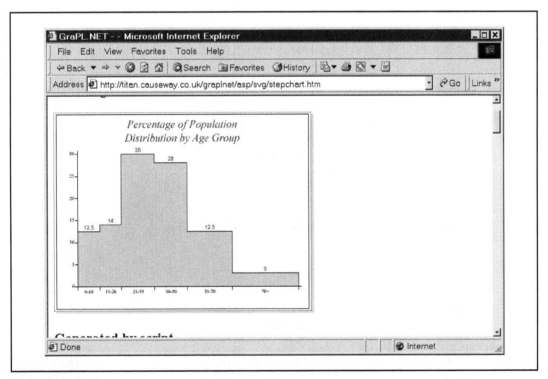

FIGURE 9-11   *The GraPL charting engine can produce SVG (as shown here), but also VML, PDF, and PNG output.* ∎

A Final Example

Let's walk through one final example, showing the script, the formatted SVG, and the SVG code that is created. This example renders a bar chart with voting results for a town called Ryedale.

The script is relatively short and somewhat readable:

```
Set grapl = Server.CreateObject("grapl.engine")   ' Connect
' Ryedale votes cast at the last General Election.
  This is a reasona ...
 With grapl
  .New 0,0,432,324
   .FrameStyle     = "Wiped,Boxed"
   .Margins        = array(42,48,36,18)
   .Heading        = "How Ryedale voted;in 2001!"
   .HeadingStyle   = "Right,Top"
   .HeadingFont    = "ARB,24,Navy"
   .Colours        = "Navy,#FAB32E,#D3342C"
   .Patterns       = "Solid"
   .XLabels        = Col_Party
   .CategoriseBy   = Col_Party
   .CategoriseInto = Col_Party
   .Style          = "Forcezero,Stacked,Values"
   .ValueFont      = "ARB,16,Navy"
   .ValueFormat    = "##,###"
   .Gap            = 0.61803
   .Axes           = "Black,1,Solid"
   .KeyStyle       = "Nokey"
   .YStyle         = "NoAxis"
   .LabelFont      = "ARB,18,Black"
  .Barchart Col_Vote2001
 End with
 Response.ContentType = "image/svg+xml"
 Response.Write grapl.RenderSVG
```

Note that the script shown here relies on some arrays of data not included directly in the script but necessary to rendering the chart shown in Figure 9-12.

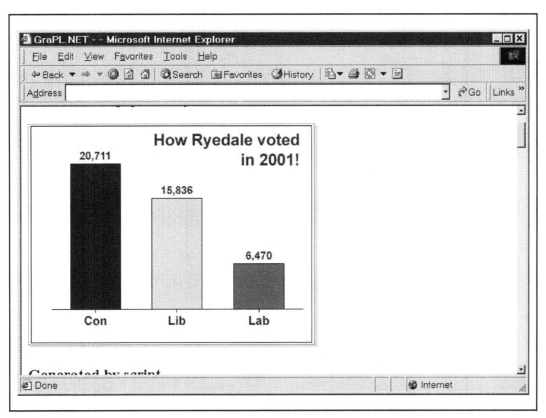

FIGURE   9-12   *The resulting image is relatively simple, and uses the values in the Col_Vote2001 array to create the three bars.* ∎

```
Col_Party = Array("Con","Lib","Lab")
 Col_Vote2001 = Array(20711,15836,6470)
 Col_Con = Array(32,28,26,30,32,25)
 Col_Lib = Array(13,12,14,14,17,14)
 Col_Lab = Array(48,54,54,49,45,55)
```

The GraPL charting engine produces the following SVG output (shown in part, and lightly edited):

```
<!DOCTYPE svg>
<svg width="436pt" height="327pt">
 <rect x="40" y="30" width="4320" height="3240"
  style="fill:silver;" />
 <rect x="3" y="3" width="4314" height="3234"
  style="fill:white; stroke-width:6; stroke:black" />
 <g shape-rendering="crispEdges" style="stroke-width:15;
  stroke:#000000; fill:#FFFFFF;">
 <rect x="48" y="40" width="4225" height="3160"  />
 </g>
 <g id="Heading">
  <text x="4100" y="328">How Ryedale voted</text>
  <text x="4100" y="616">in 2001!</text>
 </g>
 <g id="XLabels">
  <text x="1017" y="2950">Con</text>
  <text x="2250" y="2950">Lib</text>
  <text x="3483" y="2950">Lab</text>
 </g>
 <path shape-rendering="crispEdges" style="fill:none;
  stroke:#000000; stroke-width:6; " d="M 1017,2722 L 1017,2761
  M 2250,2722 L 2250,2761 M 3483,2722 L 3483,2761 "/>
 <g>
  <rect x="636" y="592" width="762" height="2128" />
  <rect x="1869" y="2720" width="762" height="0" />
  <rect x="3102" y="2720" width="762" height="0" />
 </g>
 <g>
  <rect x="636" y="592" width="762" height="2" />
  <rect x="1869" y="1093" width="762" height="1629" />
  <rect x="3102" y="2720" width="762" height="2" />
 </g>
 <g>
  <rect x="636" y="592" width="762" height="2" />
  <rect x="1869" y="1093" width="762" height="2" />
  <rect x="3102" y="2055" width="762" height="667" />
 </g>
```

```
<g>
  <rect style="fill:#FFFFFF; stroke:none" x="712" y="395"
   width="611" height="133" />
 <text x="1017" y="528">20,711</text>
</g>
<g>
  <rect style="fill:#FFFFFF; stroke:none" x="1945" y="896"
   width="611" height="133" />
 <text x="2250" y="1029">15,836</text>
</g>
<g>
  <rect style="fill:#FFFFFF; stroke:none" x="3230" y="1858"
   width="505" height="133" />
 <text x="3483" y="1991">6,470</text>
</g>
<path shape-rendering="crispEdges" style="fill:none;
 stroke:#000000;
 stroke-width:10; " d="M 360,2720 L 4140,2720 "/>
</svg>
```

Summing Up GraPL.net

GraPL.net seems to be a solid product for what it sets out to do, which is to provide Windows Active Server Page web developers a platform for dynamic image generation. We relied heavily on the examples provided, running all of the sample scripts. We then modified several of the scripts to create variant output. We did not, however, develop scripts from scratch, as the time pressures of developing the book overtook us.

So, we can't speak to how comprehensive the GraPL.net development language is, and we also have to offer the same caveat here that our testing and evaluation was limited to nonproduction environments. As a result, we have to stop short of declaring these products production ready, but we are confident that your analysis, and discussions with both the vendor and current users of the software, will help you determine whether GraPL.net and the other products can meet your production needs.

Savage Software DataSlinger

DataSlinger is a server-side product for retrieving, converting, manipulating, and serving graphical content. If AlterCast is well positioned to support graphic artists who use Adobe products in their everyday workflows, then DataSlinger is well positioned to support graphic arts, engineering, and design professionals who deal in complex vector images, especially those created on CAD-CAM systems.

Overall, we were very impressed with DataSlinger, especially its ability to work with large, complex files. Some of the samples from the vendor were large, complex illustrations, which, even in their SVG form, were several hundred kilobytes in size. As with our experience with AlterCast, we were able to install DataSlinger, get it running, do the canned demos that come with the product, and then extend it some ourselves. We were impressed with the comprehensiveness of the product, the ease of installation, and the programming interface for developing new "extenders."

Product Requirements

DataSlinger runs on both Windows and various flavors of UNIX. This broader platform support in itself suggests the company's commitment to customers engaged in more far-flung and difficult applications of computer-aided design and manufacturing.

DataSlinger comes with its own HTTP Server, or it can be configured at installation to run with IIS or the Apache server. Like AlterCast, it requires the full Java Software Development Kit (JDK) to be installed. Whereas AlterCast requires the presence of JDK 1.2.2 or higher, DataSlinger requires 1.3 or higher. (If you don't already have the JDK for Windows installed, you can download the latest version from http://java.sun.com.)

The developer of DataSlinger, Savage Software (http://www.savagesoftware.com) recommends that the software be installed on a machine with a 500-MHz processor, 40MB of available hard disk space, and 256MB of RAM. We installed DataSlinger on the same server as AlterCast and GraPL.net. (It included an AMD Athlon 1400-MHz processor and 512MB of RAM.) We then exercised all of the installed example scripts in a small network of three Windows machines, with a maximum of two users accessing the server at any one time. Finally, we ran the development tool on the same machine, and built a couple of simple extenders that we added to the server.

By default, DataSlinger runs from the 8000 port. Unlike AlterCast, which has a default home page, DataSlinger URLs are formed by embedding the command to be run, together with the target file to be processed. Thus, a URL that tells DataSlinger to convert a file from a CAD format to SVG might be formed as follows:

```
http//localhost:8000/cad2svg/filename=cad/sparkplug.dwg
```

This URL tells the DataSlinger server to apply the command cad2svg (DataSlinger calls them "scenarios") to the file sparkplug.dwg that resides in the directory cad under the document root.

DataSlinger in Action

Just as AlterCast sits on top of a core of Adobe image processing software, so does DataSlinger, again with DataSlinger's emphasis being on processing large and complex CAD files. DataSlinger is also focused on data retrieval. Like AlterCast, it can be integrated with content management systems, and also with databases. Thus, a bread-and-butter task for DataSlinger would be to retrieve a CAD file, convert it to SVG, and serve the resulting SVG data, in whole or in part, to a web site, as shown in Figure 9-13.

The process for getting DataSlinger to convert files from one format to another, or to add more complex transformation to files, is to develop what DataSlinger calls *scenarios*. Scenarios can be built through the Admin Client that comes with the software, as shown in Figure 9-14. It provides a helpful code development interface, and comes with a number of preexisting manipulators and content retrievers:

- *Manipulators* are code modules that typically perform file conversions (SVG to Flash, for example) or that add some particular functionality or transform data in some way (for example, a manipulator could embed certain additional detail in an SVG file).

- *Content retrievers* are code modules that hook DataSlinger to other data sources, and allow scenarios to make calls to these other data sources. DataSlinger comes with certain existing content retrievers, including interfaces to Oracle and MySQL.

We did not attempt to build whole new manipulators and content retrievers from scratch. Similar to what we did with AlterCast and GraPL.net, we exercised all of the provided demos and sample files. We also followed DataSlinger's guidelines for building a new scenario by linking together existing manipulators and retrievers, as shown in Figure 9-15.

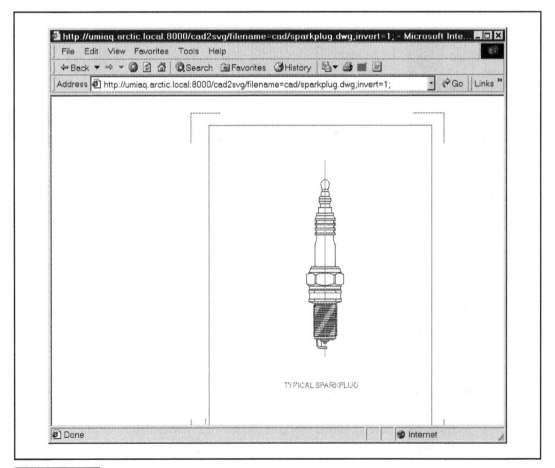

FIGURE 9-13 *DataSlinger was used to convert this CAD file to SVG, and then serve it for viewing.* ■

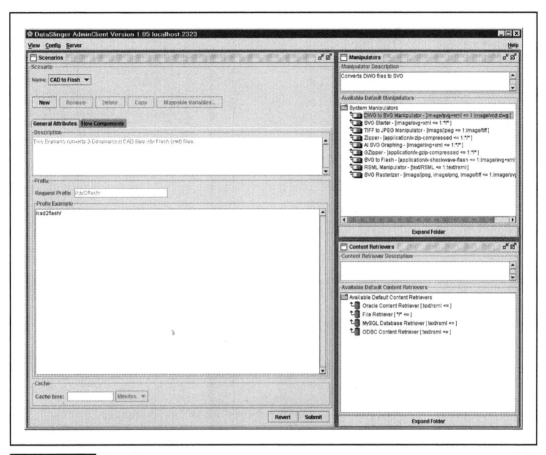

FIGURE   9-14   *The Admin Client provides a visual interface for developing new scenarios for image*
processing. ■

Specifically, we created a new scenario that would retrieve a CAD file from the
file system, first convert it to SVG, and then convert it from SVG to Flash. (Not a
terribly practical example, but one we could do!)

Creating a New DataSlinger Scenario

Once we assembled and named this new scenario, we were able to add it to the
DataSlinger server. The scenario could then be invoked by URL, in the same way

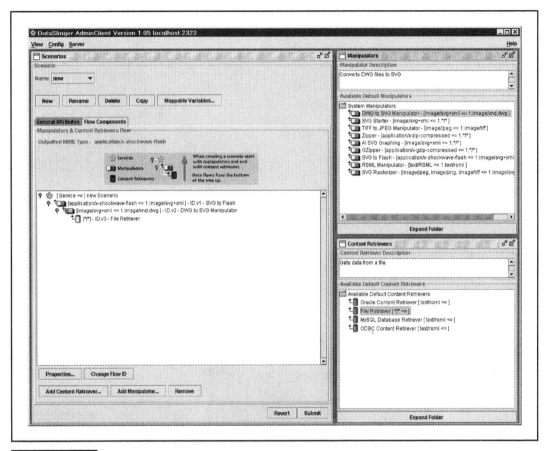

FIGURE 9-15   *The Admin Client allows you to assemble retrievers and manipulators as " flow components."* ■

the existing scenario, cad2svg, was in our first example. We named this scenario swic_swf, and Figure 9-16 shows the scenario being exercised on a moderately complex illustration of an engine.

The URL should look somewhat similar to the first DataSlinger URL listed above. We happened to run this one from the local server:

```
http://localhost:8000/swic_swf/bgcolor=CCCCCC;filename=cad/engine.dwg;
```

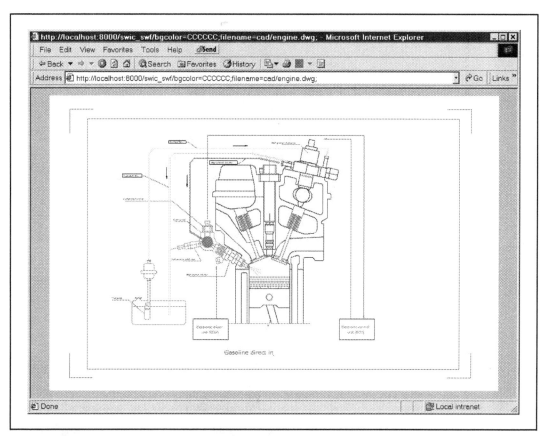

FIGURE   9-16   *The swic_swf scenario applied to an engine diagram.* ■

So, the URL tells the DataSlinger server to run the scenario swic_swf on the file engine.dwg in the directory cad below the document root. This particular URL also happens to tell the server to pass a particular background color to the converted image (bgcolor=CCCCCC), overriding the background color that may have been specified. The background color argument is possible because the SVG-to-Flash converter specifies that a particular background color can be applied during processing. This is shown in Figure 9-17, where the Admin Client reveals which properties of a manipulator can be modified during processing.

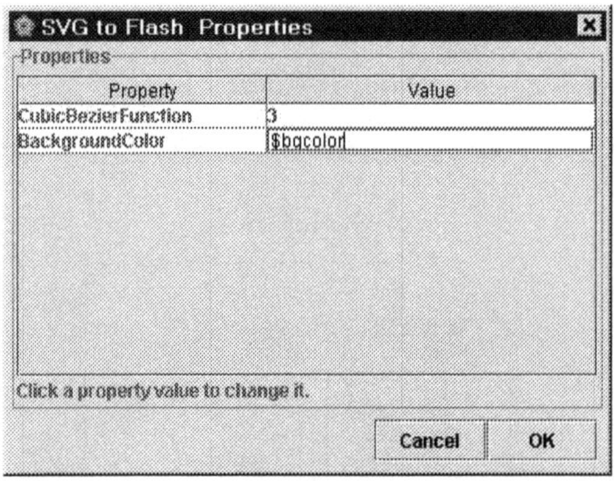

FIGURE 9-17 *The Admin Client reveals which properties of a manipulator are available during processing.* ■

Administering DataSlinger

As we mentioned, DataSlinger can be installed to work with its own HTTP server, with IIS, or with the Apache web server. Administration of the server is fairly straightforward. In the Windows environment we worked in, we started both the DataSlinger HTTP server (see Figure 9-18) and the DataSlinger server itself (see Figure 9-19) without any difficulties. We then ran them over several days without any crashes or hanging, and were able to end the processes without any difficulty.

Summing Up DataSlinger

We were impressed with DataSlinger. Like AlterCast, DataSlinger provides a great deal of general-purpose image serving and manipulation. It works on a wide variety of images, notably the larger and more complex files common in CAD/CAM

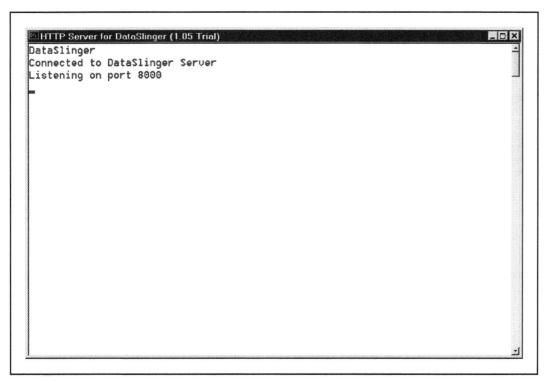

FIGURE   9-18   *The DataSlinger HTTP server maintains this status window during operation.* ■

and other design-intensive applications. Like AlterCast, it also is cross-platform
(Windows and UNIX), and, with its Java focus, has a more generic architecture
than does GraPL.net, which is a Windows-only and ASP-only product.

Perhaps of more significance is the kind of applications that Savage Software is
aiming at with the DataSlinger product. One such application is land use planning,
where municipal planners and residents can visit a web site and research local
properties.

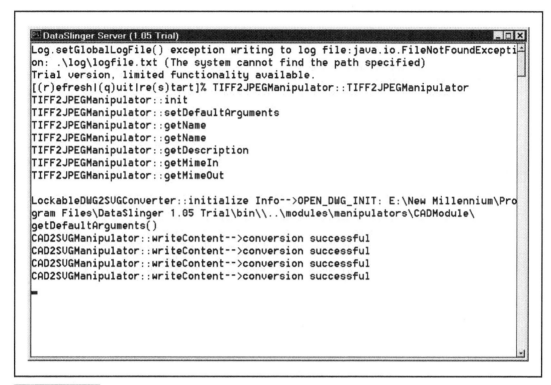

```
DataSlinger Server (1.05 Trial)                                    _ □ ✕
Log.setGlobalLogFile() exception writing to log file:java.io.FileNotFoundExcepti
on: .\log\logfile.txt (The system cannot find the path specified)
Trial version, limited functionality available.
[(r)efresh|(q)uit|re(s)tart]% TIFF2JPEGManipulator::TIFF2JPEGManipulator
TIFF2JPEGManipulator::init
TIFF2JPEGManipulator::setDefaultArguments
TIFF2JPEGManipulator::getName
TIFF2JPEGManipulator::getName
TIFF2JPEGManipulator::getDescription
TIFF2JPEGManipulator::getMimeIn
TIFF2JPEGManipulator::getMimeOut


LockableDWG2SVGConverter::initialize Info-->OPEN_DWG_INIT: E:\New Millennium\Pro
gram Files\DataSlinger 1.05 Trial\bin\\..\modules\manipulators\CADModule\
getDefaultArguments()
CAD2SVGManipulator::writeContent-->conversion successful
CAD2SVGManipulator::writeContent-->conversion successful
CAD2SVGManipulator::writeContent-->conversion successful
CAD2SVGManipulator::writeContent-->conversion successful
```

FIGURE   9-19   *The DataSlinger server also maintains a status window, and active logging of events from the server.* ■

As Figure 9-20 shows, the mapping database encompasses a large geographical area, but users are able to drill down to specific properties. Once at the specific properties, they can then display an impressive array of detail about the property, ranging from square footage to ownership history.

We do think that this kind of practical, data-intensive application will dominate with SVG, and DataSlinger seems to have robust capabilities to handle this kind of data.

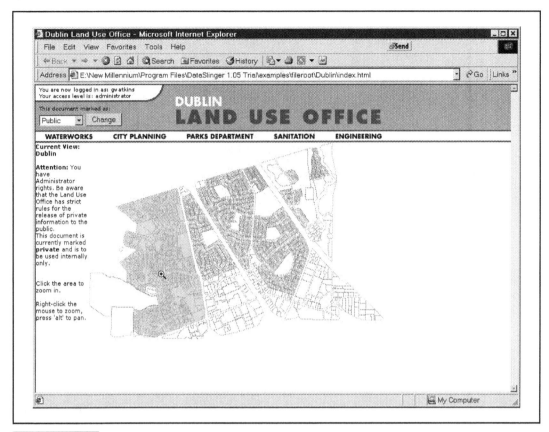

FIGURE   9-20   *In this DataSlinger-driven site, residents and municipal officials can drill down to an impressive level of detail about local land use.* ■

Conclusion

As you can tell from the tone of this chapter, we were impressed with the three products that we looked at in some detail. AlterCast and DataSlinger, especially, are full-featured, powerful, and intriguing products. We are very pleased to see such strong commercial offerings in such an early market.

Moreover, there are a number of products emerging, and significant open source efforts, such as the Batik toolkit that is being developed for the Apache HTTP server. At this writing, the SVG home page at the World Wide Web Consortium (http://www.w3.org/Graphics/SVG/SVG-Implementations.htm8#server) lists nine products for HTTP serving, and another 22 products for SVG conversion. This list will only grow.

Yet we have to admit that SVG serving technology is still very much in an early stage—not from a lack of products but, thus far, from a lack of medium-scale and large-scale enterprises that have attempted to roll out these technologies. We do think that the three products analyzed here are ready for these kinds of customers, and that implementation will accelerate by the end of 2002.

We understand that you may not yourself end up implementing a server-side product, but would likely work in concert with a web developer who would do the actual coding or scripting. From that perspective, you should know that we are confident these products are very solid choices for the developers you work with. They are extensible, and seem to be very straightforward for a developer to learn. We think a graphic designer, working in concert with a developer, will be able to create impressive, dynamic SVG-based sites.

chapter 10

SVG Futures

When we planned this book, this chapter had many potential titles, and many potential topics. At one point, SVG's use in data-driven graphics seemed most important, then its role in graphical user interface design, and then its role in cross-platform publishing. In truth, all of these potential trends are important, as well as several others.

So we arrived at this very general title for the chapter, "SVG Futures." But, in fact, such a general title is appropriate. As more people get under the hood of SVG, they find new applications, new methods, and new uses. At this writing, the first major conference on SVG is being planned in Zurich, Switzerland (SVG Open, planned for July 2002), and the scope of topics is impressive—ranging from cartography to techniques and tools to the biological sciences. Some of the individual papers suggest just how far people have gone already in their understanding and application of SVG:

- "Navimap—A software solution for online generation and broadcasting of high quality cartographic, platform independent, data"
- "Water supply network and installations: A real life application of SVG"
- "SVG for adaptive visualizations in mobile situations"
- "Using XSLT and SVG together: A survey of case studies"

This last paper is posted to the SVG Open web site and is well worth reading (http://www.svgopen.org/papers/2002/froumentin_hardy__xslt/). The authors, Max Froumentin of the W3C and Vincent Hardy of Sun Microsystems, do an excellent job of making the point that the possibilities are endless when you combine

XML data with the transformation capabilities of XSLT and the presentation capability of SVG. They show two case studies, and the one we really like, shown in Figure 10-1, shows ChessGML data (yes, as it sounds—a markup language for chess games), transformed to SVG for browser viewing.

Perhaps most impressively, the knowledge base for SVG is growing very rapidly. When we began to research this topic, only two books on SVG existed; Amazon.com now lists eight. There were then perhaps three or four good articles on the topic; there are literally dozens now. The SVG Developers mailing list at Yahoo.com has grown from 735 messages posted during May of 2001 to almost 2000 posted dur-

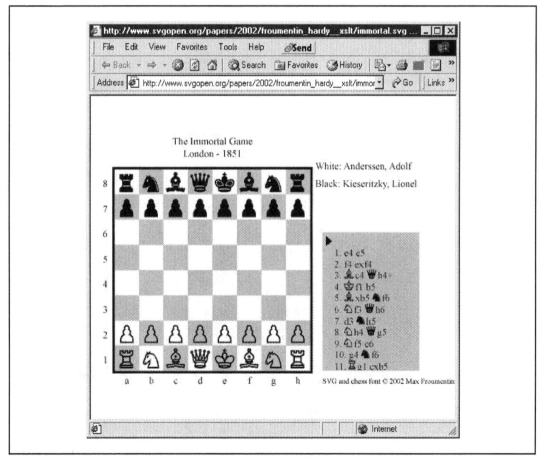

FIGURE 10-1 *ChessGML data, a dense data format not otherwise viewable in browsers, is here rendered in SVG by authors Max Froumentin and Vincent Hardy.* ∎

ing May of 2002, and it currently has 2556 members. (Even more impressive is the level of discussion on the list, which is highly practical and consistently technical, as shown in Figure 10-2.)

Your best starting point on SVG is to go to where it all began. The W3C's main page on SVG (http://www.w3.org/Graphics/SVG/Overview.htm8) is a fine bellwether. Since we started our research, the page has, conservatively, doubled in size. At this writing, it is jammed with information—links to the core documents, articles,

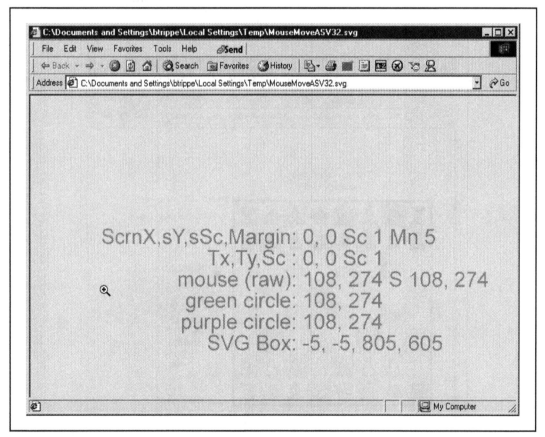

FIGURE 10-2   *This posted file is typical of the practical, detailed discussion in the Yahoo newsgroup SVG Developers (http://groups.yahoo.com/group/svg-developers/). The file shows some of the results of sample SVG code written to report mouse movements.* ■

implementations, and other resources. Announcements seem to come daily. As we are writing this chapter, the W3C has announced an online facility for converting SVG to text and HTML-tagged text (to help with searching), as shown in Figure 10-3, and Sharp has announced that it will be adding SVG support to eight mobile phones.

So, the world of SVG is fast-moving and ever-changing. The chapter we wrote this week differs from the chapter we would have written last week, and perhaps the one we would write next week. So we refuse to be more precise; *SVG Futures* it is.

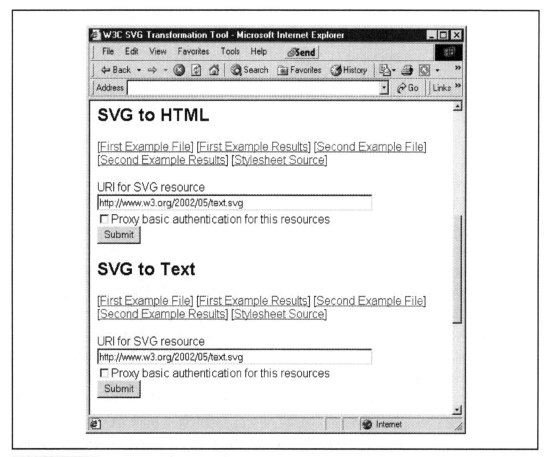

FIGURE   10-3   *The W3C has provided some facilities for converting SVG to HTML (and other forms) so that developers can experiment with making SVG searchable with standard tools. (Visit http://www.w3.org/2002/05/svg2stuff.html for more information.)* ■

SVG and Related W3C Efforts

While the sky is indeed the limit for SVG, the universe of what is happening with SVG at any one time will be bounded by the efforts at the W3C. At this writing, SVG 1.0 (http://www.w3.org/TR/SVG/) remains the official W3C Recommendation. SVG 1.1 is a W3C "candidate recommendation" as of April 30, 2002, as are the "Mobile SVG Profiles," which we will discuss shortly.

SVG 1.1 does not bring a rush of new features to SVG. Instead, it concentrates on making SVG more modular, in the same way that XHTML is intended to be more modular. In particular, SVG 1.1 takes the rather unwieldy ("monolithic") SVG 1.0 DTD and breaks it into modules that can be assembled and reassembled for different purposes. The "Mobile SVG Profiles" (http://www.w3.org/TR/SVGMobile/), known as "SVG Basic" and "SVG Tiny," then take some of these modules and build them up to make the different profiles.

SVG Tiny is intended to provide a dramatically simpler version of SVG for use with cell phones, while SVG Basic is intended for use with personal digital assistants (PDAs). (Obviously, the capabilities of the two classes of devices are beginning to, and will continue to, overlap, but the distinction makes a certain degree of sense, and gives developers targets to work against.)

Regardless of the distinction between the two devices, the overall requirement is very real. Mobile devices are indeed a growing platform for Web distribution. In announcing the mobile profiles, Dean Jackson, W3C Fellow from CSIRO, said, "Cellphones allow Internet and Web access for millions of people who don't have access to desktop machines, temporarily or otherwise. With 3GPP already incorporating Mobile SVG, we can look forward to more rich and useful content in third generation cell phones."

Jackson's point is well taken. While the drum beat of "wireless, wireless, wireless" probably inspires some to fall asleep, alternate devices for content delivery are a real, practical challenge. And if delivery to wireless devices is going to be anything but text, graphic formats are going to have to become more lightweight, more flexible, and less proprietary—that is, they are going to have to become SVG. Figure 10-4 suggests the kind of image support that mobile device vendors would like to provide.

FIGURE   10-4   *Sharp, among other wireless vendors, is already supporting SVG. Sharp's product*
SharpMotionArt is an implementation of SVG Mobile. ■

In the weeks when we were researching this chapter, there was a flurry of activity around SVG—from vendors, from developers in the field, and from the standards bodies. A few headlines that caught our attention are representative of the range of work happening in SVG:

■ Nokia announced new tools to help developers create SVG-based messages for cell phones.

- Developers introduced tools for (1) creating SVG Tiny files on Java devices and (2) creating SVG tools on Pocket PCs.

- A cell phone company announced SVG-based content for English-speaking travelers in Japan.

- Major companies like Sharp, Nokia, Texas Instruments, and IBM, as well as SVG-focused companies such as BitFlash, made various announcements about SVG support in products such as cell phones, PDAs, compact computers, and hybrid devices like the Blackberry.

SVG Tools and Trends

We feel this book has done a good job of capturing the current state of the art in SVG development and editing tools—both client-side tools, which are designed mainly for creation, and server-side tools, which offer features such as conversion, dynamic serving, and modest (to date) means of personalization. And, as our analysis showed, we are generally impressed with the tools that are out there.

However, our own work, interviews with other users, and discussions with tool vendors suggest a few directions that next-generation SVG tools will likely take. We offer the following prognostications, in order of likelihood that they will occur, with the most obvious ones coming first:

- All the tools will incorporate more and more of the *official SVG recommendations,* beginning with SVG 1.0 and then 1.1. Even the most ubiquitous tool, the Adobe Viewer, still doesn't support every feature of SVG 1.0, and it will have some further catch-up with SVG 1.1.

- Tools will also incorporate *their own namespace extensions,* similar to what Adobe does now with their namespace extensions supported by the Adobe SVG Viewer and creation tools such as Adobe Illustrator.

- *Support for the mobile profiles,* SVG Basic and SVG Tiny, will appear in more and more products. We think, for example, the best tools will allow for materials to be created in the full version of SVG, with options to "save as" the smaller profiles. We imagine such that tools will offer multiple viewers—view as full SVG, view as SVG Tiny, and so on.

- The creation tools will allow better support for collaboration. We've learned already that even a moderately complex project involving, say, a single illustrator and programmer requires the illustrator to be able to create many files, easily name them, and keep them up-to-date. This kind of *modularization and revision control*, common in a programming environment, will need to become de rigueur in tools for SVG development.

- Creation and editing tools will need *closer hooks to content management platforms* and other repositories. Just as HTML editors—and even creation tools, such as Microsoft Word—are increasingly linked to repositories, so too will tools for SVG creation and editing. Content management goes beyond the modularization and revision control mentioned earlier. Both of those are necessary but not sufficient for a full content management application, which must support the full life cycle of creation, management, and publishing.

The evolution of HTML editing tools may be a useful analog for how SVG tools will evolve. HTML editing tools went from being stand-alone "code editors" to more integrated development tools. HTML editors added WYSYWIG capabilities, layout tools, integration with scripting environments, and more—all with the goal of allowing the creative professional to create the full range of HTML without having to be a programmer. We expect SVG tools to follow a similar trajectory.

We also expect the tools to become more functional, more robust, and more scalable in a few other ways:

- The tools will support conversion to and from *a growing number of other formats*, both raster and vector.

- The tools will support *increasingly large and complex files.*

- The tools will deal with *larger volumes of files and higher throughput*, as more and larger organizations implement SVG in workflows such as manufacturing, mechanical design, and scientific analysis and illustration.

One could say that desktop tools such as Adobe Illustrator provide such robustness now, but it is a matter of volume, scale, and technical adherence to the W3C specifications. Even for conversion of raster to vector illustrations, you can use Macromedia Flash or Adobe Streamline to create .ai files to bring into Illustrator and export to SVG. However, the real issue is the quality of the output. Illustrator does a pretty good job of optimizing with symbols and simplified Bezier paths, but the really granular control you would get from an SVG native tool is not yet there. Jasc WebDraw is a good start for an SVG native tool, but it's still very young and lacks the robustness or variety of features that would be desired by a serious designer.

Finally, we do see that authoring tools will need to expand to support animation and interactivity. Or, specialized tools for animation and interactivity will need to be developed.

SVG for Application Development

Along with this trend toward more robust editing and creation tools for SVG, we (and people we interviewed) also see a trend toward SVG as a key part of how interfaces are developed. Handled correctly, SVG will help the Web realize its potential as a ubiquitous interface to all content and applications. Because SVG flexibly incorporates vector graphics, bitmap graphics, text, and style sheets, it's "scalable" in more than just the sense that the incorporated graphics can be scaled. It's also scalable in its flexibility. Because it's XML-based, SVG can be mixed with other formats—such as XHTML—and scripting languages—such as JavaScript.

This gives developers great flexibility with SVG—to develop entire web pages or individual components, such as graphics. Thus, in an application where the graphical user interface exists in the browser, or on a handheld device, the SVG can in fact be the entire interface. This puts SVG in a new, and perhaps unique, position of embodying the entire user interface in a single text file. This has tremendous potential for custom application delivery to different devices, personalization, and other situations that call for the interface to be customized on the fly.

Other Future Trends

In developing this chapter, we interviewed several experienced users of SVG and representatives from several vendors. We also read articles, sat through presentations, and read abstracts of papers. While we can't claim to have a crystal ball, we can see the following trends developing or accelerating:

- **SVG for mapping**   This is a no-brainer. But the combination of GIS data and SVG is very, very compelling. Already, several applications have been developed that combine GIS data, other mapping data, demographic data, and SVG output. See, for example, the work described at http://www.carto.net/papers/svg/index_e.html and shown here in Figures 10-5 and 10-6.

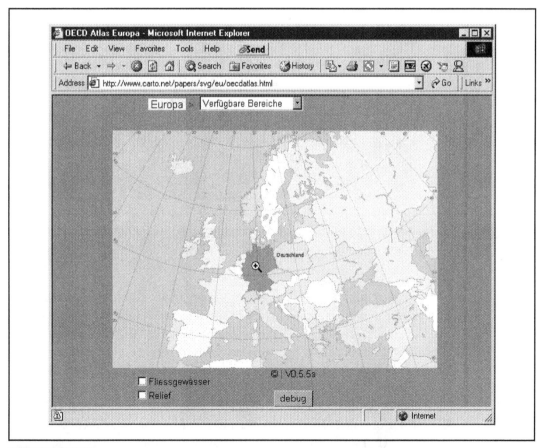

The example maps on www.carto.net are all generated from SVG.   ∎

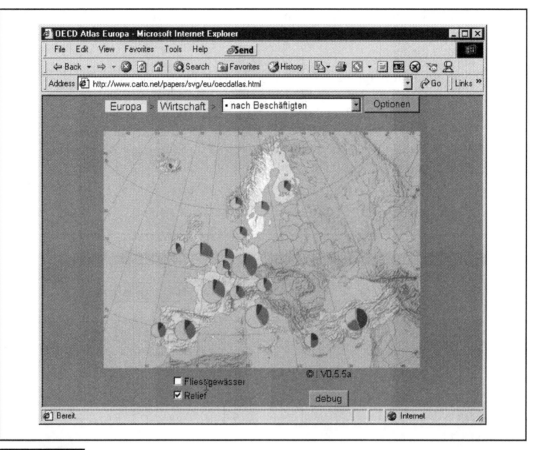

FIGURE 10-6   *The example maps on www.carto.net include demographic and statistical data that can be displayed in a variety of ways.* ■

■ **SVG for bioinformatics**   This is another area where available databases—this time of genomics data—can be combined with other data sources to produce highly meaningful SVG output. See Figure 10-7 for an example of the kinds of visualization already possible. For instance, the company Primaci Solutions (http://www.primaci.com/) has developed applications that create SVG output from BLAST data. BLAST is the National Center for Biotechnology Information (NCBI) Basic Local Alignment Search Tool. BLAST performs DNA similarity searches of all available sequence databases. (For an excellent primer on bioinformatics, see the book *Developing Bioinformatics Computer Skills* by Cynthia Gibas and Per Jambeck (O'Reilly & Associates, 2001). The opening chapter is available online at http://www.oreilly.com/catalog/bioskills/chapter/ch01.html.)

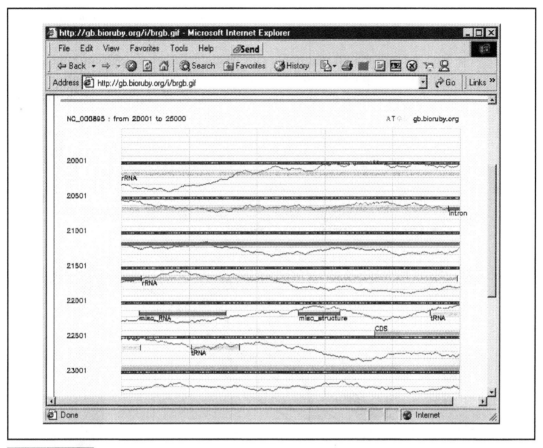

FIGURE   10-7   *Genome visualizers, such as those available from bioruby.org, will increasingly be based on SVG.* ■

- **SVG for facilities management**   Scott Michaels of Savage Software notes that, "SVG has major strengths here, in the way the data can be not just displayed but more intelligence can be created from the data display itself." He cites examples where space planners are trying to determine best routes for installing new lines and equipment, and traditional illustrations simply don't yield enough detail. Added Michaels, "I am talking about things such as relationship finding between unconnected elements in the original data set. For a standard type of facilities management application, it only makes sense to use SVG."

- **SVG for accessibility**   Because of the added metadata and element naming capabilities in SVG, web pages can be provided with highly detailed and specific alternate names and values for images, charts, and other elements.

■ **SVG for automated maintenance** Manufacturers of large equipment maintain complex illustrations related to maintenance and repair— troubleshooting diagrams, exploded views, detailed parts breakdowns, and so forth. Traditionally, these have been vector images that have gone to bitmap for printing and distribution. As shown in Figure 10-8, this can result in a significantly "dumbed-down" illustration once it is distributed on

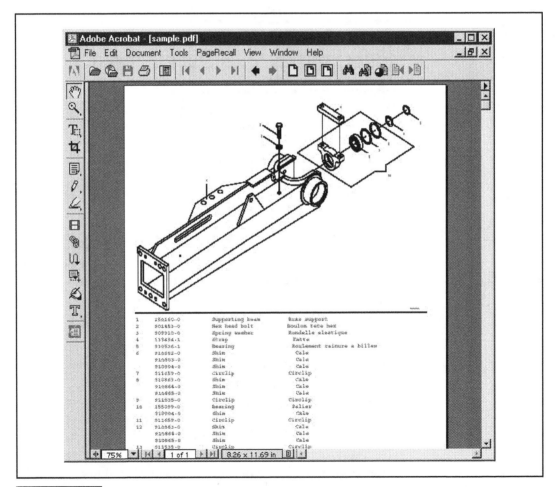

FIGURE 10-8 *Maintenance documents and web sites have traditionally had to rely on formats that were not always conducive to zooming, panning, and heavier, textual detail. SVG will improve on that.* ■

the Web or via CD-ROM. For these manufacturers, it will be highly preferable to be able to distribute a vector form of the illustration, at the very least for improved panning and zooming. It will be even better if these manufacturers can embed these illustrations within integrated maintenance tools, such as what the aviation industry likes to call *integrated electronic technical manuals* (IETMs).

- **SVG for device interfaces**   Savage Software's Michaels also foresees a trend here, where firmware-style upgrades will be done through downloadable SVG updates. According to Michaels, "You will see much more of this soon, with more hardware connecting to the computer for device upgrades. This will go beyond digital cameras [which now allow you to] download new interfaces and functionality."

- **Native printing of SVG**   This is being discussed in the W3C working group now, and will be part of the focus of SVG 2.0, with more support for more complex rendering features such as text wrapping.

As you can see, the possibilities are quite varied. Some of these—such as automated maintenance—are very specific to certain industries. Others—such as native printing and device interfaces—cut across many, perhaps all, markets.

Conclusion

By way of a conclusion, we will offer one final prognostication, but one that comes with a caveat. You will recall that earlier in the book we talked about "inline" SVG, where web pages can liberally mix XHTML, XML, and SVG in a single text stream. The current browser environment does not fully support this (with the exception of Amaya), and the path to this being supported in Internet Explorer is not yet known. Internet Explorer also still requires the separate download of an SVG Viewer.

So the caveat first—Internet Explorer, as the primary browsing environment, must come to support "inline SVG," and ideally, the liberal blending of SVG, XHTML and MathML, as the W3C has proposed. (Visit http://www.w3.org/TR/2002/WD-XHTMLplusMathMLplusSVG-20020430/ for more information.) Once this requirement is met, we are quite confident that SVG will in fact become the dominant mechanism for presenting graphical data on the Web. While bitmaps will still have their place, and Flash will be used for some animation, we do think that the vast majority of two-dimensional and three-dimensional illustrations on the Web will be rendered as SVG. We also think that a great deal of animation will also be done in SVG.

Most significant, though, will be the area of web presentation that we alluded to earlier—namely, the use of SVG to define the overall graphical user interface for applications distributed over the Web and mobile devices. We are quite confident that the open, text-based, and standards-driven approach of SVG will dominate.

For further reading and resources about SVG, see the following sections

Books

- *XML Bible,* by Elliotte Rusty Harold (John Wiley & Sons, 2001). We feel that this is the best, most comprehensive book out there. For the hands-on developer who needs lots of practical examples, sample code, and "in-the-trenches" style advice.

- *XSLT,* by Doug Tidwell (O'Reilly & Associates, 2001). XSLT is a critical new technology in content management. Doug Tidwell is an XML evangelist from IBM, and one of the leading thinkers in the field.

- *Content Management Bible,* by Bob Boiko (John Wiley & Sons, 2002). A brand-new, comprehensive book from industry guru Bob Boiko. Full of practical, real-world advice, as well as useful discussions and applications.

- *XML: A Primer,* by Simon St. Laurent (John Wiley & Sons, 2001). As several reviewers have noted, this was one of the first books on the topic, and remains one of the best. Now in its edition.

- *SVG Essentials,* J. David Eisenberg (O'Reilly & Associates, 2002). This is a programmer-oriented book that provides more code examples but fewer details on using some of the commercial products that designers rely on.

Web Sites

- http://www.xml.com has excellent ongoing coverage of SVG.

- http://www.pinkjuice.com/ includes a portfolio of SVG illustrations.

- http://www.adobe.com/svg/ is Adobe's SVG Zone. Heavily focused on Adobe products, of course, but also very useful. The developer tutorials are also feature-centric, as opposed to being pragmatic, because they were written as the Viewer was being developed.

- http://groups.yahoo.com/group/svg-developers/ is Yahoo's SVG developer mailing list. (Requires registration.)

- http://www.w3.org/Graphics/SVG/Overview.htm8 is the W3C home page for SVG.

- http://www.zvon.org/ is a technical site that bills itself as "The Guide to the XML Galaxy." It has some good reference and tutorial information on SVG.

- Kevin Lindsey's developer site, http://www.kevlindev.com, is full of excellent examples and practical guidance.

part **IV**

Appendixes

appendix A

Understanding SVG Syntax in Depth

Chapter 2 introduces you to XML, explains how to interpret and parse an XML file, and then goes on to introduce the basics of SVG syntax. The remainder of the book, of course, explores in great detail how to create and work with SVG graphics. The purpose of this appendix is to provide a ready reference to more of the syntax of the SVG 1.0 Specification. In particular, it attempts to record the specific XML syntax behind SVG, and explain each major element on its own, and give example code to use to experiment with different elements.

Material here is based on the W3C Recommendation of September 4, 2001, which can be found at http://www.w3.org/TR/SVG/. The complete DTD and extensive documentation can also be found at that link.

File Basics

Because SVG files are XML, they are text files, specifically Unicode-compliant text. The Unicode encoding ensures that SVG files can include all character sets, thus allowing SVG to be internationalized. SVG files are also a valid, registered MIME type, "image/svg+xml." The W3C recommends that SVG files be given the extension ".svg" on all platforms, and the file type of "svg " (lowercase, with a space at the end) on Macintosh HFS file systems.

SVG files must begin with two important pieces of information related to SVG being an XML file that conforms to a certain Document Type Definition, or DTD.

XML Declaration

The first line is the *XML Declaration*. This required line tells the browser, or other interpreting software, that the data that follows is XML:

```
<?xml version="1.0" standalone="no"?>
```

The string

```
version="1.0"
```

declares that the XML data conforms with Extensible Markup Language (XML) 1.0 (W3C Recommendation of October 6, 2000).

The string

```
standalone="no"
```

is a somewhat more complicated matter. The word *standalone* refers to whether the XML file "stands alone" or whether it references external DTDs ("no" means it does not stand alone and references external DTDs). The default value is "no," and, in fact, the XML declaration can be validly expressed as

```
<?xml version="1.0">
```

SVG files do rely on a DTD that would normally not be included in the SVG file itself, so standalone would logically be set to "no."

Document Type Declaration

The next line is the *Document Type Declaration*, which is another bit of formal XML syntax. In short, the Document Type Declaration declares two things—the root element of the XML data that follows, and the identity and, often, the location of the DTD that will be used to parse the XML.

```
<!DOCTYPE svg PUBLIC "-//W3C//DTD SVG 1.0//EN"
    "http://www.w3.org/TR/2001/REC-SVG-20010904/DTD/svg10.dtd">
```

Let's break down what the Document Type Declaration will typically look like in an SVG file:

`<!DOCTYPE svg`	Begins the Document Type Declaration and declares the root element to be svg.

PUBLIC "-//W3C//DTD SVG 1.0//EN"	Indicates that the DTD being used is a PUBLIC DTD, owned by the W3C, with the identifier DTD SVG 1.0, and that it is written in English (EN).
http://www.w3.org/TR/2001/ REC-SVG-20010904/DTD/svg10.dtd	Provides the URL where the DTD can be accessed for processing.

Everything Else

Typically, all the SVG markup and data will then be placed between the start and end tags of the root element, svg. In a simple drawing, the SVG tag includes the width and height dimensions, and the end SVG tag will then be the last text in the file:

```
<svg width="200" height="200">
(ALL MARKUP AND DATA GOES HERE)
</svg>
```

In practice, an SVG document can be as simple as a single object described inside of a single SVG element, or it can be a complex set of nested objects. We provide a variety of examples in the other sections of the book. The remainder of this appendix deals with the specific syntax of the elements themselves.

The SVG Element

Because SVG files are XML documents, and XML documents are usually hierarchical, one useful way of understanding them is to begin by looking at the parent element. The element type declaration for the SVG element reads as follows:

```
<!ELEMENT svg (desc|title|metadata|defs|
path|text|rect|circle|ellipse|line|polyline|polygon|
                use|image|svg|g|view|switch|a|altGlyphDef|
                script|style|symbol|marker|clipPath|mask|
                linearGradient|radialGradient|pattern|
                filter|cursor|font|
```

```
animate|set|animateMotion|animateColor|animateTransform|
               color-profile|font-face )* >
```

If you put your XML thinking cap back on, you will recall that this syntax tells you that an SVG element can consist of some or all of the elements listed (desc, title, metadata, and so forth), in any order, and they can be liberally repeated. So, as you have seen in the other chapters, an SVG file can consist of a single text element, or a single rect element, or a single path element, or a liberal intermingling of these and other elements listed previously. In fact, the SVG element is a bit of a catchall, as perhaps it should be since illustrations themselves are likely to contain many different elements—in many different orders and configurations.

Attributes for the SVG Element

In addition to the elements that can be contained within the SVG element, the SVG element itself can be ornamented with a wide variety of attributes. The attribute list syntax for the SVG element reads as follows:

```
<!ATTLIST svg
  xmlns CDATA #FIXED "http://www.w3.org/2000/svg"
  id ID #IMPLIED
  xml:base CDATA #IMPLIED
  requiredFeatures %FeatureList; #IMPLIED
  requiredExtensions %ExtensionList; #IMPLIED
  systemLanguage CDATA #IMPLIED
  xml:lang NMTOKEN #IMPLIED
  xml:space (default|preserve) #IMPLIED
  externalResourcesRequired (false | true ) #IMPLIED
  class CDATA #IMPLIED
  style CDATA #IMPLIED
  %PresentationAttributes-All;
  viewBox %ViewBoxSpec; #IMPLIED
  preserveAspectRatio %PreserveAspectRatioSpec; 'xMidYMid meet'
  zoomAndPan (disable | magnify) 'magnify'
  %graphicsElementEvents;
  %documentEvents;
  version %Number; #FIXED "1.0"
```

```
x %Coordinate; #IMPLIED
y %Coordinate; #IMPLIED
width %Length; #IMPLIED
height %Length; #IMPLIED
contentScriptType %ContentType; "text/ecmascript"
contentStyleType %ContentType; "text/css" >
```

Obviously, this is a great deal of detail, and we won't attempt to explain each and every attribute. In other words, this is nothing you will commit to memory. Indeed, you are best off learning how to read the DTD and interpret it, and then returning to it when you need to interpret or understand certain details. To help you begin to understand it, it's worth looking at some of the simpler and more often used attributes that you will commonly encounter and want to use. Even these, though, require digging into the DTD syntax.

The attribute zoomAndPan is a good example of how attributes are declared. The intention of the attribute is to allow the designer or developer to allow or inhibit panning and zooming on a given SVG illustration. If you look at the DTD, zoomAndPan is defined as follows:

```
zoomAndPan (disable | magnify) 'magnify'
```

As defined, this means the SVG element can include a zoomAndPan attribute that can choose from the values "disable" or "magnify" (if none is chosen, the DTD tells it to default to "magnify"). The intention of the attribute is to allow the designer or developer to allow or inhibit panning and zooming on a given SVG illustration. Thus, valid markup for an SVG element could be

```
<svg zoomAndPan="magnify">
```

or

```
<svg zoomAndPan="disable">
```

As another example, we've seen how you can apply height and width attributes to the SVG tag. Unfortunately, while the underlying thinking is simple, the DTD is a little dense in how it defines these attributes:

```
width %Length; #IMPLIED
height %Length; #IMPLIED
```

The DTD writer snuck in a little bit of shorthand here, using the parameter entity "%Length;" that has as its replacement text the string "CDATA." Thus, you could swap in the replacement text "CDATA" for "%Length;" in the attribute declaration for width and height and correctly read it as

```
width CDATA #IMPLIED
height CDATA #IMPLIED
```

This is the DTD's way of saying that the width and height attributes can contain "CDATA" or character data. In the markup itself, the attributes might be expressed as

```
<svg width="200" height="200">
```

or

```
<svg width="200mm" height="200mm">
```

Armed with your understanding of the three attributes (zoomAndPan, width, and height), you could now create a valid SVG element with the following attributes:

```
<svg width="200" height="200" zoomAndPan="magnify">
```

To understand the remaining attributes, we have provided an expansion of the remaining parameter entities used in this section of the DTD. (See Table A-1.)

Parameter Entity	Expansion Text
%stdAttrs;	"id ID #IMPLIED xml:base %URI; #IMPLIED"
%testAttrs;	"requiredFeatures %FeatureList; #IMPLIEDrequiredExtensions %ExtensionList; #IMPLIEDsystemLanguage %LanguageCodes; #IMPLIED"

TABLE   A-1   *An Expansion of the Remaining Parameter Entities Used in this Section of the DTD* ■

Parameter Entity	Expansion Text
%langSpaceAttrs;	"xml:lang %LanguageCode; #IMPLIED xml:space (default|preserve) #IMPLIED"
%Boolean;	"(false | true)"
%ClassList;	"CDATA"
%StyleSheet;	"CDATA"
%PresentationAttributes-All;	(The entire collection of presentation attributes is summarized in Table A-2.)
%ViewBoxSpec;	"CDATA"
%PreserveAspectRatioSpec;	"CDATA"
%graphicsElementEvents;	"onfocusin %Script; #IMPLIED onfocusout %Script; #IMPLIED onactivate %Script; #IMPLIED onclick %Script; #IMPLIED onmousedown %Script; #IMPLIED onmouseup %Script; #IMPLIED onmouseover %Script; #IMPLIED onmousemove %Script; #IMPLIED onmouseout %Script; #IMPLIED onload %Script; #IMPLIED"
%documentEvents;	"onunload %Script; #IMPLIED onabort %Script; #IMPLIED onerror %Script; #IMPLIED onresize %Script; #IMPLIED onscroll %Script; #IMPLIED onzoom %Script; #IMPLIED"
%Number;	"CDATA"
%Coordinate;	"CDATA"
%Length;	"CDATA"
%ContentType;	"CDATA"
%Script;	"CDATA"
%URI;	"CDATA"
%FeatureList;	"CDATA"
%ExtensionList;	"CDATA"
%LanguageCodes;	"CDATA"
%LanguageCode;	"NMTOKEN"

TABLE A-1   *An Expansion of the Remaining Parameter Entities Used in this Section of the DTD (continued)* ■

Presentation-Oriented Attributes: %PresentationAttributes-All;

Beginning with the SVG element itself, many SVG elements can be liberally ornamented with presentation-oriented attributes dealing with colors, fills, strokes,
fonts, gradients, and the like. These attributes can be applied at the parent level
(beginning with the SVG element itself) or on various container or graphic elements. The parameter entity %PresentationAttributes-All; is used to collect a long
list of parameter entities, each of which includes a number of attributes. These are
summarized in Table A-2.

Parameter Entity	Expansion Text
%PresentationAttributes-All;	"%PresentationAttributes-Color; %PresentationAttributes-Containers; %PresentationAttributes-feFlood; %PresentationAttributes-FillStroke; %PresentationAttributes-FilterPrimitives; %PresentationAttributes-FontSpecification; %PresentationAttributes-Gradients; %PresentationAttributes-Graphics; %PresentationAttributes-Images; %PresentationAttributes-LightingEffects; %PresentationAttributes-Markers; %PresentationAttributes-TextContentElements; %PresentationAttributes-TextElements; %PresentationAttributes-Viewports;"
%PresentationAttributes-Color;	"color %Color; #IMPLIED color-interpolation (auto | sRGB | linearRGB | inherit) #IMPLIED color-rendering (auto | optimizeSpeed | optimizeQuality | inherit) #IMPLIED
%PresentationAttributes-Containers;	"enable-background %EnableBackgroundValue; #IMPLIED "
%PresentationAttributes-feFlood;	"flood-color %SVGColor; #IMPLIED flood-opacity %OpacityValue; #IMPLIED "

TABLE A-2 *Collection of Presentation Attributes* ■

Parameter Entity	Expansion Text
%PresentationAttributes-FillStroke;	"fill %Paint; #IMPLIED fill-opacity %OpacityValue; #IMPLIED fill-rule %ClipFillRule; #IMPLIED stroke %Paint; #IMPLIED stroke-dasharray %StrokeDashArrayValue; #IMPLIED stroke-dashoffset %StrokeDashOffsetValue; #IMPLIED stroke-linecap (butt | round | square | inherit) #IMPLIED stroke-linejoin (miter | round | bevel | inherit) #IMPLIED stroke-miterlimit %StrokeMiterLimitValue; #IMPLIED stroke-opacity %OpacityValue; #IMPLIED stroke-width %StrokeWidthValue; #IMPLIED "
%PresentationAttributes-FilterPrimitives;	"color-interpolation-filters (auto | sRGB | linearRGB | inherit) #IMPLIED "
%PresentationAttributes-FontSpecification;	"font-family %FontFamilyValue; #IMPLIED font-size %FontSizeValue; #IMPLIED font-size-adjust %FontSizeAdjustValue; #IMPLIED font-stretch (normal | wider | narrower | ultra-condensed | extra-condensed | condensed | semi-condensed | semi-expanded | expanded | extra-expanded | ultra-expanded | inherit) #IMPLIED font-style (normal | italic | oblique | inherit) #IMPLIED font-variant (normal | small-caps | inherit) #IMPLIED font-weight (normal | bold | bolder | lighter | 100 | 200 | 300 | 400 | 500 | 600 | 700 | 800 | 900 | inherit) #IMPLIED "
%PresentationAttributes-Gradients;	"stop-color %SVGColor; #IMPLIED stop-opacity %OpacityValue; #IMPLIED "

TABLE A-2 *Collection of Presentation Attributes* (continued) ∎

Parameter Entity	Expansion Text
%PresentationAttributes-Graphics;	"clip-path %ClipPathValue; #IMPLIED clip-rule %ClipFillRule; #IMPLIED cursor %CursorValue; #IMPLIED display (inline | block | list-item | run-in | compact | marker | table | inline-table | table-row-group | table-header-group | table-footer-group | table-row | table- column-group | table-column | table-cell | table-caption | none | inherit) #IMPLIED filter %filterValue; #IMPLIED image-rendering (auto | optimizeSpeed | optimizeQuality | inherit) #IMPLIED mask %MaskValue; #IMPLIED opacity %OpacityValue; #IMPLIED pointer-events (visiblePainted | visibleFill | visibleStroke | visible| painted | fill | stroke | all | none | inherit) #IMPLIED shape-rendering (auto | optimizeSpeed | crispEdges | geometricPrecision | inherit) #IMPLIED text-rendering (auto | optimizeSpeed | optimizeLegibility | geometricPrecision | inherit) #IMPLIED visibility (visible | hidden | inherit) #IMPLIED "
%PresentationAttributes-Images;	"color-profile CDATA #IMPLIED "
%PresentationAttributes-LightingEffects;	"lighting-color %SVGColor; #IMPLIED "
%PresentationAttributes-Markers;	"marker-start %MarkerValue; #IMPLIED marker-mid %MarkerValue; #IMPLIED marker-end %MarkerValue; #IMPLIED "

TABLE   A-2   *Collection of Presentation Attributes* (continued) ■

Parameter Entity	Expansion Text
%PresentationAttributes-TextContentElements;	"alignment-baseline (baseline | top | before-edge | text-top | text-before-edge | middle | bottom | after-edge | text-bottom | text-after-edge | ideographic | lower | hanging | mathematical | inherit) #IMPLIED baseline-shift %BaselineShiftValue; #IMPLIED direction (ltr | rtl | inherit) #IMPLIED dominant-baseline (auto | autosense-script | no-change | reset| ideographic | lower | hanging | mathematical | inherit) #IMPLIED glyph-orientation-horizontal %GlyphOrientationHorizontalValue; #IMPLIED glyph-orientation-vertical %GlyphOrientationVerticalValue; #IMPLIED kerning %KerningValue; #IMPLIED letter-spacing %SpacingValue; #IMPLIED text-anchor (start | middle | end | inherit) #IMPLIED text-decoration %TextDecorationValue; #IMPLIED unicode-bidi (normal | embed | bidi-override | inherit) #IMPLIED word-spacing %SpacingValue; #IMPLIED "
%PresentationAttributes-TextElements;	"writing-mode (lr-tb | rl-tb | tb-rl | lr | rl | tb | inherit) #IMPLIED "
%PresentationAttributes-Viewports;	"clip %ClipValue; #IMPLIED overflow (visible | hidden | scroll | auto | inherit) #IMPLIED "

TABLE A-2 *Collection of Presentation Attributes* (continued) ∎

Description of Major Elements

The following sections define each major element, provide a working example of code, and outline the XML content model for each element. Each "example of valid syntax" has been tested against the Adobe viewer, so you should be able to create stand-alone SVG files with these examples by placing them in the following template of code and saving them to a file named, "*.svg."

```
<?xml version="1.0" standalone="no"?>
<!DOCTYPE svg PUBLIC "-//W3C//DTD SVG 1.0//EN"
    "http://www.w3.org/TR/2001/REC-SVG-20010904/DTD/svg10.dtd">
```

```
<svg width="200" height="200">
(INSERT "example of valid syntax" code here)
</svg>
```

a Analogous to the "a" element in HTML; the "a" element is used for linking. In the following example, the "a" element is used to link a rect object to an external URL.

Example of Valid Syntax:

```
<a xlink:href="http://www.nmpub.com">
<rect fill="rgb(0,0,255)" stroke="rgb(0,0,0)" stroke-width="1"
x="50" y="85" width="108" height="56"/>
</a>
```

Content Model:

```
<!ELEMENT a     (#PCDATA|desc|title|metadata|defs|
path|text|rect|circle|ellipse|line|polyline|polygon|
use|image|svg|g|view|switch|a|altGlyphDef|
script|style|symbol|marker|clipPath|mask|
linearGradient|radialGradient|pattern|filter|cursor|font|animate|
set|animateMotion|animateColor|animateTransform|
color-profile|font-face )* >
```

animate The animate element can be used to animate a single attribute or property. The following example shows a blue circle, originally rendered at a radius of 30. The animate element is then used to shrink the circle to 0, and then increase it to 60 over a 5-second period.

Example of Valid Syntax:

```
<circle id="a0001" cx="100" cy="100" r="30" fill="rgb(0,0,255)"/>
<animate attributeName="r" begin="1s" dur="5s" xlink:href="#a0001"
from="0" to="60">
</animate>
```

Content Model:

```
<!ELEMENT animate (%descTitleMetadata;) >
```

Note *The entity %descTitleMetadata; has a long, cumbersome syntax, but basically allows for the elements "title," "desc," and "metadata" to appear in any order.*

animateColor   The animateColor element is used specifically to bring animation effects to colors. In the following example, a red circle with a blue border is changed to an entirely red circle over a period of several seconds.

Example of Valid Syntax:

```
<circle id="a0002" cx="50" cy="50" r="40" fill="rgb(0,0,255)"
stroke="rgb(255,0,0)" stroke-width="4"/>
<animateColor attributeName="fill" xlink:href="#a0002" begin="1s" dur="5s"
fill="freeze" from="rgb(0,0,255)" to="rgb(255,0,0)"/>
```

Content Model:

```
<!ELEMENT animateColor (%descTitleMetadata;) >
```

animateMotion   The animateMotion element is used to move objects along a straight line or arbitrary path. In the following example, the blue circle with the red outline is moved across the page.

Example of Valid Syntax:

```
<circle id="a0002" cx="50" cy="50" r="40" fill="rgb(0,0,255)"
stroke="rgb(255,0,0)" stroke-width="4"/>
<animateMotion path="M40 40 L40 40" xlink:href="#a0002" begin="1s" dur="5s"
fill="freeze"/>
```

Content Model:

```
<!ELEMENT animateMotion (%descTitleMetadata;,mpath?) >
```

animateTransform   The animateTransform element is used to apply animation to one or more of the various transformations available in SVG, notably scaling, rotation, and skewing. In the following example, the small blue rectangle is rotated 30 degrees.

Example of Valid Syntax:

```
<rect id="a0003" x="50" y="50" width="10" height="10" fill="rgb(0,0,255)"/>
<animateTransform attributeName="transform" xlink:href="#a0003"
type="rotate"
begin="1s" dur="5s" from="0" to="30"/>
```

Content Model:

```
<!ELEMENT animateTransform (%descTitleMetadata;) >
```

circle   The circle element is used to create a circle based on a defined center point and a radius. In the following example, the center of a solid blue circle is positioned at x,y position 100,100, with a radius of 50.

Example of Valid Syntax:

```
<circle cx="100" cy="100" r="50" fill="rgb(0,0,255)"/>
```

Content Model:

```
<!ELEMENT circle %descTitleMetadata; , (animate|set|animateMotion|
animateColor|animateTransform)*) >
```

clipPath   The clipPath element allows you to define an area for clipping. Anything within the clipped area will be displayed; anything outside of it will not be displayed. In the following example, a blue rectangle of 100 × 100 has a clip-path of 50 × 72 applied to it.

Example of Valid Syntax:

```
<clipPath id="cp0001">
<rect x="50" y="75" width="50" height="72"/>
</clipPath>
<rect x="50" y="50" width="100" height="100" fill="rgb(0,0,255)" clip-
path="url(#cp0001)"/>
```

Content Model:

```
<!ELEMENT clipPath (%descTitleMetadata;,
                    (path|text|rect|circle|ellipse|line|polyline|
                    polygon|use|animate|set|animateMotion|
                    animateColor|animateTransform)*) >
```

defs   The defs element is used as a container element to group together elements that will later be used in a drawing. It has the same content model as the "g" element, allowing for many objects to be liberally included. It is often used in combination with the use element, which then can place the element in the drawing. In the following example, the defs element includes descriptions of two squares, a red one and a blue one. The use tag is then used to place the blue square twice and the red square once.

Example of Valid Syntax:

```
<defs>
    <rect id="a0001" width="20" height="20" fill="rgb(0,0,255)"/>
    <rect id="a0002" width="20" height="20" fill="rgb(255,0,0)"/>
</defs>
<use xlink:href="#a0001" x="20" y="20"/>
<use xlink:href="#a0001" x="50" y="50"/>
<use xlink:href="#a0002" x="100" y="100"/>
```

Content Model:

```
<!ELEMENT defs (desc|title|metadata|defs|
path|text|rect|circle|ellipse|line|polyline|polygon|
                  use|image|svg|g|view|switch|a|altGlyphDef|
                  script|style|symbol|marker|clipPath|mask|
                  linearGradient|radialGradient|pattern|
                  filter|cursor|font|
                  animate|set|animateMotion|animateColor|
                  animateTransform|color-profile|font-face)* >
```

desc　The desc element is used to provide a texutal description of the whole drawing or major elements of it. The text in the desc element is not displayed as part of the drawing, but could otherwise be used by an agent or rendering device. The desc element is also potentially useful for accessibility (given appropriate rendering software). The <title> and <desc> elements could be displayed as ToolTips, or as with the Adobe SVG Viewer, the <title> element immediately within the outermost <svg> displays as the title in the browser window (when viewing the SVG directly—not embedded in HTML).

Example of Valid Syntax:

```
<svg width="200" height="200">
<desc>Test image for showing use of the &quot;defs&quot; element.
```

```
Renders one blue
square and one red square.</desc>
<defs>
    <rect id="a0001" width="20" height="20" fill="rgb(0,0,255)"/>
    <rect id="a0002" width="20" height="20" fill="rgb(255,0,0)"/>
</defs>
<use xlink:href="#a0001" x="20" y="20"/>
<use xlink:href="#a0001" x="50" y="50"/>
<use xlink:href="#a0002" x="100" y="100"/>
</svg>
```

Content Model:

```
<!ELEMENT desc (#PCDATA)* >
```

ellipse   The ellipse element is one of the basic graphical shapes in an SVG document. It defines an ellipse based on a center point and two radii (rx and ry). The following example shows a solid blue ellipse.

Example of Valid Syntax:

```
<ellipse fill="rgb(0,0,255)" stroke="rgb(0,0,0)" stroke-width="1" cx="100"
cy="80" rx="48" ry="20"/>
```

Content Model:

```
<!ELEMENT ellipse (%descTitleMetadata;,(animate|set|animateMotion|
animateColor|animateTransform)*) >
```

filter   The filter element is used to contain a set of filter primitives that can later be applied to an image. SVG supports a wide range of filters that are commonly used in illustration programs, including blend, composite, flood, diffuse lighting, and so on. In the following example, a normal and lighten blend filter are applied to text and a background image. This is a simplified version of the blending modes documented in the SVG 1.0 Specification (http://www.w3.org/TR/SVG/filters.html).

Example of Valid Syntax:

```
<svg width="200" height="200">
    <defs>
```

```
    <filter id="normal">
            <feBlend mode="normal" in2="BackgroundImage"
in="SourceGraphic"/>
        </filter>
        <filter id="lighten">
            <feBlend mode="lighten" in2="BackgroundImage"
in="SourceGraphic"/>
        </filter>
    </defs>
    <rect fill="none" stroke="rgb(0,0,255)" x="1" y="1" width="498"
height="498"/>
    <g enable-background="new">
        <rect x="100" y="20" width="200" height="200" fill="rgb(0,0,255)"/>
        <g font-size="32" fill="rgb(136,136,136)" fill-opacity="0.8">
            <text x="30" y="90" filter="url(#normal)">Normal</text>
            <text x="30" y="160" filter="url(#lighten)">Lighten</text>
        </g>
    </g>
</svg>
```

Content Model:

```
<!ELEMENT filter (%descTitleMetadata;,(feBlend|feFlood|
  feColorMatrix|feComponentTransfer|
  feComposite|feConvolveMatrix|feDiffuseLighting|feDisplacementMap|
  feGaussianBlur|feImage|feMerge|
  feMorphology|feOffset|feSpecularLighting|
  feTile|feTurbulence|animate|set)*) >
```

g   The "g" or group element is used as a container object to group related graphi-cal objects. The "g" element can be very useful in creating structure in a large or complex illustration. Groups can be given unique IDs for later referencing, and they can also be assigned <title> and <desc> elements for further identification and processing. In the following example, four rectangles are separated into two differ-ent groups.

Example of Valid Syntax:

```
<g>
<rect fill="rgb(1,1,255)" stroke="rgb(0,0,0)" stroke-width="1" x="32" y="32"
```

```
width="44" height="40"/>
<rect fill="rgb(1,1,255)" stroke="rgb(0,0,0)" stroke-width="1" x="116" y="32"
width="44" height="40"/>
</g>
<g>
<rect fill="rgb(255,13,1)" stroke="rgb(0,0,0)" stroke-width="1" x="32" y="124"
width="52" height="44"/>
<rect fill="rgb(255,13,1)" stroke="rgb(0,0,0)" stroke-width="1" x="120" y="128"
width="44" height="40"/>
</g>
```

Content Model:

```
<!ELEMENT g (desc|title|metadata|defs|
path|text|rect|circle|ellipse|line|polyline|polygon|
                use|image|svg|g|view|switch|a|altGlyphDef|
                script|style|symbol|marker|clipPath|mask|
                linearGradient|radialGradient|pattern|
                filter|cursor|font|
                animate|set|animateMotion|animateColor|
                animateTransform|color-profile|font-face)* >
```

image   The image element is used to include other image files into a defined rectangle. These could include bitmap formats such as JPEG and vector formats such as SVG. The W3C SVG specification says that "conforming SVG viewers need to support at least PNG, JPEG, and SVG format files." The Adobe SVG viewer also supports GIF files. The following example creates a rectangle and embeds a JPG file within the rectangle.

Example of Valid Syntax:

```
<image x="68" y="75" width="64" height="56" xlink:href="C:\My Documents\
msb.jpg"/>
```

Content Model:

```
<!ELEMENT image %descTitleMetadata;,(animate | set | animateMotion |
 animateColor | animateTransform)*) >
```

line   The line element is a primary SVG element that draws a line between two x,y coordinates. The following example draws a line from x,y 16,63 to x,y 128,63.
Example of Valid Syntax:

```
<line fill="none" stroke="rgb(0,0,0)" stroke-width="2" x1="16" y1="63" x2=
"128" y2="63"/>
```

Content Model:

```
<!ELEMENT line (%descTitleMetadata;,(animate|set|animateMotion|
animateColor|animateTransform)*) >
```

linearGradient   The linearGradient element allows you to define a gradient along a line. The stop element, defined separately, is an important child element of a linearGradient. Also, gradientUnits is an important attribute. The two possible values of gradientUnits, userSpaceOnUse and objectBoundingBox, can significantly optimize how an SVG illustration uses gradients. For instance, Adobe Illustrator 10 generates gradients using userSpaceOnUse only. This means that even though an object may use the exact same gradient (in the authoring app), the gradient will be defined twice in the SVG. If a designer uses gradients on a lot of objects, particularly if they are from the same Illustrator swatch or style, the SVG can be significantly improved by removing the excess gradient definitions, and changing the gradientUnits to objectBoundingBox, as in the following example. In this example, a gradient from black to white is first defined inside of a <defs> element and then applied to a line.
Example of Valid Syntax:

```
<defs>
    <linearGradient id="black-white" x1="0%" y1="0%" x2="100%" y2="0%"
        spreadMethod="pad" gradientUnits="objectBoundingBox">
        <stop stop-color="rgb(0,0,0)" offset="0%" stop-opacity="1"/>
        <stop stop-color="rgb(255,255,255)" offset="100%" stop-opacity="1"/>
    </linearGradient>
</defs>
<line fill="none" stroke="url(#black-white)" stroke-width="2" x1="28" y1="80"
x2="156" y2="80"/>
```

Content Model:

```
<!ELEMENT linearGradient (%descTitleMetadata;,(stop|animate|set|
animateTransform)*) >
```

path   The path element is one of the basic graphical objects in an SVG document. It allows you to outline a shape that can be filled, stroked, or used as clipping path. In the following example, the key attribute to a path element is the path *data* (d="....”), which includes primitives such as *moveto* (indicated by the letter “M,” *line* (the letter “L”).

Example of Valid Syntax:

```
<path d="M123.5 23 L175.701 42.9254 L131.614 99.0002 L175.5 163" fill="none"
stroke="rgb(0,0,0)" stroke-width="1"/>
```

Content Model:

```
<!ELEMENT path (%descTitleMetadata;, animate|set|animateMotion|animateColor|
animateTransform)*) >
```

polygon   The polygon element is one of the basic graphical objects in an SVG document, defining a closed shape composed of connected line segments. In the following example, a blue triangle is drawn as a polygon.

Example of Valid Syntax:

```
<polygon fill="rgb(0,0,255)" stroke="rgb(0,0,0)" stroke-width="1"
points="76,63.6795 96,98.3205 56,98.3205" transform="matrix(1 0 0 2.19393 0 -
96.7084)"/>
```

Content Model:

```
<!ELEMENT polygon (%descTitleMetadata;, animate|set|animateMotion|
animateColor|animateTransform)*) >
```

polyline   Like the polygon element, the polyline element defines a set of connected lines, but a polyline element is typically open while a polygon element is typically closed. The following example draws a series of gray lines.

Example of Valid Syntax:

```
<polyline fill="none" stroke="rgb(128,128,128)" stroke-width="5" points=
"350,250 450,250 450,375 650,175 650,375 750,375"/>
```

Content Model:

```
<!ELEMENT polyline (%descTitleMetadata;,
animate|set|animateMotion|animateColor|animateTransform)*) >
```

rect   The rect (rectangle) element is one of the basic graphical objects in an SVG document. The following example shows a blue rectangle.

Example of Valid Syntax:

```
<rect fill="rgb(0,0,255)" stroke="rgb(0,0,0)" stroke-width="1" x="52" y="59"
width="104" height="60"/>
```

Content Model:

```
<!ELEMENT rect (%descTitleMetadata;,
animate|set|animateMotion|animateColor|animateTransform)*) >
```

script   The script element is equivalent to the script element in HTML, and is used as a container for scripts that can act on the entire SVG document.

Example of Valid Syntax:

```
<script type="text/javaccript"> <![CDATA[
(SCRIPT TEXT GOES HERE)
]]> </script>
```

Content Model:

```
<!ELEMENT script (#PCDATA) >
```

stop   Colors on a gradient are defined by a set of stop elements. In the following example, a linear gradient from black to white is defined in two stop colors.

Example of Valid Syntax:

```
<defs>
<linearGradient id="black-white" x1="0%" y1="0%" x2="100%" y2="0%"
```

```
spreadMethod="pad" gradientUnits="objectBoundingBox">
 <stop stop-color="rgb(0,0,0)" offset="0%" stop-opacity="1"/>
 <stop stop-color="rgb(255,255,255)" offset="100%" stop-opacity="1"/>
</linearGradient>
</defs>
<line fill="none" stroke="url(#black-white)" stroke-width="2" x1="28" y1="80"
        x2="156" y2="80"/>
```

Content Model:

```
<!ELEMENT stop (animate|set|animateColor)* >
```

style   The style element is equivalent to the HTML style element and allows you to include style sheets.

Example of Valid Syntax:

```
<style type="text/css"><![CDATA[
      circle {
         fill: blue;
         stroke: black;
         stroke-width: 5
      }
]]></style>
```

Content Model:

```
<!ELEMENT style (#PCDATA) >
```

symbol   Similar to the desc element defined above, the symbol element can be used to define graphical objects that are not rendered until they are later referenced by a use element. However, symbols are different from objects referenced by the <use> element. A symbol element typically has the attributes viewBox and preserveAspectRatio to allow the symbol to be scaled to fit within a rectangular viewport, defined by the referencing use element. With such use, a graphical symbol can be treated as a template object.

Example of Valid Syntax:

```
<symbol>
      <rect id="a0001" width="20" height="20" fill="rgb(0,0,255)"/>
```

```
            <rect id="a0002" width="20" height="20" fill="rgb(255,0,0)"/>
</symbol>
<use xlink:href="#a0001" x="20" y="20"/>
<use xlink:href="#a0001" x="50" y="50"/>
<use xlink:href="#a0002" x="100" y="100"/>
```

Content Model:

```
<!ELEMENT symbol (desc|title|metadata|defs|
path|text|rect|circle|ellipse|line|polyline|polygon|
            use|image|svg|g|view|switch|a|altGlyphDef|
            script|style|symbol|marker|clipPath|mask|
            linearGradient|radialGradient|pattern|filter|
            cursor|font|
            animate|set|animateMotion|animateColor|
            animateTransform|color-profile|font-face)* >
```

text   The text element is one of the basic graphical elements in an SVG document, defining a region of text in a document. The following example shows 24-pt Arial Black, bolded.

Example of Valid Syntax:

```
<text fill="rgb(0,0,0)" font-size="24" font-family="Arial Black" font-
weight="bold" x="24px" y="67px">This is text.</text>
```

Content Model:

```
<!ELEMENT text (#PCDATA|desc|title|metadata|
            tspan|tref|textPath|altGlyph|a|animate|set|
            animateMotion|animateColor|animateTransform)* >
```

textPath   The textPath element allows text to follow an arbitrary path, instead of just a straight line. The following example shows text following a (crude) path.

Example of Valid Syntax:

```
<path id="p0001" d="M28.5 107 L72.5 87 L108.932 85.0982 L160.5 107" fill=
"none" stroke="rgb(0,0,0)" stroke-width="1"/>
```

```
<text font-size="16">
<textPath xlink:href="#p0001">textPath allows this.</textPath>
</text>
```

Content Model:

```
<!ELEMENT textPath (#PCDATA|desc|title|metadata|tspan|tref|altGlyph|a|
animate|
set|animateColor)* >
```

title   The title element can be applied to an entire SVG document, a container element, or an individual graphical element. Like the desc element, the title element will not be rendered as part of the drawing, but can otherwise be acted on by the application or other software agent. It is especially useful for lengthy and complex SVG documents. The title element is also potentially useful for accessibility (given appropriate rendering software). The <title> and <desc> elements could be displayed as ToolTips, or as with the Adobe SVG Viewer, the <title> element immediately within the outermost <svg> displays as the title in the browser window (when viewing the SVG directly—not embedded in HTML).

Example of Valid Syntax:

```
<svg width="200" height="200">
<title>This document demonstrates text following an arbitrary path.</title>
<path id="p0001" d="M28.5 107 L72.5 87 L108.932 85.0982 L160.5 107" fill=
"none"
         stroke="rgb(0,0,0)" stroke-width="1"/>
<text font-size="16">
<textPath xlink:href="#p0001">textPath allows this.</textPath>
</text>
</svg>
```

Content Model:

```
<!ELEMENT title (#PCDATA)* >
```

tspan   The tspan element allows you to isolate text for specific treatment, such as font change or alignment. The tspan element also allows for multiline text selection in an SVG illustration. In the following example, the tspan element is used to enclose some text for bolding.

Example of Valid Syntax:

```
<text font-family="Arial" font-size="24" x="20" y="20" fill="rgb(0,0,0)">
Tspan can be used to <tspan style="font-weight:bold">bold</tspan>  text.
</text>
```

Content Model:

```
<!ELEMENT tspan (#PCDATA|desc|title|metadata|tspan|tref|altGlyph|
a|animate|set|animateColor)* >
```

use   The use element can be used in concert with elements such as defs and symbol to instantiate graphical objects that have previously been defined but not yet rendered. As such, the use element is very powerful for applications such as complex drawings that require objects to be defined, used, and reused. The following example shows how the use element is used with the symbols element.

Example of Valid Syntax:

```
<symbol>
   <rect id="a0001" width="20" height="20" fill="rgb(0,0,255)"/>
   <rect id="a0002" width="20" height="20" fill="rgb(255,0,0)"/>
</symbol>
<use xlink:href="#a0001" x="20" y="20"/>
<use xlink:href="#a0001" x="50" y="50"/>
<use xlink:href="#a0002" x="100" y="100"/>
```

Content Model:

```
<!ELEMENT use (%descTitleMetadata;,(animate|set|animateMotion|animateColor|
animateTransform)*) >
```

appendix B

Example Files

This appendix lists the SVG code for three of the example graphics used in Part 2. These SVG files, and other SVG example images from throughout this book, can be found online at www.svgfordesigners.com.

Chapter 3: splash.svg

```
<?xml version="1.0" standalone="no"?>
<!DOCTYPE svg PUBLIC "-//W3C//DTD SVG 1.0//EN"
     "http://www.w3.org/TR/2001/REC-SVG-20010904/DTD/svg10.dtd">
<svg width="600" height="440">
     <defs>
          <filter id="AI_Shadow_2" y="-15%" x="-15%" width="140%"
height="130%"
               filterUnits="objectBoundingBox">
               <feGaussianBlur in="SourceAlpha" result="blur"
```

```
stdDeviation="6"/>
                <feOffset in="blur" result="offsetBlurredAlpha" dy="8"
dx="8"/>
                <feMerge>
                    <feMergeNode in="offsetBlurredAlpha"/>
                    <feMergeNode in="SourceGraphic"/>
                </feMerge>
        </filter>
        <linearGradient id="XMLID_4_" gradientUnits="userSpaceOnUse"
x1="300.5"
                y1="440.5" x2="300.5" y2="0.5005">
                <stop offset="0.5787" style="stop-color:rgb(255,255,255)"/>
                <stop offset="0.6339" style="stop-color:rgb(252,251,253)"/>
                <stop offset="0.6883" style="stop-color:rgb(242,239,247)"/>
                <stop offset="0.7424" style="stop-color:rgb(225,219,236)"/>
                <stop offset="0.7963" style="stop-color:rgb(201,192,222)"/>
                <stop offset="0.8501" style="stop-color:rgb(170,156,203)"/>
                <stop offset="0.9039" style="stop-color:rgb(133,112,180)"/>
                <stop offset="0.9565" style="stop-color:rgb(89,61,154)"/>
                <stop offset="1" style="stop-color:rgb(48,13,129)"/>
        </linearGradient>
    </defs>
    <path d="M600.5 440.5 L0.5 440.5 L0.5 0.5 L600.5 0.5 z"
        style="fill:url(#XMLID_4_);stroke:rgb(0,0,0)"/>
    <text
        transform="matrix(1 0 0 1 113.75 308.323) translate(0 1)
translate(0 10) translate(0 10) translate(0 10) translate(0 10) translate(0
10) translate(0 10) translate(0 10) translate(0 10) translate(0 10)
translate(0 -1) translate(0 -10) translate(14 -46)"

        style="filter:url(#AI_Shadow_2)">
<tspan x="1.59907e-295px" y="0px"
style="fill:rgb(48,13,129);font-family:'Myriad-Bold';font-size:48">Tri-State
Greyhound</tspan>
        <tspan x="0" y="48"
style="fill:rgb(48,13,129);font-family:'Myriad-Bold';font-size:48">Adoption
League</tspan>
        </text>
    <g
        transform="matrix(1 0 0 1 -12 -29) translate(0 1) translate(0 10)
translate(0 10) translate(0 10) translate(0 10) translate(0 10) translate(0
```

```
10) translate(0 10) translate(0 10) translate(0 10) translate(0 -1)
translate(0 -10) translate(14 -46)"

            style="filter:url(#AI_Shadow_2)">
        <path
            d="M291.3 225.8 C262.8 217.7 230 207.8 217.5 203.6 C211.1
201.5 211.4 199.6 205.7 195.8
                C198.6 191.1 187.4 186.4 156.3 184.1 C113.2 181 82.9
232.1 49.5 224.2 C59.9
                227.8 66.2 226.6 66.2 226.6 C66.2 226.6 59.5 233.3 45.9
232.6 C45.9 232.6
                50.7 248.9 55.2 254.6 C62.5 263.6 57.6 273.2 58.1 287.8
C58.8 310.8 83.5 316.5
                90.6 336.3 C94.7 321.2 114.3 290.9 137.2 274.9 C137.2
274.9 159.4 290.5
                187.6 273 C212.9 257.3 250.6 262.3 257.3 261.5 C268 260.2
282.6 242.6 287.3
                238.4 C289.7 236.1 290.3 239.1 291.3 225.8 z"

style="fill:none;stroke:rgb(0,0,0);stroke-width:5;stroke-miterlimit:1"/>
        <path
            d="M228.5 258.3 C202.9 255.3 195.9 257.4 180.1 268.2 C173
273.1 144.5 279.2 132.8 252.5
                C131.3 257.8 131.5 265.7 125.6 270.1 C123.8 271.4 112.4
283.8 110.2 285.5
                C107 288.1 105.1 292.1 97.3 295.6 C98.5 295.6 101.5 296
101.5 296 C101.4 293.7
                115.6 284.7 112.1 292 L88.7 320 L90.1 324 C98.6 308.9
110.3 295.2 112.6
                293.3 C116.4 290.1 115.2 288.5 120.4 284.4 C124.4 280.5
128.1 278 129.9 272.4
                C134.5 258.2 136.4 268.8 139.4 270.6 C142 272.1 150.1
275.5 160.9 276.2 C176.6
                277.2 186.8 266.7 193.4 263.3 C200.4 259.7 206.9 259
228.3 259.4 z"/>
        <path
            d="M174.3 205.4 C147.6 205.6 138.5 255.9 71.6 229.5 C58.2
237.2 54.7 236.3 54.7 236.3
                C152.7 258.9 154.2 202.8 175.3 209.3 C174.6 207.5 174.3
205.4 174.3 205.4 z"/>
        <path
```

```
            d="M211.1 208.6 C211.1 208.6 184.5 206.9 178.1 210.7 C194
213.3 199.3 214.1 200.1 219
                    C202.4 211.7 211.1 208.6 211.1 208.6 z"/>
        <path
                d="M182.8 257.1 L184.7 258.7 C184.7 258.7 196.4 250.2 210.6
251.1 C225.4 252.1 225.7
                    255.6 241.4 258 C258.3 260.6 262.5 254.5 266.7 251.4
C270.5 248.6 282 238 283.4
                    236.1 C284.2 235 284.9 235.8 284.9 227.8 L278.8 225.7
C278.8 225.7 275.2
                    230.4 271.7 231.4 C280.9 235.1 278.3 238.6 273.9 242.3
C269.5 246 260.1 255.5
                    248 254.5 C242.7 254.1 223.7 249.9 221.2 248.9 C214.3
246.1 201.1 244.6
                    193.3 250.6 C184.6 257.4 182.8 257.1 182.8 257.1 z"
                style="stroke:rgb(0,0,0);stroke-miterlimit:1"/>
    </g>
    <text
        transform="matrix(1 0 0 1 225.69 88.5) translate(0 1) translate(0
10) translate(0 10) translate(0 10) translate(0 10) translate(0 10)
translate(0 10) translate(0 10) translate(0 10) translate(0 10) translate(0
-1) translate(0 -10) translate(14 -46)"

        style="filter:url(#AI_Shadow_2)">
<tspan x="1.58724e-295px" y="0px"
style="fill:rgb(48,13,129);font-family:'Myriad-Roman';font-size:18;letter-
spacing:9">WELCOME</tspan>
            </text>
</svg>
```

Chapter 4: navbar.svg

```
<?xml version="1.0" encoding="utf-8"?>
<!— Generator: Adobe Illustrator 10, SVG Export Plug-In . SVG Version: 3.0.0
```

```
Build 76)  —>
<!DOCTYPE svg PUBLIC "-//W3C//DTD SVG 1.0//EN"    "http://www.w3.org/TR/2001/
REC-SVG-20010904/DTD/svg10.dtd" [
     <!ENTITY ns_flows "http://ns.adobe.com/Flows/1.0/">
     <!ENTITY ns_extend "http://ns.adobe.com/Extensibility/1.0/">
     <!ENTITY ns_ai "http://ns.adobe.com/AdobeIllustrator/10.0/">
     <!ENTITY ns_graphs "http://ns.adobe.com/Graphs/1.0/">
     <!ENTITY ns_vars "http://ns.adobe.com/Variables/1.0/">
     <!ENTITY ns_imrep "http://ns.adobe.com/ImageReplacement/1.0/">
     <!ENTITY ns_sfw "http://ns.adobe.com/SaveForWeb/1.0/">
     <!ENTITY ns_custom "http://ns.adobe.com/GenericCustomNamespace/1.0/">
     <!ENTITY ns_adobe_xpath "http://ns.adobe.com/XPath/1.0/">
     <!ENTITY ns_svg "http://www.w3.org/2000/svg">
     <!ENTITY ns_xlink "http://www.w3.org/1999/xlink">
]>
<svg
     xmlns:x="&ns_extend;" xmlns:i="&ns_ai;" xmlns:graph="&ns_graphs;"
i:viewOrigin="-68.1885 344.8564" i:rulerOrigin="0 0" i:pageBounds="0 480 640 0"
     xmlns="&ns_svg;" xmlns:xlink="&ns_xlink;" xmlns:a="http://ns.adobe.com/
AdobeSVGViewerExtensions/3.0/" width="841" height="40"
     viewBox="0 0 841 40" overflow="visible" enable-background="new 0 0 841
40" xml:space="preserve">
     <style type="text/css">
     <![CDATA[
@font-face{font-family:'Myriad-Bold';src:url("data:;base64,\
```

Note   *Embedded font omitted*

```
]]>
     </style>
     <metadata>
         <variableSets  xmlns="&ns_vars;">
             <variableSet  varSetName="binding1" locked="none">
                 <variables></variables>
                 <v:sampleDataSets  xmlns="&ns_custom;"
xmlns:v="&ns_vars;"></v:sampleDataSets>
             </variableSet>
         </variableSets>
     </metadata>
     <filter  y="-15%" x="-15%" width="140%" height="160%" id="AI_Shadow_2"
```

```
filterUnits="objectBoundingBox">
         <feGaussianBlur  in="SourceAlpha" result="blur" stdDeviation="6"></
feGaussianBlur>
         <feOffset  in="blur" result="offsetBlurredAlpha" dy="4" dx="4"></
feOffset>
         <feMerge>
             <feMergeNode  in="offsetBlurredAlpha"></feMergeNode>
             <feMergeNode  in="SourceGraphic"></feMergeNode>
         </feMerge>
     </filter>
     <g id="Layer_1" i:layer="yes" i:dimmedPercent="50"
i:rgbTrio="#4F008000FFFF">
         <g i:knockout="Off" filter="url(#AI_Shadow_2)">
             <linearGradient id="XMLID_3_" gradientUnits="userSpaceOnUse"
x1="390.6494" y1="28.2495" x2="390.6494" y2="4.2495">
                 <stop  offset="0.1124" style="stop-color:#FBC391"/>
                 <stop  offset="0.2809" style="stop-color:#FFFFFF"/>
                 <stop  offset="1" style="stop-color:#FF6400"/>
                 <a:midPointStop  offset="0.1124"
style="stop-color:#FBC391"/>
                 <a:midPointStop  offset="0.5" style="stop-color:#FBC391"/>
                 <a:midPointStop  offset="0.2809"
style="stop-color:#FFFFFF"/>
                 <a:midPointStop  offset="0.5" style="stop-color:#FFFFFF"/>
                 <a:midPointStop  offset="1" style="stop-color:#FF6400"/>
             </linearGradient>
             <path i:knockout="Off" fill="url(#XMLID_3_)"
d="M690.649,16.25c0,6.627-5.373,12-12,12h-576c-6.627,0-12-5.373-12-12

c0-6.627,5.373-12,12-12h576C685.276,4.25,690.649,9.622,690.649,16.25z"/>
             <path i:knockout="Off" fill="none"
d="M690.649,16.25c0,6.627-5.373,12-12,12h-576c-6.627,0-12-5.373-12-12

c0-6.627,5.373-12,12-12h576C685.276,4.25,690.649,9.622,690.649,16.25z"/>
         </g>
         <switch i:knockout="Off" i:objectNS="&ns_flows;"
i:objectType="pointText">
             <foreignObject requiredExtensions="&ns_flows;" x="0" y="0"
width="1" height="1" overflow="visible">
                 <flowDef  xmlns="&ns_flows;">
                     <region>
```

```
                                     <path d="M135.094,22.448"/>
                           </region>
                           <flow  xmlns="&ns_flows;"  fill="#FF0096"
font-family="'Myriad-Bold'" font-size="16" text-align="center"
text-align-last="center">
                                       <p><span>HOME</span></p>
                           </flow>
                     </flowDef>
                     <x:targetRef  xlink:href="#XMLID_4_" />
               </foreignObject>
               <a xlink:href="home.html">
                     <text id="XMLID_4_" transform="matrix(1 0 0 1 112.8066
22.4482)"><tspan x="0" y="0" fill="#FF0096" font-family="'Myriad-Bold'"
font-size="16">HOME</tspan></text>
                  </a>
            </switch>
            <switch i:knockout="Off" i:objectNS="&ns_flows;"
i:objectType="pointText">
                  <foreignObject requiredExtensions="&ns_flows;" x="0" y="0"
width="1" height="1" overflow="visible">
                        <flowDef  xmlns="&ns_flows;">
                           <region>
                                 <path d="M257.958,22.448"/>
                           </region>
                           <flow  xmlns="&ns_flows;"  fill="#FF0096"
font-family="'Myriad-Bold'" font-size="16" text-align="center"
text-align-last="center">
                                       <p><span>NEW ARTICLES</span></p>
                           </flow>
                     </flowDef>
                     <x:targetRef  xlink:href="#XMLID_5_" />
               </foreignObject>
               <a xlink:href="new.html">
                     <text id="XMLID_5_" transform="matrix(1 0 0 1 205.3506
22.4482)"><tspan x="0" y="0" fill="#FF0096" font-family="'Myriad-Bold'"
font-size="16">NEW ARTICLES</tspan></text>
                  </a>
            </switch>
            <switch i:knockout="Off" i:objectNS="&ns_flows;"
i:objectType="pointText">
                  <foreignObject requiredExtensions="&ns_flows;" x="0" y="0"
```

```
width="1" height="1" overflow="visible">
                    <flowDef   xmlns="&ns_flows;">
                         <region>
                              <path d="M380.821,22.448"/>
                         </region>
                         <flow   xmlns="&ns_flows;"   fill="#FF0096"
font-family="'Myriad-Bold'" font-size="16" text-align="center"
text-align-last="center">
                                   <p><span>ARCHIVES</span></p>
                         </flow>
                    </flowDef>
                    <x:targetRef   xlink:href="#XMLID_6_" />
               </foreignObject>
               <a xlink:href="archive.html">
                    <text id="XMLID_6_" transform="matrix(1 0 0 1 344.6289
22.4482)"><tspan x="0" y="0" fill="#FF0096" font-family="'Myriad-Bold'"
font-size="16">ARCHIVES</tspan></text>
               </a>
          </switch>
          <switch i:knockout="Off" i:objectNS="&ns_flows;"
i:objectType="pointText">
               <foreignObject requiredExtensions="&ns_flows;" x="0" y="0"
width="1" height="1" overflow="visible">
                    <flowDef   xmlns="&ns_flows;">
                         <region>
                              <path d="M503.685,22.448"/>
                         </region>
                         <flow   xmlns="&ns_flows;"   fill="#FF0096"
font-family="'Myriad-Bold'" font-size="16" text-align="center"
text-align-last="center">
                                   <p><span>ABOUT US</span></p>
                         </flow>
                    </flowDef>
                    <x:targetRef   xlink:href="#XMLID_7_" />
               </foreignObject>
               <a xlink:href="about.html">
                    <text id="XMLID_7_" transform="matrix(1 0 0 1 466.6367
22.4482)"><tspan x="0" y="0" fill="#FF0096" font-family="'Myriad-Bold'"
font-size="16">ABOUT US</tspan></text>
               </a>
          </switch>
```

```
            <switch i:knockout="Off" i:objectNS="&ns_flows;"
i:objectType="pointText">
                <foreignObject requiredExtensions="&ns_flows;" x="0" y="0"
width="1" height="1" overflow="visible">
                    <flowDef  xmlns="&ns_flows;">
                        <region>
                            <path d="M626.548,22.448"/>
                        </region>
                        <flow  xmlns="&ns_flows;"  fill="#FF0096"
font-family="'Myriad-Bold'" font-size="16" text-align="center"
text-align-last="center">
                            <p><span>CONTACT US</span></p>
                        </flow>
                    </flowDef>
                    <x:targetRef  xlink:href="#XMLID_8_" />
                </foreignObject>
                <a xlink:href="contact.html">
                    <text id="XMLID_8_" transform="matrix(1 0 0 1 581.3838
22.4482)"><tspan x="0" y="0" fill="#FF0096" font-family="'Myriad-Bold'"
font-size="16">CONTACT US</tspan></text>
                </a>
            </switch>
        </g>
</svg>
```

Chapter 5: brindle.svg

```
<?xml version="1.0" encoding="iso-8859-1"?>
<!DOCTYPE svg PUBLIC "-//W3C//DTD SVG 20000303 Stylable//EN" "http://
www.w3.org/TR/2000/03/WD-SVG-20000303/DTD/svg-20000303-stylable.dtd">
<!— Creator: CorelDRAW —>
<svg xml:space="preserve" x="-2.62152in" y="-3.1311in" width="5.43908in"
height="2.09296in" style="shape-rendering:geometricPrecision;
text-rendering:geometricPrecision; image-rendering:optimizeQuality"
     viewBox="-2622 0 5440 2093">
 <defs>
  <style type="text/css">
   <![CDATA[
    .str0 {stroke:#1F1A17;stroke-width:3}
    .fil2 {fill:none}
    .fil1 {fill:#2A1F74}
    .fil0 {fill:#D92624}
   ]]>
  </style>
 </defs>
 <g id="Layer 1">
  <path id="95286848" class="fil0" d="M-2339 1391m300 -234c0,0 0,0 0,0 0,-31
-8,-55 -25,-73 -17,-18 -41,-27 -71,-26 0,34 0,69 0,103 0,34 0,69 0,103 30,0
54,-9 71,-28 17,-20 25,-46 25,-79zm-100 233c0,0 0,0 0,0 -49,0 -98,0 -147,0
0,-126 0,-252 0,-378 0,-125 0,-251 0,-377 49,-1 99,-2 148,-6 20,-1 39,-2
56,-1 19,0 36,3 53,7 17,5 33,12 49,24 26,19 45,44 59,74 13,30 19,62 19,95
0,34 -6,65 -19,93 -13,28 -34,51 -63,73 21,9 39,24 52,43 14,19 25,40 32,63
7,24 11,47 11,70 -1,51 -12,93 -34,126 -23,33 -53,57 -90,72 -37,15 -79,22
-126,22zm95 -549c0,0 0,0 0,0 0,-29 -9,-50 -24,-66 -16,-16 -38,-22 -67,-20
0,62 0,124 0,186 29,-1 51,-11 66,-29 16,-18 25,-42 25,-71zm190 550m204 -2c0,0
0,0 0,0 -50,0 -100,0 -151,0 0,-132 0,-264 0,-396 0,-132 0,-264 0,-396 51,-7
101,-14 152,-22 25,-4 53,-7 83,-8 30,-1 60,3 88,14 28,10 51,31 69,61 19,31
29,75 29,133 0,48 -9,92 -26,132 -18,39 -45,73 -82,99 21,63 44,126 65,189
22,64 45,128 67,193 -53,0 -106,1 -159,1 -22,-64 -45,-128 -67,-190 -22,-63
-44,-124 -66,-186 -1,0 -1,0 -2,0 0,63 0,126 0,188 0,63 0,125 0,188zm0
-681c0,0 0,0 0,0 0,36 0,72 0,108 0,36 0,73 0,109 9,0 18,0 26,-1 35,-4 59,-18
74,-41 16,-24 23,-53 23,-88 0,-20 -3,-38 -10,-53 -6,-15 -17,-26 -32,-33
-16,-7 -35,-8 -60,-4 -7,1 -14,2 -21,3zm333 681m53 -881c0,0 0,0 0,0 50,-9
100,-19 151,-28 0,151 0,303 0,454 0,152 0,303 0,455 -51,0 -101,0 -151,0
0,-147 0,-294 0,-440 0,-147 0,-294 0,-441zm205 880m53 -928c0,0 0,0 0,0 48,-9
97,-18 145,-27 31,91 63,183 94,276 31,95 63,190 95,286 0,0 1,-1 1,-2 -8,-47
-12,-97 -12,-148 1,-74 0,-148 0,-222 0,-73 0,-147 0,-221 51,-8 101,-16
151,-24 0,169 0,337 0,505 0,168 0,336 0,504 -47,0 -95,0 -142,0 -32,-98
```

```
-63,-196 -94,-293 -31,-95 -62,-189 -93,-283 -1,1 -2,2 -2,3 2,32 5,64 7,96
0,13 0,26 1,39 0,73 0,146 0,219 0,74 0,147 0,220 -50,0 -101,0 -151,0 0,-155
0,-309 0,-464 0,-155 0,-309 0,-464zm527 927m188 -1c0,0 0,0 0,0 -45,0 -90,0
-134,0 0,-170 0,-340 0,-511 0,-170 0,-340 0,-511 37,-4 76,-8 114,-13 5,0
16,-3 34,-4 19,-2 40,-2 67,2 25,5 52,16 80,34 29,18 54,46 78,84 25,38 45,90
60,155 16,65 23,146 24,244 0,101 -10,191 -31,269 -21,77 -55,139 -102,183
-48,44 -111,66 -190,68zm17 -185c0,0 0,0 0,0 30,1 55,-9 75,-31 20,-21 36,-50
48,-84 11,-35 19,-71 24,-110 5,-39 8,-75 8,-108 0,-34 -3,-71 -7,-111 -5,-38
-13,-76 -24,-111 -12,-35 -27,-63 -47,-85 -20,-21 -47,-31 -77,-29 0,112 0,223
0,335 0,111 0,223 0,334zm332 185m53 -1056c0,0 0,0 0,0 50,1 101,2 151,5 0,142
0,285 0,428 0,142 0,285 0,427 53,1 106,2 159,3 0,64 0,129 0,193 -104,0 -207,0
-310,0 0,-176 0,-352 0,-528 0,-176 0,-352 0,-528zm325 1056m53 -1033c0,0 0,0
0,0 101,12 202,25 304,40 0,62 0,123 0,185 -51,-7 -102,-13 -153,-19 0,74 0,148
0,221 45,4 90,8 135,12 0,62 0,123 0,185 -45,-3 -90,-6 -135,-8 0,76 0,152
0,229 51,1 103,3 155,4 0,62 0,124 0,185 -102,0 -204,0 -306,0 0,-173 0,-345
0,-517 0,-173 0,-345 0,-517zm344 1034m188 0c0,0 0,0 0,0 -45,0 -90,0 -135,0
0,-163 0,-326 0,-489 0,-163 0,-326 0,-489 38,6 76,13 114,19 5,1 17,2 35,5
18,4 40,10 66,20 26,11 52,27 81,50 28,22 54,52 78,90 24,38 44,85 59,144 16,57
24,127 24,210 1,86 -9,161 -30,227 -21,65 -56,117 -103,155 -48,37 -110,57
-189,58zm16 -169c0,0 0,0 0,0 30,2 55,-6 75,-24 21,-18 37,-43 48,-72 12,-30
20,-62 25,-96 5,-33 7,-65 7,-94 0,-30 -2,-63 -7,-98 -4,-35 -13,-69 -24,-102
-11,-33 -27,-62 -47,-85 -20,-23 -46,-38 -77,-43 0,103 0,205 0,307 0,102 0,205
0,307zm332 171m295 -852c0,0 0,0 0,0 34,6 67,20 99,40 32,21 61,49 86,86 26,36
46,81 61,136 15,53 23,117 23,192 0,75 -8,138 -23,190 -15,52 -35,94 -61,127
-25,32 -54,55 -86,71 -32,16 -65,24 -99,24 -34,0 -66,-8 -99,-25 -31,-16
-60,-42 -86,-78 -25,-36 -45,-83 -60,-142 -15,-59 -24,-130 -24,-213 0,-83
9,-153 24,-209 15,-55 35,-99 60,-130 26,-31 54,-52 86,-62 32,-11 65,-13
99,-7zm-107 423c0,0 0,0 0,0 0,14 0,33 1,56 1,23 4,48 8,75 4,26 10,51 17,75
8,24 18,43 32,58 13,16 29,24 49,25 20,0 37,-7 50,-21 13,-14 24,-32 32,-54
7,-23 13,-46 17,-71 3,-25 6,-49 7,-70 1,-23 2,-41 2,-54 0,-15 -1,-34 -2,-56
-1,-23 -4,-47 -7,-72 -4,-26 -10,-50 -17,-73 -8,-23 -19,-43 -32,-58 -13,-16
-30,-27 -50,-29 -20,-3 -36,2 -49,15 -13,12 -24,29 -32,51 -7,22 -13,46 -17,71
-4,26 -7,50 -8,74 -1,23 -1,43 -1,58zm402 430m297 -425c0,0 0,0 0,0 82,3 165,5
247,6 0,19 0,39 0,59 1,32 -1,66 -5,100 -4,34 -11,68 -22,100 -10,32 -24,61
-43,87 -18,26 -42,47 -70,62 -29,16 -64,24 -105,24 -41,0 -76,-9 -107,-25
-31,-16 -57,-38 -78,-66 -21,-28 -38,-59 -51,-94 -13,-35 -22,-72 -28,-109
-6,-38 -9,-74 -9,-110 0,-36 2,-74 8,-112 5,-38 14,-74 26,-108 12,-34 29,-64
50,-90 20,-26 47,-45 78,-59 31,-12 68,-18 111,-15 39,2 74,13 103,29 30,16
55,37 75,64 21,28 37,59 47,95 -49,18 -98,36 -147,54 -2,-14 -6,-28 -10,-43
-5,-15 -12,-29 -23,-40 -10,-11 -25,-18 -44,-19 -20,-2 -37,3 -51,14 -14,12
-24,27 -33,47 -8,20 -14,42 -18,65 -5,24 -7,46 -8,68 -2,22 -2,40 -2,55 0,17
```

```
0,35 1,58 1,22 3,44 7,67 4,24 10,45 19,65 8,21 19,37 34,49 15,13 33,20 55,20
19,0 35,-6 47,-16 12,-11 20,-25 26,-41 7,-17 11,-33 13,-51 2,-17 4,-32 3,-46
-32,0 -64,-1 -96,-2 0,-47 0,-95 0,-142z"/>
  <path id="95286936" class="fil1" d="M-2217 1525l0 33c-10,-7 -19,-11 -27,-11
-9,0 -17,3 -22,9 -6,6 -9,14 -9,24 0,9 2,17 6,23 2,3 6,8 11,13 4,5 10,12 18,19
14,14 23,26 28,36 5,10 7,22 7,37 0,19 -5,35 -16,48 -11,12 -25,18 -42,18 -15,0
-27,-4 -37,-12l0 -33c12,9 23,13 33,13 9,0 16,-3 21,-9 6,-6 8,-15 8,-25 0,-9
-2,-18 -6,-25 -2,-3 -5,-7 -8,-12 -4,-4 -9,-9 -14,-15 -9,-8 -16,-16 -22,-22
-5,-7 -9,-12 -12,-17 -5,-10 -8,-22 -8,-37 0,-19 5,-35 15,-46 11,-12 25,-18
42,-18 12,0 23,3 34,9z"/>
  <path id="95286936" class="fil1" d="M-2124 1520l33 0 0 177c0,18 2,31 5,36
3,6 10,9 20,9 10,0 16,-2 19,-7 4,-6 5,-16 5,-33l0 -182 33 0 0 182c0,28 -4,46
-12,56 -10,11 -25,16 -46,16 -22,0 -38,-7 -48,-21 -6,-10 -9,-28 -9,-56l0
-177z"/>
  <path id="95286936" class="fil1" d="M-1918 1520l44 0c22,0 37,5 47,16 10,11
15,28 15,52 0,34 -10,55 -30,65 -10,4 -24,7 -43,7l0 111 -33 0 0 -251zm33
111c14,0 24,-3 29,-9 6,-6 9,-16 9,-30 0,-15 -3,-26 -8,-33 -5,-7 -14,-11
-25,-11l-5 0 0 83z"/>
  <path id="95286936" class="fil1" d="M-1735 1520l45 0c22,0 37,5 47,16 10,11
15,28 15,52 0,34 -10,55 -30,65 -10,4 -24,7 -43,7l0 111 -34 0 0 -251zm34
111c14,0 24,-3 29,-9 6,-6 8,-16 8,-30 0,-15 -2,-26 -7,-33 -6,-7 -14,-11
-25,-11l-5 0 0 83z"/>
  <path id="95286936" class="fil1" d="M-1551 1520l34 0 0 222 55 0 0 29 -89 0
0 -251z"/>
  <path id="95286936" class="fil1" d="M-1389 1520l34 0 0 251 -34 0 0 -251z"/>
  <path id="95286936" class="fil1" d="M-1265 1520l90 0 0 28 -56 0 0 80 50 0 0
29 -50 0 0 85 56 0 0 29 -90 0 0 -251z"/>
  <path id="95286936" class="fil1" d="M-1008 1525l0 33c-10,-7 -19,-11 -28,-11
-9,0 -16,3 -22,9 -5,6 -8,14 -8,24 0,9 2,17 6,23 2,3 5,8 10,13 5,5 11,12 19,19
13,14 23,26 28,36 5,10 7,22 7,37 0,19 -5,35 -16,48 -11,12 -25,18 -42,18 -15,0
-27,-4 -37,-12l0 -33c12,9 23,13 32,13 10,0 17,-3 22,-9 5,-6 8,-15 8,-25 0,-9
-2,-18 -6,-25 -2,-3 -5,-7 -9,-12 -3,-4 -8,-9 -14,-15 -8,-8 -15,-16 -21,-22
-5,-7 -10,-12 -12,-17 -6,-10 -8,-22 -8,-37 0,-19 5,-35 15,-46 10,-12 24,-18
42,-18 12,0 23,3 34,9z"/>
  <path id="95286936" class="fil1" d="M-795 1520l91 0 0 28 -57 0 0 80 51 0 0
28 -51 0 0 115 -34 0 0 -251z"/>
  <path id="95286936" class="fil1" d="M-501 1652c0,44 -5,76 -15,94 -10,19
-26,28 -49,28 -25,0 -42,-10 -52,-30 -10,-20 -15,-54 -15,-105 0,-44 5,-76
15,-94 10,-19 26,-28 50,-28 21,0 37,7 47,21 7,10 12,24 15,41 3,17 4,41
4,73zm-35 3c0,-43 -2,-72 -6,-86 -4,-15 -12,-22 -24,-22 -12,0 -20,7 -24,20
-4,13 -6,40 -6,80 0,36 2,62 6,76 4,14 12,20 24,20 11,0 19,-6 23,-19 5,-12
```

```
7,-35 7,-69z"/>
  <path id="95286936" class="fill" d="M-416 1520l45 0c18,0 32,4 41,13 12,11
17,29 17,52 0,18 -3,33 -9,44 -6,10 -14,17 -26,20l47 122 -35 0 -46 -123 0 123
-34 0 0 -251zm34 111c13,0 23,-3 28,-9 6,-6 8,-16 8,-31 0,-8 0,-14 -1,-20
-2,-5 -3,-10 -6,-13 -2,-4 -5,-6 -9,-8 -4,-2 -9,-2 -14,-21-6 0 0 83z"/>
  <path id="95286936" class="fill" d="M-123 1520l36 0 17 54c0,2 1,4 1,6 1,2
1,4 2,6 6,20 11,37 13,50 2,-13 4,-23 5,-28l5 -23 2 -8 14 -57 35 0 -43 143 0
108 -34 0 0 -108 -53 -143z"/>
  <path id="95286936" class="fill" d="M203 1652c0,44 -5,76 -14,94 -10,19
-27,28 -50,28 -24,0 -42,-10 -52,-30 -9,-20 -14,-54 -14,-105 0,-44 4,-76
14,-94 10,-19 27,-28 50,-28 21,0 37,7 47,21 7,10 12,24 15,41 3,17 4,41
4,73zm-35 3c0,-43 -2,-72 -6,-86 -4,-15 -12,-22 -24,-22 -12,0 -20,7 -24,20
-4,13 -6,40 -6,80 0,36 2,62 6,76 5,14 13,20 24,20 12,0 19,-6 24,-19 4,-12
6,-35 6,-69z"/>
  <path id="95286936" class="fill" d="M289 1520l33 0 0 177c0,18 2,31 5,36 3,6
10,9 20,9 10,0 16,-2 19,-7 4,-6 5,-16 5,-33l0 -182 33 0 0 182c0,28 -4,46
-12,56 -10,11 -25,16 -46,16 -22,0 -38,-7 -48,-21 -6,-10 -9,-28 -9,-56l0
-177z"/>
  <path id="95286936" class="fill" d="M495 1520l44 0c19,0 32,4 41,13 12,11
17,29 17,52 0,18 -3,33 -9,44 -6,10 -14,17 -25,20l46 122 -34 0 -47 -123 0 123
-33 0 0 -251zm33 111c14,0 23,-3 28,-9 6,-6 8,-16 8,-31 0,-8 0,-14 -1,-20
-1,-5 -3,-10 -6,-13 -2,-4 -5,-6 -9,-8 -4,-2 -9,-2 -14,-21-6 0 0 83z"/>
  <path id="95286936" class="fill" d="M868 1639l61 0 0 10c0,49 -4,82 -12,99
-9,17 -25,26 -48,26 -24,0 -41,-10 -51,-29 -10,-20 -15,-52 -15,-99 0,-52 5,-87
16,-105 11,-16 27,-24 48,-24 17,0 30,3 39,11 9,8 16,22 22,40l-32 13c-1,-6
-3,-12 -5,-17 -1,-4 -3,-8 -5,-10 -5,-5 -11,-8 -19,-8 -11,0 -19,7 -23,21 -4,15
-6,41 -6,78 0,39 2,64 6,78 4,13 12,20 24,20 11,0 18,-5 23,-14 4,-11 6,-27
6,-50l0 -6 0 -5 -29 0 0 -29z"/>
  <path id="95286936" class="fill" d="M1015 1520l44 0c19,0 32,4 41,13 12,11
17,29 17,52 0,18 -3,33 -9,44 -6,10 -14,17 -25,20l46 122 -34 0 -47 -123 0 123
-33 0 0 -251zm33 111c14,0 23,-3 28,-9 6,-6 8,-16 8,-31 0,-8 0,-14 -1,-20
-1,-5 -3,-10 -6,-13 -2,-4 -5,-6 -9,-8 -4,-2 -9,-2 -14,-21-6 0 0 83z"/>
  <path id="95286936" class="fill" d="M1207 1520l90 0 0 28 -56 0 0 80 49 0 0
29 -49 0 0 85 56 0 0 29 -90 0 0 -251z"/>
  <path id="95286936" class="fill" d="M1359 1520l36 0 17 54c0,2 1,4 1,6 1,2
2,4 2,6 7,20 11,37 13,50 2,-13 4,-23 5,-28l5 -23 2 -8 14 -57 35 0 -43 143 0
108 -34 0 0 -108 -53 -143z"/>
  <path id="95286936" class="fill" d="M1560 1520l34 0 0 98 49 0 0 -98 34 0 0
251 -34 0 0 -124 -49 0 0 124 -34 0 0 -251z"/>
  <path id="95286936" class="fill" d="M1893 1652c0,44 -5,76 -14,94 -10,19
-27,28 -50,28 -24,0 -42,-10 -52,-30 -9,-20 -14,-54 -14,-105 0,-44 4,-76
```

```
14,-94 10,-19 27,-28 50,-28 21,0 37,7 47,21 7,10 12,24 15,41 3,17 4,41
4,73zm-35 3c0,-43 -2,-72 -6,-86 -4,-15 -12,-22 -24,-22 -12,0 -20,7 -24,20
-4,13 -6,40 -6,80 0,36 2,62 6,76 5,14 13,20 24,20 12,0 19,-6 24,-19 4,-12
6,-35 6,-69z"/>
  <path id="95286936" class="fil1" d="M1979 1520l33 0 0 177c0,18 2,31 5,36
3,6 10,9 20,9 10,0 16,-2 19,-7 4,-6 5,-16 5,-33l0 -182 33 0 0 182c0,28 -4,46
-12,56 -10,11 -25,16 -46,16 -22,0 -38,-7 -48,-21 -6,-10 -9,-28 -9,-56l0
-177z"/>
  <path id="95286936" class="fil1" d="M2185 1520l31 0 34 100c10,28 18,59
26,91 -3,-20 -5,-37 -6,-53 -2,-16 -2,-31 -2,-44l0 -94 34 0 0 251 -32 0 -38
-113c-3,-11 -7,-21 -10,-32 -3,-11 -6,-23 -8,-35 0,-2 -1,-4 -1,-6 -1,-2 -1,-4
-2,-7 0,3 1,5 1,7 0,2 0,4 0,5l2 26 2 31c0,1 0,4 0,6 0,3 0,5 0,9l2 109 -33 0 0
-251z"/>
  <path id="95286936" class="fil1" d="M2392 1520l42 0c13,0 23,1 32,4 8,3 15,8
22,14 9,11 16,24 20,41 4,16 6,40 6,70 0,27 -3,50 -7,67 -4,17 -11,30 -21,39
-13,11 -35,16 -66,16l-28 0 0 -251zm34 221c21,0 35,-6 41,-18 8,-13 11,-37
11,-73 0,-39 -3,-65 -10,-80 -7,-14 -19,-22 -38,-22l-4 0 0 193z"/>
  <g>
   <rect id="95286056" class="fil2 str0" x="-2620" y="1" width="5436"
height="2090"/>
   <rect id="95286144" class="fil2 str0" x="-2520" y="101" width="5236"
height="1890"/>
  </g>
  <rect id="95286584" class="fil2 str0" x="-2420" y="201" width="5036"
height="1690"/>
 </g>
</svg>
```

INTERNATIONAL CONTACT INFORMATION

AUSTRALIA
McGraw-Hill Book Company Australia Pty. Ltd.
TEL +61-2-9415-9899
FAX +61-2-9415-5687
http://www.mcgraw-hill.com.au
books-it_sydney@mcgraw-hill.com

CANADA
McGraw-Hill Ryerson Ltd.
TEL +905-430-5000
FAX +905-430-5020
http://www.mcgrawhill.ca

**GREECE, MIDDLE EAST,
NORTHERN AFRICA**
McGraw-Hill Hellas
TEL +30-1-656-0990-3-4
FAX +30-1-654-5525

MEXICO (Also serving Latin America)
McGraw-Hill Interamericana Editores S.A. de C.V.
TEL +525-117-1583
FAX +525-117-1589
http://www.mcgraw-hill.com.mx
fernando_castellanos@mcgraw-hill.com

SINGAPORE (Serving Asia)
McGraw-Hill Book Company
TEL +65-863-1580
FAX +65-862-3354
http://www.mcgraw-hill.com.sg
mghasia@mcgraw-hill.com

SOUTH AFRICA
McGraw-Hill South Africa
TEL +27-11-622-7512
FAX +27-11-622-9045
robyn_swanepoel@mcgraw-hill.com

**UNITED KINGDOM & EUROPE
(Excluding Southern Europe)**
McGraw-Hill Education Europe
TEL +44-1-628-502500
FAX +44-1-628-770224
http://www.mcgraw-hill.co.uk
computing_neurope@mcgraw-hill.com

ALL OTHER INQUIRIES Contact:
Osborne/McGraw-Hill
TEL +1-510-549-6600
FAX +1-510-883-7600
http://www.osborne.com
omg_international@mcgraw-hill.com